Women Through the Lens

Women Through the Lens

GENDER AND NATION
IN A CENTURY OF CHINESE CINEMA

Shuqin Cui

UNIVERSITY OF HAWAI'I PRESS

HONOLULU

Library of Congress Cataloging-in-Publication Data
Cui, Shuqin.
Women through the lens : gender and nation in a century of Chinese cinema / Shuqin
Cui.
p.   cm.
Includes bibliographical references and index.
ISBN 0-8248-2532-2 (hardcover : alk. paper)
ISBN 978-0-8248-3296-4 (pbk. : alk. paper)
1. Motion pictures—China—History.   2. Women in motion pictures.   3. Sex role in
motion pictures.   I. Title.
PN1993.5.C4 C85 2003
791.43'0951—dc21
2002010919

Chapters 2 and 6 of the present work appeared in slightly
different versions as noted below. "Stanley Kwan's Center Stage:
The (Im)possible Engagement between Feminism and Postmodernism," by
Shuqin Cui, from *Cinema Journal* 39:4, pp. 60–80,
copyright © 2000 by the University of Texas Press, all rights reserved;
and "Gendered Perspective: The Construction and Representation
of Subjectivity and Sexuality in *Ju Dou*," by Shuqin Cui, in
Transnational Chinese Cinemas: Identity, Nationhood, Gender,
ed. Sheldon Hsiao-peng Lu, pp. 303–329, copyright © 1997
by the University of Hawai'i Press, all rights reserved.

Illustrations reprinted by permission of
the China Film Archive, Beijing.

Designed by Argosy

Printed by The Maple-Vail Book Manufacturing Group

謹以此書獻給我的父母與女兒
To my parents and daughter

Analysis of socialist cinema in a postsocialist context uncovers how the "red classics" of the Maoist era were transformed and packaged for market consumption and ideological instruction. The attempt of the state-controlled mass culture to adapt to a new, market-driven popular culture reveals how and why a state cinema managed to lead and satisfy a mass market audience. Socialist aesthetics follow the dictates of ideology to provide model characters for the betterment of a mass audience. The central position of the proletariat as both film topic and viewing audience confines representation and perception to totalitarian motives. Owing to the empowerment of socialist rhetoric, a background power, either the Communist Party's current policy or a political event, provides a solution whenever the film narrative reaches an impasse.

While important to revolutionary filmmaking, gender relations are established more on the basis of class than of sex. The question of whether gender difference persists in the absence of sexual difference calls for a broadened feminist perspective. Careful analysis of a socialist classic—Xie Jin's *The Red Detachment of Women,* for example—shows how woman becomes a discursive device and semiotic code in the master narrative of communist revolution. Often, woman is subordinated first to the patriarchal tradition, then to the communist collective. By emphasizing her status as the "oppressed class sister," communist discourse legitimizes woman's emancipation. Nevertheless, erasing her gender difference to demonstrate equality with men conceals the political suppression of women for the purposes of a collective, sexless nation-state.

Investigation of new wave films shows how a national cinema can project itself onto international screens by articulating nation and gender in images and allegorical narratives. Creators of the new cinema, labeled too simplistically as the fifth generation of film directors, have attracted international attention with *signs* of China. Their eagerness to redefine Chinese history and their passion for cinematic innovation transform national experience into visual allegories. These allegories, I argue, highlight woman as a visual signifier of national history and as a sexual image for the world's gaze. When the female image entices international viewers yet frustrates local perception, however, the concept of the gaze has to be reconsidered as a matter of regional as well as sexual differences. In Zhang Yimou's *Ju Dou,* for instance, the off-screen sound effects and point-of-view structure reveal socially defined gender positions, while the mise-en-scène and closed film form visually suppress sexual transgressions. Yet the image of Zhang's female lead conveys both sexual and national codes, drawing the international gaze to her "beautifully" suffering body. Chen Kaige's *Farewell My*

Concubine, to give another illustration, shows the impossibility of escape from the authoritarian power of history as the two male figures assume an array of historical, gendered, and professional positions. Woman's entrance into the male-dominated cultural territories of opera and history endangers men and threatens death for the female self.

This study also discusses self-representation by Chinese women directors in order to uncover a feminine film practice in film history. In China, female directors have "enjoyed" legitimate participation in the mainstream production system. Their sociopolitical visibility, however, requires the concealment of a gendered self. The suppression of the feminized self, a sacrifice made to compete with men, has hampered the development of a possible women's cinema. In addition, the lack of interest in feminist theory and the absence of a tradition of feminist filmmaking work against the development of a women's cinema. As demonstrated in my analysis of two films, we do hear the female voice and see her point of view, but the voice remains uncertain and the perspective ambiguous. In Hu Mei's *Army Nurse,* the first-person, voice-over narration and accompanying flashbacks suggest a female desire to assert a woman's voice against the dominant discourse of communist ideology. The voice, however, speaks to the conflict between social expectations and personal desire. In Huang Shuqin's *Human, Woman, Demon,* interactions between stage opera and private drama delineate the female protagonist's identity crisis rather than her self-assurance.

Although their films may embody a clear sense of female consciousness, few female directors are willing to embrace feminism's theoretical principles. To emphasize difference means to acknowledge social inferiority, and to identify oneself as a feminist would move a director from the center to the margins of film production. Questions repeatedly raised by Western feminist critics (Have you ever encountered problems because of your gender in the process of making films? What Western feminist ideas or films have influenced your filmmaking?) typically receive a flat "no" in response. Yet the explicit rejection of Western feminism does not indicate the absence of a female consciousness or poetics of film style in Chinese women's self-representations. Rather, when viewed in a distinct sociocultural setting, the issues of difference and feminism take on new meanings.

THEORETICAL APPROACH

The question of sexual difference has been a central concern in feminist theoretical writings on cinema. Differences between men and women or differences among women serve as a means for feminist film critics to explore gender relations as they appear in cinematic representations. The inquiry into sexual difference typically posits a film structure described as a patriarchal system of visual pleasure based on a dichotomy of subject and object, the viewer and the viewed. For almost two decades, feminist film theory has been dominated by responses, revisions, and challenges to issues raised by Laura Mulvey in her 1975 essay, "Visual Pleasure and Narrative Cinema."[7] Taking woman and representation as a key issue and Freudian concepts of sexuality and the unconscious as a point of departure, Mulvey situates gender relations in a cinematic system of the look and pleasure. In her thesis, the division between viewing subject and viewed object assumes masculine and feminine positions; a dichotomy of man as active bearer and woman as passive object of the look constitutes the basis of a patriarchal film form. Around the axis of this dominant dichotomy, interaction between textual production and film spectatorship generates sexual difference in accordance with a patriarchal unconscious.

In an effort to move beyond the concept of sexual difference and the system of the look, feminist film criticism poses further questions regarding the construction of gender. Teresa de Lauretis claims that gender is both product and process of its representation and self-representation.[8] The process of representation depends on a sociocultural construct and a semiotic apparatus, where the former emphasizes social relations while the latter assigns meanings and effects to individuals within any given social order. The idea of self-representation indicates a subjective position where women might take a place in the process of representation. The construction of gender is also affected by investigating what is repressed in discourse and what escapes dominant representation. In de Lauretis' reformulated gender structure, it is the system of representation and sociocultural construction rather than sexual opposition between men and women that produces gender differences.

Taking the problem of representation as a fundamental question of gender difference, feminist film criticism has advocated readings of representations different from those offered by conventional studies. Two major forms of reading (deconstructive and constructive) from primarily a feminist point of view propose to open up new ways of thinking about film theory and practice. First, a deconstructive rereading of classical cinema takes the form of textual analysis, demystifying the contradictions that Doane, Mellencamp, and Williams identify as "symptomatic of the repression of women in patriarchal culture."[9] The specific engagement of reading "against the grain" means to provoke viewers into an awareness of how classical films work to support and sustain the idea of men as producers and spectators of representation, with women as images to be represented and viewed.

Among feminist interpretations, Tania Modleski's reading of Alfred Hitchcock's films unravels a crisis of masculine subjectivity by examining an ambivalent male attitude toward representations of woman and the implication of that attitude for film spectatorship. The ambivalence in Hitchcock's films, Modleski observes, arises as the male character and the director both identify with and fear femininity. Represented as a figure victimized by patriarchy, woman functions simultaneously as a mirror image and a mechanism of displacement. By identifying with the mirror image, the masculine conscious and unconscious are able to generate a male identity. Denial of this identification, however, allows men to project fear and loss exclusively onto woman, "who does the suffering for both of them."[10] Thus the dialectic of identifying with and fearing femininity conveys a male masochism.

Second, a constructive defining of "women's cinema" indicates a female consciousness that desires to read and represent women, underscoring the existence of a tradition of female cinematic writing. The contrast between the deconstructive rereading of classical cinema and the constructive defining of women's films lies in the implication that whereas the former aims to dismantle the male-dominated cinema system, the latter tries to build an alternative form of female discourse. In representing and reading women's films within the canon of conventional theories, feminist film critics have faced controverted questions: Can a women's cinema be defined? If so, how? Is it possible to sweep aside existing forms of discourse in order to develop a new form of cinematic language? What are the possibilities for an alternative feminist cinematic practice?[11]

The constructive concern for women's cinema entails the rediscovery of long ignored female directors and examination of recent female film productions outside or within the commercial and cultural constraints of Hollywood. Ambivalence and contradiction are crucial issues for the theorizing of women's cinema—as Claire Johnston shows in her study of Dorothy Arzner, whom Johnston redefines as a woman director making films that critique Hollywood's cinematic conventions from within. For Sandy Flitterman-Lewis, ambivalence and contradiction stem from the director's distance from the Hollywood model and her continuing investment in narrative cinema. For Wendy Dozoretz, an autobiographical investment in film practice creates the possibility of female inscription on film.[12] In sum, the contradictions central to feminist film criticism on contemporary women's cinema focus on the problems of theorizing women's desire, identifying female aesthetics, and establishing a subject position for women as cinematic spectators.

meaning in the relation between the party, the revolutionary savior, and woman, its subaltern. Difference appears as well in the contrast between socialist model heroes and the masses waiting for political enlightenment.

When Chinese new cinema finally gains access to international screens, the world order has become a rapidly evolving transnational system. International relations, capital flow, market economics, and geopolitics all interact within a transnational framework. As international audiences sample the global marketplace, the concept of film spectatorship moves beyond the positioning of either men or women in a subject viewing position. In a transnational framework, cinematic spectatorship involves "a cooperative Orientalism" in which filmmakers consciously exhibit national allegories for viewers who embrace the representations as expected symbols of Chineseness. Thus the film directors acquire transnational capital for further productions, and the international market receives more non-Western cultural products. As national cinema engages capitalism, worldwide distribution, and diverse audiences, it needs to be seen anew in relation to the relevant conventional theories and practices. Are all third world texts necessarily political allegories, as Fredric Jameson has proposed? Or what does Edward Said's theory of Orientalism have to say to this new situation?[21]

The possibility of seeing gender difference and cinematic spectatorship from a transnational perspective arises from or depends on certain representations. Visual representations that embody national identities and attract international audiences rely on history for meaning and women for pleasure. Chen Kaige's *Farewell My Concubine*, for instance, positions both heterosexual and homosexual relations against national history and the tradition of Peking opera, successfully winning a market for an exotic, erotic product. Due to its stunning visual beauty and female sexuality, Zhang Yimou's *Ju Dou* lures the audience into pleasure in looking. The visual pleasure, in contrast to Laura Mulvey's assumption, involves psychological torment as the woman responds directly to the gaze with her bruised body. Zhang's visual mise-en-scène of a concealed iron house, a sexually abused woman, and a sadistic or impotent man has become his trademark. Is this the entire picture of Chines cinema? Few would bother to pursue the question so long as the films coming from China meet the criteria of international film festivals and the expectations of international viewers. Under conditions where officials control mainstream production inside China and the elite attract capital, efforts at self-representation face tremendous difficulties when trying to bring either a feminine voice or a female poetics to film practices. Problems like these are exposed only when seen from transnational feminist perspectives.

FILM AS TEXTUAL SYSTEM

Critical attention to Chinese cinema, while largely a response to interest in cultural differences, as well as in national allegories, has frequently given short shrift to film as a visual medium. The language systems and semiotic dynamics that make the medium distinct from other art forms have not received enough attention. In considering how the meanings of gender and nation are constructed through visual representations, this study takes textual analysis as a basic methodology. The primary assumption of textual analysis, according to Stephen Heath, "is the will to treat films as texts, as units of discourse."[22] Nonetheless, to treat film as text entails multiple perspectives. Christian Metz, for instance, sees textual analysis as a means to explore the mesh of cinematic codes, images and sounds, and extra cinematic codes. For Jacques Derrida, textual analysis involves the practice of deconstruction, a process of "unpacking" texts to reveal the "unspoken premises while being alert to the discursive heterogeneity." For Roland Barthes, the concept emphasizes a distinction between work and text. The work he defines as a completed product that carries intended meanings, while the text refers to an imagined space where meanings arise from interactions between writing and reading. From a Bakhtinian perspective, textual analysis involves both text and context, where "the artistic text," as Robert Stam summarizes, "is not to represent real-life existents but rather to stage the conflicts through the coincidences and competitions of languages and discourses."[23]

Guided primarily but not exclusively by these analytical suggestions, my readings of six exemplary films demonstrate the textual process of producing cultural work. I take special interest in understanding how a visual language system participates in constructing the meaning of nation and gender. The essential elements of the visual medium include series of cinematic devices, elaborated with respect to cinematography, mise-en-scène, editing, sound, and color. These are the areas where narrative meanings as well as semiotic structures can be articulated. Any presumption that film analysis can be adequately approached through the mere viewing of a film followed by interpretations of narrative meaning is simplistic.

Stanley Kwan's *Center Stage*, for instance, presents metanarratives complicated by a silent screen star's personal drama and the process of remaking her films and therefore connects history and representation. A deconstruction of the film's metastructure enables us to see the concept of history as an unfolding process of textualization. The use of Maggie Cheung, a contemporary Hong Kong star, to impersonate Ruan Lingyu, the star of early Chinese films, forges an intertextual connection. This casting links past to present and postsocialist China to postcolonialist Hong Kong. Alternations between the original and the remake of the archival films show history reconstructed from fragments of a vanished past. Moreover, self-reflexive exposure to the filmmaking process, such as uncovering the shooting procedure or revealing the camera or the director, displays to the audience how cinema as an ideological and mechanical apparatus turns history into textual production or reproduction.

By way of contrast, Xie Jin's *Red Detachment of Women* exemplifies the norm of socialist aesthetics. A close reading of the film enables the audience to see how the ideology of national revolution transforms woman from an oppressed victim into a model proletarian. The film's characterization reproduces class conflicts between the exploiters and their victims, while the gender difference between male political mentors and female subalterns is masked. The matrix of transformation from oppressed female into revolutionary heroine requires that woman reject her sexual/gender identity and submit to a degendered, collective entity. The film's visual devices include extreme close-ups to centralize the heroes or heroines and montage editing to reinforce class conflict. Contrasts in lighting draw spatial divisions between land ruled by the oppressors or liberated by the communists.

In Zhang Yimou's *Ju Dou*, the use of off-screen sound effects and a point-of-view structure unravels a social order that allows a husband to abuse a woman's body while his nephew possesses her body visually. The directorial designation of the mise-en-scène and closed film form illustrates a confined social system within which sexual desire can be practiced only through incestual transgressions. In Chen Kaige's *Farewell My Concubine*, the spatial division between on-stage opera and off-stage realities juxtaposes the protagonists' life stories to fifty years of Chinese history. The metaphor of castration, the ritual practice of corporal punishment, and the use of costuming and makeup elaborate the gender identity of the female impersonator. In Hu Mei's *Army Nurse*, a first-person, voice-over narration in conjunction with a flashback structure conveys a female desire to assert a woman's voice against the dominant discourse of communist ideology. A female point of view insists on a woman's consciousness—to see as a desiring subject. In Huang Shuqin's *Human, Woman, Demon*, spatial transitions and interactions between stage opera and personal drama delineate the female protagonist's identity crisis. Here the use of conceptual montage reinforces a sense of crisis by arranging different images of an individual within a single frame.

In order to further examine gender and nation in cinematic representation, this study also stresses the conceptual distinction between narrative and narration. This distinction was underscored by Gerard Genette, introduced to film studies by Seymour Chatman, and applied by Edward Branigan, among others. In his investigation into how meaning is produced in classical cinema, for instance, Branigan expounds his arguments about point of view and subjectivity through the contrast between narration and narrative. Narrative, according to Branigan, refers to what the film presents to us—that is, "what is told." Narration concerns how the film constructs its representation—that is, "the telling." The contrast between the told and the telling, then, is represented by a subjective point-of-view structure. Branigan further defines narration as a textual activity of giving and ordering a narrative. Subjectivity refers to "a specific instance or level of narration where the telling is attributed to a character in the narrative and received by us as if we were in the situation of a character."[24] In other words, narration and cinema become subjective when both the storytelling and the reader's perception are mediated through a film character's perspective and tailored by way of the director's point of view.

The process of narration, according to Branigan, brings together a number of textual systems. First, the establishment of an *origin*, occupied at times by either camera or character, marks the creation of a *space* from which representation is derived. Then, the *character* in the space transmits a vision (glance, sight, look, or gaze) from his/her point to an object to be revealed or represented. In addition, *time* links the units of the representation, and *frame* divides what is represented from what is not. The final element, *mind*, is a coherence of representation or intelligibility evident in the organization of the narrative.[25] As a result, the process of narration forms a subjectivity when all the textual elements are imposed on a character and transformed through the character's point of view. The character functions to lend coherence to the narrative and to the viewer's comprehension of meaning. Finally, the spectator's position with respect to space forges an identification with the character.

Yet another function of narration in the visual arts is the positioning of the viewer with respect to visual space. In other words, when the production of space is correlated with a character, a character point of view will control the telling and viewing of the story. Here the emphasis is on a dialectical relationship between narration and perception, or narrator and spectator. First, the establishment of space introduces a point of origin and invites the viewer's vision into the space from which narration derives. Second, the attribution of space in constructing a character point of view regulates the viewer's access to the diegetic world. Therefore, the spectator's absorption of the film, Branigan suggests, is the experience of being this character. In sum, character subjectivity, in relation to both the telling and the viewing, constitutes a communication between the film world and the spectator's consciousness of that world.

Beyond the distinction between narrative and narration, the concept of enunciation functions as another productive instance in the process of a textual system. "The concept of enunciation refers . . . to the entire cinematic process, comprising both 'author' and 'spectator' in the desiring production of the text."[26] Addressing the spectator as the reading or viewing subject, the director's system of enunciation is first to design series of images in terms of various cinematic strategies. In order to maintain the film's power to fascinate the audience, the controller of enunciation (director and camera) will conceal itself in the operations of film production but leave the screen images to speak to the spectators' desires and invite their comprehension. In the apparent absence of authorship and a source of origin, the spectator will assume the position of subject of enunciation and conceive the cinematic signs as a representation of history or reality. Effacement of the markers of enunciation, as Christian Metz explains, is so "that the viewer may have the impression of being that subject himself, but an empty, absent subject, a pure capacity for seeing."[27]

The concept of enunciation, with certain modifications, helps to explain the encounter between the discourse of Chinese texts and the imagination of Western audiences. In the process of meaning production, commitment to representation and obsession with visuality have motivated many Chinese filmmakers to transform a national or cultural experience into cinematic images. The structuring of a cinematic world involves a subjective and socioculturally specific process. After distribution to the Western film market, however, the film becomes a discursive and visual text removed from its context of production and left for spectators' various interpretations. It is in the perception of the audience that meaning is constituted. An audience will, for instance, obtain impressions of China's modern history from cinematic images in Chen Kaige's *Farewell My Concubine*, Zhang Yimou's *To Live*, or Tian Zhuangzhuang's *The Blue Kite*. The political clamoring on the sound track and the images of Red Guard violence are signs of the Cultural Revolution. Editing strategies that crosscut between different historical moments suggest the expanse of China's history. But when the signs function in the eyes of the audience only as the referents of "history," their implied meanings remain unrecognized. Decades of sociopolitical upheavals for Chinese people can be reduced to momentary spectacles of political violence shorn of connotation.

As a further example of the audience as the subject of enunciation, viewers might comprehend China's patriarchal oppression of women in a compositional shot such as the one in Zhang Yimou's *Ju Dou* that shows the husband sitting astride his wife like an animal and abusing her. Seeing a woman in the foreground, a dynamic image in the film's production of meaning, the audience may experience a visual pleasure: the Asian woman as a heroine who "suffers so beautifully and sexually."[28] In addition, the male presence concealed from the screen in Zhang's *Raise the Red Lantern* or rendered sexually impotent in *Ju Dou* may be read by the audience in terms of political allegory—that is, how the power regime in China still dominates even though it is now impotent or old. The experience of interpreting meaning from non-Western cinematic texts positions the spectator as the subject of the production of film discourse. As a result, the spectator engages in an imaginary "I-you" relation with the film text. The production of a national cinema and its Western reception, in this "I-you" relation, might dissolve cultural specificity in the pleasure of the spectacle.

Nevertheless, a Western audience need not take an "I-you" stance with every Chinese film. When films such as Hu Mei's *Army Nurse* or Huang Shuqin's *Human, Woman, Demon* raise the possibility of a feminine language (not feminist yet) in film production, they do not have the appeal of spectacular films. When I screen these two movies in a film class on the subject of gender and representation, students receive them as examples of romance or B-level movies. Searching for an explanation to this reaction, I find that, on the one hand, a core representation of female experience apart from historical epics or spectacular scenarios denies the audience's desire for viewing pleasure. On the other hand, viewers have difficulty interpreting the films unless they are willing to bring a gender consciousness to bear. The system of enunciation thus stresses the construction of both a textual system and a viewing subject. It is through a reciprocal encounter—the film's power to fascinate the audience and the audience's expectation of familiar signs—that cinematic meaning is produced.

As a result, a framework of sociocultural context, a method of close textual analysis, a perspective of transnational feminism, and a consideration of film spectatorship make possible the analysis of the cinematic production of meaning. From these bases we are able to examine gender, nation, and representation in Chinese cinema from multiple points of view.

Part One

Early Production

Chapter One

From Shadow-Play
to a National Cinema

IN THE LATE NINETEENTH AND early twentieth centuries, external and internal forces compelled China to begin the task of building a modern nation. One of these forces was Western imperialism. China's engagement with the West was double-sided. On the one hand, the West had humiliated the nation through military victories and exploitative treaties, but on the other, it offered China the alluring prospects of political progress and scientific achievement. Both sides of this dichotomy contributed to the process of Chinese modernization. The former created a need for national redemption and the latter a need for national reform. During this historical period, *wen*, writing and culture, became the primary medium for the construction of national narratives and the central vehicle for providing moral instruction (*wenyi zaidao*). At about the same time, motion pictures, which had been introduced into China in 1896, started to attract public attention, but only as an entertainment form and a commercial enterprise and not as a means for national enlightenment. It was not until the 1930s that political and cultural activists realized that cinema could play the same role as *wen* in the construction and representation of a modern nation.

Recent scholarly inquiry holds that the concept of a national cinema should not be defined simply in terms of the films produced by and within a particular nation-state. Issues such as distribution and exhibition, audience reception, cultural discourses, textual construction, and sociocultural context must also be considered.[1] Moreover, these issues, I believe, must be further located within a transnational framework, in which the borderlines among nations and among cinemas are interactive rather than fixed. Of particular importance to this study is the relationship between gender and nation, which presents a necessary point of departure for an understanding of the projection of the nation in Chinese cinema. As Anne McClintock has argued, "Nationalism is constituted from the very beginning as a gendered discourse and cannot be understood without a theory of gender power."[2] Early Chinese cinema was transformed and subordinated to the representation of the nation. This study will examine how and why the female sign became integrated into the process of nationalizing women and thereby engendering the nation.

SHADOW-PLAY AS ATTRACTION

Chinese cinema originated neither as a technical innovation nor as an independent art form. Its history needs to be seen as a mixture of foreign novelty and domestic adaptation. Foreign-produced films—French in 1896, American in 1897, and other imports—came to China as "foreign shadow-plays" (xiyang yingxi) and later as "electric shadows" (dianying). At first, the shadow magic shows took place in public spaces such as teahouses, theater houses, and amusement parks. The moving images, comic skits, exotic scenes, or dance numbers were not the only attractions; they shared the stage with opera, acrobatics, storytelling, and a variety of traditional Chinese performances. Viewers would enjoy the shows with tea or snacks and carry on conversations. The open-air setting and collective viewing in public space offered the local audience the comfort of tradition and a glimpse of unfamiliar cultures. This particular mode of exhibition/reception was a salient characteristic of early film culture in China: the public consumption of a variety of amusing attractions.[3]

The emergence of movie theaters and feature films in major cities led to a change in the mode of distribution, presentation, and reception. After a Spanish showman, Antonio Ramos, opened his first movie theater, Hongkew Cinema, in Shanghai in 1908, the number of theaters increased to 233 in seven cities by 1929. Shanghai alone housed 53 movie theaters, with a total seating capacity of 37,110. However, theaters varied in quality and served different audiences. First-run theaters with sound equipment and modern features reached foreign residents and the middle and upper classes, while smaller and less grand ones catered to ordinary citizens. In addition, a few theaters were allowed to screen domestic productions. According to data from the U.S. Department of Commerce, "Of the estimated 450 feature films exhibited in China in 1929, fully 90 per cent were of American origin. . . . American films predominate in the Chinese market." The report further states that "practically all the larger motion-picture producers in the United States and Europe have agents or distributors in Shanghai. The best pictures produced anywhere are released in Shanghai almost as soon as they are in the country of production."[4] These foreign shadow-plays, supported by transnational capital, constituted an occupying culture of moving images rather than armed forces.

In response to the dominance of foreign distribution and exhibition, domestic production emerged first to meet local needs, then to counter foreign competitors. A curiosity about pictures in motion and the desire to make films brought about China's first silent film sequences: *Conquering Jun Mountain* (Ding Junshan, 1905). These were staged opera parts performed in front of a stationary camera by the well-known actor Tan Xinpei. After a successful screening in Daguanlou Theater in Beijing, the film's producers, Ren Qingtai, the owner of Fengtai Photography Studio, and his photographer, Liu Zhonglun, continued to make "shadow opera" pieces.[5] They invited famous opera actors, selected visually striking acts, and transformed them into shadow-plays, a national version of a foreign form. It was more than a coincidence that China's first sound film, *Sing-Song Girl Red Peony* (Genü Hongmudan, 1930), took the life of a well-known female opera singer as its narrative and used four popular opera arias to structure the film. For the first time, Peking opera was heard from the screen. At this stage, however, sound meant spoken language and musical numbers rather than a sound track. The connection between staged opera and its visual projection raises the questions of why the theater tradition served as a resource for early filmmaking and why shadow-play emerged as a conceptual interpretation.

In seeking explanations, film scholars inside and outside China have taken shadow-play as a point of departure for the study of early cinema. Through reading a 1926 publication, *On the Writing of Yingxi Script*, Chen Xihe argues that the notion of shadow-play generates a theoretical/aesthetic system where ethical principles are the nexus and functional effect is the system.[6] Zhong Dafeng, in his "Historical Survey of Yingxi Theory," proposes that the concept of shadow-play embodies a theatrical form on the one hand and a narrative ontology on the other.[7] Both describe an early cinema that emphasizes social function and moral instruction. Moreover, they see shadow-play's theatrical centrality and functional capacity running throughout Chinese film history. From a different perspective, Mary Farquhar and Chris Berry see shadow-opera films as "a cinema of attractions . . . a sort of hailing of the viewer into public spaces."[8]

As a way of continuing this examination, I wish to argue that the concept of shadow-play—the transformation of theatrical performances or

dramatic plays into screen images—recognizes both the cinematic apparatus itself and the film narratives it constructs. Nonetheless, with emphasis
given to the play rather than to the shadow projection, the concept has
inscribed a film tradition—its production and perception—with Chinese
narrative conventions and theatrical structures. In this respect, film practice at its early stage showed that "an effort was already being made to
impose 'Chineseness' on film."[9] As Chen Xihe and Zhong Dafeng have per-
suasively explained, the national characteristics derive from a tradition of
theater and literature strong on ethical doctrines and educational intent.
Questions concerning the adaptation of Western forms for the telling of
native stories and the lack of regard for the visual system have yet to be
explored. The view of shadow-play as attraction, however, allows an alternative vision toward early filmmaking in China.

From the start, foreign and domestic productions offered various
attractions. How the attraction is constituted and to whom it appeals, however, require elaboration. A "cinema of attractions," as Tom Gunning
explains, "directly solicits spectator attention, inciting visual curiosity, and
supplying pleasure through an exciting spectacle."[10] The cinematic apparatus, spectacular actions, and addressed spectatorship are the key components of attraction. Accordingly, the aspects of attraction evident in early
Chinese shadow-opera films are drawn mainly from the theatrical tradition.
Peking opera, a national theater (guoju), is a popular performative form for
a popular spectatorship. Its features of spectacle include the colors of costume and makeup, eye-catching acrobatic and martial arts, performing figures, and symbolic gestures, along with spoken and sung text. When
producing his shadow-opera films, for instance, Ren Qingtai would select
the most spectacular operatic numbers, motifs familiar to Chinese audiences. But in the process of turning opera into film in a single shot with a
stationary camera, the filmmakers had no means of screen space and camera movement, let alone editing. As a result, figures or props could suddenly
disappear from the screen. Thus, while the performative attractions
appealed to the Chinese audience from the very beginning, the medium of
cinema remained unexamined. This emphasis on performative spectacle
over the process of projection was common in the earliest domestic film
production.

The rise of narrative films in domestic production marked the transition from shadow-opera films to early cinema. The narratives often concerned sociocultural issues and followed the forms of civilized plays or
popular stories of the time. Although domestic productions lacked the quality and budget of foreign imports, they appealed to local audiences with

familiar subjects, narrative structures, and modes of narration. The films included discursive categories and visual tropes that employed gender relations and female images to signify Chineseness. However, the process of *being* or *becoming* national cannot be isolated from transnational interactions, as illustrated in films made by two important figures, Zheng Zhenqiu and Zhang Shichuan.[11] The first narrative film in Chinese film history, *The Difficult Couple* (Nanfu nanqi, 1913), for instance, centers on the theme of arranged marriage, a culturally specific subject. Interestingly, the production involved cooperation between Americans and Chinese; the former supplied capital and facilities while the latter selected the theme. Again, a static camera position, a frontal perspective, and an unchanging long shot framed the characters and scenes as photographed pictures. Mechanical recording could show how an arranged marriage unfolds but could not reveal the psychological and emotional dimensions of the couple's lives. Nevertheless, the subject of arranged marriage made the film a social critique. The presentation of two young people, strangers who are forced into marriage, illuminated the injustice of tradition. Thus the film prompted the audience to consider a moral question.

In addition, the figure of a virtuous wife and good mother was meant to embody social and moral conventions. *The Orphan Rescues Grandfather* (Guer jiuzu ji, 1923), an important early production, established a primary structure for the family melodrama genre. A dutiful wife and filial daughter-in-law is accused of adultery and driven out of her father-in-law's household. In a theatrical coincidence, no one recognizes her pregnancy until the death of her husband. She rears her son alone and enrolls him in a school apparently financed by the boy's grandfather. At a critical moment, when the old man's adopted son attempts to murder him for his fortune, the young boy intervenes. Realizing that he has a virtuous daughter-in-law and loyal grandson, the old man chooses her to inherit the family fortune. The woman donates the money for building schools. Thus a woman presented first as an unfaithful wife and the cause of a family crisis ascends to the feminine ideals of enduring suffering and bearing an heir. The financial reward for her chastity transforms the immoral female body into a symbol of rectitude.

In contrast to portraying a virtuous woman, *A Woman in Shanghai* (Shanghai yi furen, 1925) presents the figure of the fallen woman. The film shows how an innocent country girl comes to metropolitan Shanghai to seek her fortune. Succumbing to temptation and a madam's wiles, she is lured into prostitution. Although she lives by selling her body, she helps her former fiancé get married and frees another street girl from life in a brothel. The film contends that a woman is made a prostitute by social forces. Films such as these identify themselves as national or Chinese through the female image and body. As a gendered category and narrative trope, woman is defined as the embodiment of sociocultural meanings: the female figure appears as the victim of tradition, the self-sacrificing paragon of virtue, and the fallen angel with a heart of gold.

Social function and moral instruction are embedded within the narratives of these films. Unlike the cultural otherness of foreign shadow-plays, Chinese narratives draw on native experience and thus encourage self-examination. Yet the question of whether films "might have had a specific social function is less a question of subject matter and its dramatization than of modes of representation and address—of the ways in which films solicited their viewers."[12]

Studying the relation between subject matter and mode of narration in early films reveals a primary narrative ontology. Zheng Zhenqiu uses film as a vehicle of indoctrination. In his mind, the finest art should contain social criticism and school an audience about how to distinguish good from evil. To this extent, women, children, and the poor become his most persuasive signifying figures. In addition, years of experience in the theater and as a critic taught Zheng the significance of theatrical effect on audience reception. Films he scripted or directed are dramatically centered on binary opposites. Conflicts between the moral and the evil, virtue and villainy, and poor and rich drive linear but dramatic narratives. Characters, acting more as exempla than as particular psychological entities, teach the audience correct behavior. Crises are often mediated through moral education and theatrical endings. The film world, sensational and sentimental, absorbs the audience into a temporary emotional engagement and release.

In response to Zheng's designated film world, Zhang Shichuan established a three-shot structure: an establishing shot introduces the setting, a medium shot places the protagonist in a social/familial milieu, and a close-up conveys intense moments. Parallel editing, crosscutting, and flashback serve the linear narrative and sustain the melodramatic effect. Cinematography, editing, and sound effects had no autonomous position in early film history but remained subordinated to narrative need. The films made cooperatively by Zheng and Zhang are not the only illustrations. Owing to the commercial climate at the end of the 1920s, martial arts and ghost/spirit films flourished alongside the full-length features of conventional drama.

Early filmmaking was a commercial enterprise for a few studios, provided a form of entertainment for urban audiences, and allowed a measure of personal experimentation. But for various reasons, early cinema did not serve the nationalistic apparatus in a significant way. Certainly, foreign interests dominated the distribution and exhibition of films. However, before we brand early Chinese cinema as an artifact of Western cultural imperialism, we should remember that national reforms in the early twentieth century depended on modern literature as the primary medium of national salvation. Intellectuals and writers shared a faith that *wen* "could play a significant role in influencing minds in the process of national renewal" because of its metanarrative functions: at once social and personal, moral and psychological, political and ideological.[13] As a result, the literary and cultural productions of May Fourth discourse show little evidence of writing for or about cinema. Nevertheless, because of its distance from mainstream discourse, early cinema was able to remain a popular cultural form more engaged in national narratives than in national ideologies. Its perception as shadow-play, its theatrical structure, and its appeal to local audiences marked early cinema with Chinese characteristics. Such "independence" or "uniqueness" might seem temporary or arbitrary in a nation continually in the throes of unsettling change.

TRANSITION

The 1930s saw the transformation of early Chinese cinema into a socionational practice. The concept of nation and society became a subject central to filmmaking, a transition that calls for critical explanation. The official Chinese discourse underscores communist leadership and leftist involvement in film production.[14] Film scholars analyze narrative forms inherited from literary and theatrical aesthetics, as well as visual qualities and the influence of foreign films.[15] More important, careful consideration is also given to nationalism and the social conditions of the period. A significant aspect that has yet to receive sufficient exploration, however, is the question of the role of gender in relation to the idea of nationhood in early cinema.

In a nation caught in the throes of constant turmoil, film production could hardly remain as a form of mass entertainment or commercial enterprise. In the 1930s, China experienced social upheavals and foreign invasion: Japanese aggression challenged China's national sovereignty, socioeconomic crises drove the population deeper into poverty, and power struggles between communist and nationalist forces stirred constant civil strife.[16] Widespread social disorder and the dominance of foreign films directly exposed Chinese audiences to the hegemony of foreign power. This dual spectacle, national and visual, showed progressive filmmakers the power of cinema, the visual medium, to expose social problems and construct national discourses. "Chinese national cinema," Sheldon Lu indicates, "has grown to be a key apparatus in the nation-building process. It is an indispensable cultural link in the modern Chinese nation-state, an essential political component of Chinese nationalism."[17] The process of reevaluating the subjects, visual forms, and social implications of film drew film circles and left-wing groups together for the first time. The engagement between the two marked the ascendancy of socio-ideological discourse over film production.

The collaboration between filmmakers and cultural activists focused on the question of what and how to *write* for and about film. The leftists, who lacked experience in film production but had strong ideological convictions, began their participation in the film business by writing screenplays and film reviews. The concept of realism furnished a theoretical ground and narrative frame, while national issues and social problems became primary subjects. By dramatizing the misfortunes of the poor and the corruption of the wealthy, writers highlighted class antagonisms. The leftists' screenplays and film reviews, however, did not reflect simple observation or provide accurate representation of the national and social reality: they transformed that reality into visual representation through writing. The engagement between writing and film allowed leftists to seek legitimate positions in the film industry and practice discursive modes for the construction of a national cinema.

Wild Torrents (Kuang liu, 1932) is considered the first leftist film production in Chinese film history. In May 1931, a terrible flood invaded Wuhan and sixteen other provinces along the Yangtze River. Film director Cheng Bugao and his two cameramen visited the scene to film the disaster. The documentary reveals a striking contrast between the flood victims crying for their lives and the insensitive wealthy people viewing the spectacle from a balcony. Xia Yan, the leading figure of the leftist group, took the documentary footage as source material and transformed the images into a written script. The writing task thus required that the visual scene prompt the creation of a progressive written text. Depiction of social and class conflict between the powerful and the vulnerable sets the tone. The tale of peasants fighting the flood while the landlord's family indulges in leisure activities dramatizes the subject to theatrical effect. After the written text sets the subject and narrative frame, the filming procedure, in turn, undergoes a subversive mission to visualize the text in a socially specific and politically progressive manner. The director follows the written text in using parallel editing to bring class conflict into sharp contrast. In addition, the alternation of documentary footage and staged mise-en-scène blurs the real with the imaginary. The screening of *Wild Torrents* announced the leftist presence in the film industry and indicated that writing would be the predominant force in film creation.

The ability to assert authorship or authority over film through writing enabled the leftist film participants to expand their influence. They turned to the tradition of May Fourth literature for further inspiration. *Spring Silkworms* (Chuncan, 1933) became the first film adaptation in this mode. Xia Yan, in rewriting Mao Dun's story into a screenplay, tried to preserve the realism of the literary text. Striving to remain faithful to a realistic style, the film director chose a visual form close to that of the documentary. In the scripting of the film, therefore, literature determined not only the thematic subject, but also the visual form. The difficulty in finding forms appropriate for socionational topics, however, led leftist film writers to turn to Soviet cinema, especially Sergei Eisenstein's concept of montage.[18] Another of Xia Yan's scripts, *Twenty-Four Hours in Shanghai* (Shanghai ershisi xiaoshi, 1933), uses montage to dramatize the clash between workers and the ruling class. Using temporal and spatial contrasts as a means of social and ideological construction, the script calls on the film to produce a series of montage effects: the female factory workers exhausted after work, the factory owner's mistress rising from her bed, the poor family despairing over an injured child, the upper classes enjoying themselves in a dance hall. The insertion of socionational discourse through subjective writing, followed by visual interpretation, was characteristic of early Chinese cinema.[19]

Social consciousness and the narrative composition of progressive cinema were not the only discourse in film production in the 1930s. A countervoice that was raised but suppressed remains a controversial topic in Chinese film history. The advocates of soft-core cinema, with Liu Naou as the notable representative, precipitated a debate on fundamental issues of filmmaking. Liu's primary argument elevated visual form over social efficacy. Liu Naou argues that the question of *how* to construct a film subject is more important than *what* the subject is about. If cinema is the combination of science and art that manipulates a mechanism of time and space, then the mode of representation or visual form should provide the criteria for judging film aesthetics. Liu finds fault with the leftist film critics, charging that they ignore the concept of *motion* in depending on literary and theatrical modes for visual representation and scripting cinema with social and class ideologies. Liu ends his article by declaring that "The star system in the United States is losing its momentum. The director system in Europe is facing difficulty finding new inspiration. The era now should be given to the cinematographer."[20]

The debate between the opposing groups did not simply pit content against form; it also stirred a conflict between proponents of nationalism and advocates of modernity. In his research on soft-core films, Leo Ou-Fan

Lee comments that Liu Naou's "ecstatic panegyric to the cinema had a lot to do with his obsession with this hallmark of western modernity, which he considered to be the true essence of modern life."[21] Western modernity in the fields of art and cinema grew out of the avant-garde movements in the West from 1912 to 1930, when German Expressionism, the Soviet montage school, and French Impressionism called for an autonomous art free of illustration and storytelling.[22] Giving primacy to film aesthetics, filmmakers turned away from commercial interests to explore cinema as a serious art. Their experiments in modernism reflect specific cultural and aesthetic trends in Western history. Meanwhile, the possibility of creating an absolute art cinema in China, with no avant-garde tradition, and in the 1930s, with the nation plunged in crises, was doubtful.

Filmmakers and critics from the soft-core school did make a serious attempt to put aesthetic ideas into production practice.[23] *The Girl in Disguise* (Huashen guniang, 1936), an apolitical drama with a focus on gender transgression, stands out as a representative example. The film does not imitate Western avant-garde texts; instead, it demonstrates how to inscribe ethical and gender issues through visual means. Parents in a well-off family disguise their daughter as a boy to please the grandfather. When the "boy" goes to Shanghai to visit the old man, her masqueraded identity causes a series of comic turns: a girl falls in love with "him," while "he" becomes interested in another young man. The film's plot twists and high-quality cinematography proved successful with audiences and generated box office profits.

Leftist film critics responded fiercely to soft-core film productions such as this. Laden with ideology, their accusations stressed that such films showed no awareness of the national situation or social problems; they made no commitment to national enlightenment and mass education. As a result, films and filmmakers, directly or indirectly, in the eyes of leftists were traitors or imperialist collaborators. Rereading the debates of the two groups in the 1930s, we consistently hear the swelling voice of nationalism on the one hand and the insistent call for aesthetic modernity on the other.

GENDER AND REPRESENTATION

The desire to insert national subjects and social criticism into film production led the progressive activists to search for an appropriate system of representation. From the May Fourth cultural and literary innovations, they borrowed gender issues and female images. Since then, the confluence of women, nation, and representation has never ceased to attract political and discursive attention. The call for women's salvation did not emerge from female consciousness or as an independent movement; instead, it arose in the urgency of sociocultural reform. Activists who pursued anti-traditionalism and anti-imperialism, for instance, discovered the female gender as the "oppressed other" of social injustice and a potential object of national enlightenment. From this socionational perspective, women, taken as a universal category, represented gendered identity as well as social class. Reformers believed that by fusing the notions of gender and nation they could replace gender awareness with national consciousness, bring about women's emancipation through national salvation, and supplant gender difference with equal rights in humanity. "Women's emancipation in China," as Li Xiaojiang observes, "is the direct product of social revolution and national salvation, not the result of a feminist movement."[24]

The significance of woman's usefulness in the construction of national discourse derived specifically from her gendered position. First, in her personal repression, woman bore signs and codes signifying larger socionational issues. Exposing the state of the nation through the sufferings of its people placed woman in a position of exhibition. As a displayed object, she not only provided physical evidence of and persuasive witness to social oppression, but also affirmed the legitimacy of male intellectuals' cultural mission. In fact, the voice that spoke for women's issues came from male intellectuals rather than from women themselves. As initiators of women's emancipation, men took a leading and subjective position. With images of themselves as progenitors of a cultural awakening and mentors of repressed women, men reinforced the unequal foundations of gender relations: an enlightened savior stooping to help an unawakened female figure. Empowered by their leading roles, men justified recruiting women to serve the mission of national salvation.

By displaying women's suffering in the cause of national revolution, male intellectuals practiced social reform without reexperiencing their own victimization; their goal of saving others served the purpose of saving themselves. As the male avant-garde launched the dual task of emancipating women and awakening the nation, women carried a double burden as victim and signifier of the nation-state. Representing women's suffering and at the same time searching for a self-identity became possible when female silence awaited the savior's voice, ensuring that women would be spoken for in a male discourse. Using a language of his own to speak for others, the male narrator could shape his narrative from a subjective perspective.

In Lu Xun's literary career, for instance, two female corpses, Xianglin's wife and Juansheng's Zijun, haunt the living through their silent deaths. In

"New Year's Sacrifice," Xianglin's wife, a traditional female figure, is presented as an oppressed other to critique the patriarchal system. Her narrative enacts the ancient hierarchy in gender relations: in traditional China, women embodied no public identity other than as counterparts to men. Their absolute subordination observed the three obediences: to the father in youth, to the husband in marriage, and to the son in widowhood. The encounter between the woman and the I-narrator reveals a barrier between the oppressed other and the intellectual speaker. As Xianglin's wife approaches the scholar to ask a philosophical question concerning the existence of a soul in one's afterlife, this female voice is met with ignorance and denial. To employ woman in a narrative discourse on social injustice and as a gendered other for a problematic male self indicates a dilemma facing modern Chinese intellectuals: the desire to speak for women and the problem of doing so. The narrator's solution to the crisis is to let the female protagonist become a human sacrifice. The death of the woman generates a narrative of self-examination while denouncing a dark society through her body and her silence.

The corpse that lies beside Xianglin's wife is the figure of a "new woman," Zijun. The dead body ironically signifies what a woman can become after she breaks out of the patriarchal house. Lu Xun's "Regret for the Past" continues to use female configurations to explore the problematic intellectual. The story presents a popular May Fourth romantic relationship with the male character, Juansheng, as the enlightened instructor and the female figure, Zijun, as his follower. A commitment to gender equality and a taste for works of foreign literature are the ties that bind them together. Thinking herself enlightened and emancipated, Zijun announces to the world that "I am myself; no one has the right to interfere in my life!" She resolutely breaks away from the patriarchal household and lives with the man she loves. The idealistic assumptions weave beautiful illusions, yet the reality of daily life exposes the distance between the male mentor and his female student. While the man struggles to support the family through writing, the woman is left to indulge herself only in the worries of what meal she can prepare for the day. Estrangement between the writing male and the domestic female plants the seeds of tragedy. Zijun chooses death as the closure of the new woman's journey toward emancipation. Upon this dead body, Juansheng—writer, narrator, and character in the story—deposits his sorrows and regrets, not so much for Zijun as for himself.[25]

The deaths of the two female characters—one traditional, one modern—indicate a self-contradiction in identity construction. While literary authors contemplated the question of what else they could create for the female other, film producers wondered how to put the female image on the silver screen and into an urban milieu.

PROSTITUTE: THE OTHER'S OTHER

The question of how urban space and modernity relate to nationalism has attracted critical attention recently. Taking the metropolis of Shanghai as spatial focus, scholars have asked, "What makes Shanghai modern and what constitutes its modern qualities in a matrix of meaning constructed by both Western and Chinese cultures?"[26] My particular interest, however, concerns woman's relation to the city, the nation, and modernity. A superimposition becomes apparent as the female figure is situated against an urban backdrop. The presence of her body in urban space refers to "the city of darkness," home to forces of evil and cruel exploitation, or to "the city of light," center of modern enlightenment and commercial prosperity.[27] Yet the absence of a female subjectivity limits woman to different gendered roles; she lacks an autonomous identity. Progressive scriptwriters and filmmakers, however, believed that the female image would illustrate national themes emphasizing resistance to foreign aggression and agency within modern society. Their search for and construction of the gendered other in a city raises a series of important questions: How is woman defined in a metropolis as the repressed gender? What is missing or neglected when the female image becomes the focus of the metropolitan spectacle? How should we understand the role of woman in the process of constructing a national cinema, thereby a nation-state? It is to these questions that we now turn.

In the urban milieu of the 1930s, particularly in Shanghai, the camera lens finally seized the image of the streetwalker and conferred on her a significant identity: "the other of the oppressed other." The prostitute, whom Shannon Bell calls "the other within the categorical other women," embodies doubly disprivileged identities: a fallen whore compared to other women and a sexual commodity exchanged among men.[28] After Xianglin's wife, symbol of tradition, and Zijun, a modern Nora, fade from the scene, the presence of this socially oppressed and sexually commercialized figure, the prostitute, provides another icon for the written and visual media. Framed within the modern city yet configured according to May Fourth conventions, representations of the prostitute embody social and class implications. The discourse producers—the modern reformers—offer the image of the prostitute as an emblem of a humiliated nation and oppressive society. Films display her body to expose social indignity yet reveal in her the heart of a virtuous woman. In the visual configuration of the prostitute, taking

Goddess, 1934

the classical film *Goddess* (Shennü, 1934) as an example, we see how she is torn between virtue and vice, or between mind and body. She is at once a shameful streetwalker and a compassionate mother.

An explanation for this dichotomy can be found first in the naming of the prostitute. For instance, the title, *Goddess,* refers to a self-sacrificing prostitute-mother. The opening mise-en-scène introduces her dual identity unambiguously. A sculpture of a mother kneeling to nurse her baby illustrates the ideal of motherly love. Subtitles define the image: "She is the prostitute in the night street and a holy mother as she holds her baby in her arms." The linguistic transition from prostitute to goddess occurs as the filmmaker alternates between use of the prostitute body in a narrative of social critique and as a way to comment on female chastity as essential to traditional values. Thus the prostitute becomes at once a discursive indicator of social problems and a visual image for cinematic articulation, mobilized accordingly through spatial transgressions.

The female body serves as a sexual metaphor and a social indicator in an urban setting. *Goddess,* for example, uses spatial and temporal terms to position woman to be simultaneously a lowly prostitute and a good mother:

the spatial division between city street and domestic house and the temporal division between day and night. In the opening sequence, an establishing shot introduces metropolitan Shanghai alive with brilliant neon lights. The camera then enters a private room, panning across dresses hung on a wall and nursing bottles set on a table until it stops at the image of a woman with a baby in her arms. As the woman applies makeup, leaves the sleeping baby in its cradle, and joins the crowd in the city street, we realize that the contrast in the mise-en-scène and the crosscut between public and domestic space introduce her dual identities of prostitute and mother.

The city street becomes the public setting where social transactions and gender differences intertwine. Strolling in the street and framed in the screen, the prostitute presents a sexual commodity to male customers; chased by the police, she poses a moral danger to society; trapped in the hands of a local ruffian, she becomes man's possession. Her representational efficacy, however, could also serve socionational discourses. During the 1920s and 1930s, the prostitute was widely represented as a victimized, disorderly, dangerous embodiment of social trouble. Reformers regularly decried prostitution as the exploitation of women and hence as a national disgrace. The image of the prostitute as a sign of social decay, according to Gail Hershatter, can be traced to the belief of Chinese cultural reformers that "a system which permitted the treatment of women as inferior human beings would inevitably give rise to a weak nation."[29] Although integration of the prostitute into national discourse created a forum for social discussion, the audience was not allowed to hear the prostitute's own voice.

The configuration of the prostitute, while assuming her commodified sexual identity and her role as metaphor for the ambitions of male reformers, raised questions of perception because of her "immoral code" or lowly status. The problem of how to move the mass audience to identify with the plight of the prostitute became a serious concern for directors. They responded with a cinematic strategy that brought the female figure back home from the street and lifted her from a lowly prostitute to a virtuous mother. Thus, while she is not sexually clean, her heart is pure. This doubly defined prostitute body continually comes to terms in spatial transformations. In a close-up in *Goddess*, the camera frames the woman's legs and feet, tapping impatiently. A pair of men's feet enters the screen to meet the woman's, and both pairs then walk together off-screen. The suggested destination should be clear, yet the actual destination is unexpected. In a superimposition, the two pairs of feet fade from the screen, followed by the woman stepping into her home. The economic shift from "doing business" to returning home, or from streetwalker to mother, is unmistakable.

In order to make the prostitute-mother character sympathetic, the film indicates why she sells her body: the economic pressure to make a living and the devotion to her son's education. When her son asks why the neighbors call him "the son of a bitch," the prostitute-mother expresses her belief that education will help her son rise above his social origins. The psychological anxiety about money is revealed again by a superimposition. Within the same frame, we see the mise-en-scène of the mother with the sleeping boy in her arms. The imagined metropolis, the bright neon lights, and the figure of the mother appear simultaneously. The image is one of a woman willing to sacrifice her body for the sake of her child's education. "Culturally required self-sacrifice," as Rey Chow indicates, "was the major support of traditional Chinese culture."[30]

The spatial transformation from public to domestic blurs the social-gender lines between prostitute and mother. The prostitute body offers a visual image for progressive cinema while the maternal character represents traditional values. The prostitute presents a multifaceted female identity that serves different desires and signifies much more than sex as a commodity. As a screen image of sexual desire, the prostitute body becomes an object for male possession and pleasure in viewing. As a discursive code for social problems, the prostitute body calls for social reform and a progressive representation. As a venerated mother imbued with moral virtue, the maternal figure encourages sympathetic recognition as a traditional icon. Several important films share such themes. *Women* (Nüren, 1934) categorizes women into different social and gender stereotypes. *Life* (Rensheng, 1934) depicts the course of a female life from orphan to prostitute as it explores philosophical questions apart from class conflict and social causes. *Street Angel* (Malu tianshi, 1937) uses the contrasting figures of woman as angel and woman as whore to signify national crisis and ethical values. While early filmmaking produced representations of the oppressed, such as prostitutes, it also sought to create visual images of the new woman.

THE NEW WOMAN:
A PROBLEMATIC IDENTITY

An explicit illustration of May Fourth enlightenment involved identification with a Western figure introduced by male intellectuals—Ibsen's Nora—and a self-identity created in Sophia, the work of a woman author.[31] The figure of the new woman, however, remains ambiguous and problematic because neither the master narratives nor women themselves have responded successfully to the question of what a woman can be *after* she leaves a patriarchal household. In literary and cultural critiques by male intellectuals, Ibsen's Nora stood as a symbol for their mission of modernizing Chinese women. According to their presumptions, Nora's conscious decision to become an individual human being rather than a man's doll and to leave her husband's house set an ideal model for Chinese women to follow. Yet "the sound of a slamming door," as Lu Xun remarked, "is an unsatisfactory answer to the dilemmas posed by women's search for emancipation."[32] As long as she remained excluded from the economic sphere, a Chinese Nora faced the dilemma of either returning to her husband's house or submitting to prostitution:

> Nowadays, a Nora's departure from the family is not necessarily disastrous. Because her personality and action still appear original, she may gain compassion from some people who will help her survive. However, her freedom is already limited if she needs to rely on people's compassion. Furthermore, if one hundred Noras left home, compassion would diminish. If there were thousands and thousands of them, these Noras would merely provoke aversion. The best solution for them is to hold economic power in their own hands.[33]

In women's self-representations, a model new woman, Sophia, strove to overcome the traditional roles of wife, mother, and daughter. However, the questions of what a female subjectivity might mean or what a woman might become apart from a man's other create psychological confusion. From Ding Ling's "The Diary of Miss Sophia," for instance, we hear the constant refrain of "Can I name what I really need?"[34] The new woman is perplexed and disturbed by the contradiction between what the cultural enlightenment promised and what it in fact delivered. In her predicament—unable to return to tradition but incapable of truly assuming the identity of "new woman"—lie the "primary social and historical reasons to understand modern women writers and their writings."[35] Moreover, while writing may provide a means for revealing female desire and despair, the writing woman faces the absence or ambiguities of a female discourse. Enlightened to seek emancipation yet confined to personal exploration, the new woman is further entrapped within the question of an "inexplicable self."[36]

The problem of Nora's unfulfilled promise stems from the fact that the new woman's gender consciousness reflected the impetus of its time and the May Fourth revolution. The cultural enlightenment inspired the new woman to flee the patriarchal house, yet social reality showed her only illusions. Whenever adopting the identity of symbolic emancipation resulted in personal mystification, the new woman turned to writing to seek an explanation. As the object of emancipation discourse, however, the new woman could write about personal experience but not about the subject of enlightenment or the nation. As the writing mainly served to clarify personal confusion, it was denied a place in the construction of national history and literary tradition. In comparison to the elite women authors, women in the mass majority remained the incarnation of China's social reality and national condition. The "universal category of woman" or collective identity legitimated her position as the subject of representation.[37] As the signifier of the nation-state, however, she was doomed to subordination. In other words, as long as she was bound to the system of signification, no universal woman could exist other than in relation to men or the nation.

Unlike the literary canon in the early twentieth century, where women's writing and publication offered female voices and authorship, women in films remained mainly as images. As a sexual symbol, the actress appeared on magazine covers or commercial calendars. As a screen image, she played numerous roles designed for her: the oppressed or the progressive, a prostitute or a modern woman. In real life, the actress or star, while bestowed with a glamorous image, hardly enjoyed an autonomous identity as a new woman. Women in films remained under the male or national gaze; they held no positions in writing or filming. In addition, progressive filmmaking in the 1930s demanded that modern female images embody class difference and social conscience in the form of proletarian politics. The image makers, however, faced the problem of how to create a new woman, about which they had little comprehension. They turned, therefore, to broad categories—woman as either petty bourgeois intellectual or model proletarian. Each further confused the concept of "the new woman."

The classic film *The New Woman* (Xin nüxing, 1935; dir. Cai Chusheng) self-reflexively uncovers the dilemma. The first question, as the film title suggests, asks who or what is the new woman. The film presents three types of female figures and situates them in socially and politically defined gender categories. The stereotyped identities are clearly drawn, yet the question of what it means to be a new woman in the urban milieu and in visual representation remains ambiguous and problematic. One of the three female leads, Mrs. Wang, a cultured, pleasure-seeking woman, depends on her wealthy husband for a life of leisure. A Ying, a progressive worker, has a part-time job in a factory and teaches music in the workers' union. Wei Ming, independent and well educated, teaches music in a private school. In addition, she writes and composes in her spare time. The film presents the three women as examples of progressive, conservative, and moderate types. The film focuses on Wei Ming because she is neither

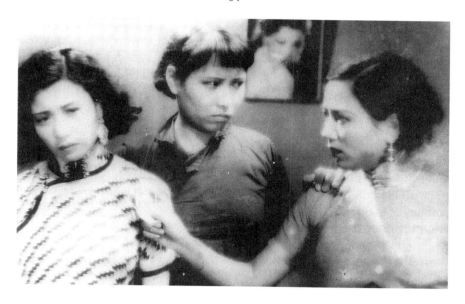

The New Woman, 1935

a revolutionary figure nor a man's ornament. The dilemma that woman faces and the director attempts to explain indicates an ambivalence toward problems of representation.

Finding it difficult to define the new woman, film directors such as Cai Chusheng turned to May Fourth conventions for inspiration. The subjective insertion of the new woman cliché for the construction of gender identity became a conspicuous narrative strategy. *The New Woman*, for instance, relies on flashback to unfold the female protagonist's past. Wei Ming's life fragments, through montage and flashback, form a collective picture of the May Fourth era. The new woman fell in love with her school sweetheart, and an unexpected pregnancy shamed her parents. She escaped from the household with her lover, married happily, and had a baby. Nonetheless, the husband later abandoned her. The woman put the baby in her sister's care and left Beijing for Shanghai to seek an independent life. The use of flashback attempts to relocate the female protagonist in relation to the May Fourth narratives and thus confer new woman status on her.

Although the film marks the woman with a new identity, the questions remain: Who will the Chinese Nora become after she leaves home? What is the meaning of "the new woman" in an urban milieu? Metropolitan

Shanghai attracts women who seek career opportunities but transforms them into sexual commodities. The modern woman who presents a model of independence and professionalism also assumes a gender position akin to the prostitute's as the target of man's sexual desire. The female protagonist is torn between modern personae—teacher/writer—and sexual consort of powerful men. Wei Ming writes stories and composes music, we are told. She fantasizes that if words can be sold for money, then she will rely on writing to make a living. Yet she fails to realize that her writing—like her body—registers value only when sold as a sexual commodity because agreement to publish her work depends on a sexual exchange. At the moment when her daughter is dying of pneumonia and the only way to collect money is to become a one-night prostitute, she realizes that writing means nothing more than selling one's body.

The woman writer belongs to the category of "the new woman." The correlation between writing and prostitution, however, reveals a directorial ambiguity in representation. In the process of pursuing progressive discourse, the image makers understood the significance of portraying woman as an oppressed member of society and presenting her as a visual spectacle. On the one hand, she is lavishly displayed on the dust jackets of new books, signifying "modern femininity" as a popular commodity. On the other hand, she struggles against the gender-coded strictures of urban modernity, often forced into prostitution. When the writer is separated from the written work and publication becomes a sexual transaction, the writing process remains a void that social convention and male discourse rush to fill.

In order to mediate the inadequate character of the new woman, *The New Woman* introduces a revolutionary female contrast, A Ying. The counterpart figure, complete with masculine physical features and political ideologies, serves to distinguish differences among women themselves. A Ying is also portrayed as a writing woman. However, she writes revolutionary songs for the purpose of enlightening the mass of working sisters. The film attempts to establish a model woman for others to follow. She is a strong figure able to identify herself first as a human being, then as a woman and a progressive cultural worker dedicated to the national cause. Unfortunately, this sexless revolutionary figure is little more than a visual cliché speaking political rhetoric. Neither the Nora type nor the revolutionary model can define the modern woman.

It is the death of the female protagonist that ends the narrative and conceals the embarrassment in representation. Crosscuts between Wei Ming on her deathbed and the factory women marching link the individual woman's sacrifice to women's collective enlightenment. Thus Wei Ming's suicide raises the question of women and death in relation to socionational themes. Ai Xia (Wei Ming in the film), whom Ruan Lingyu reenacts in *The New Woman*, was a talented actress in the 1930s. She committed suicide after scripting and playing a leading role in the film *A Modern Woman*. Her life and death, while providing the original source for *The New Woman*, prefigured the demise of Ruan, who ended her life with sleeping pills shortly after the film was released. Death by suicide, in the name of new woman and in the form of a remake, intertwines tragedy with representation and inquiry. The inquiry into who killed Wei Ming, a film character, extends to the question of who killed Ai Xia and Ruan Lingyu, women in real life.

Here the decision to end one's life cannot be defined simply as a personal tragedy; it is also the inescapable consequence of cinematic representation. Both Ai Xia and Ruan Lingyu chose death as silent resistance and a form of final dignity. The direct factors behind the deaths of Ai Xia and Ruan resulted from public intrusion into their personal lives. When personal stories become the subject of social gossip and public spectacle, the cinematic representation assumes a privileged position of interpreting death and upholding justice. First, the film director uses the female death as a subversive challenge to an oppressive society, therefore investing the film with progressive tones. Second, representation of the suicide dramatizes the antagonism between a silent film and news media to suggest that cinematic showing is "more authentic than the journalistic telling."[38] In either form, woman is altered to meet the needs of a representational medium.

WOMAN AND NATION
IN MELODRAMATIC FORM

Despite foreign influences and domestic experiments, Chinese cinema began and remains within a melodramatic tradition. "Film melodrama," defined broadly, "seeks to engage the emotions of the audience and provide thrills; often [the films] are characterized by the liberal use of music to underscore the developing plot."[39] From a political perspective, melodrama has been defined as a Western concept that presents a "theater of social misfortune in which personal virtue is contested, hidden, misrecognized, or subverted, a form of theater that seeks within the confining and largely recalcitrant parameters of the old society to restore and recenter the ethical imperatives required of the bourgeois age."[40] The modern version of melodrama "embodies the negotiation between the traditional ethical system and the new nation-state ideology."[41]

As a mode of political and emotional expression, melodrama provides representations that attempt to explain a threatening social reality. Paul Pickowicz, applying the Western notion of melodrama in the context of early Chinese cinema, sees the nature of leftist filmmaking as a "marriage between classic melodrama and elementary Marxism."[42] Chinese cinema, Pickowicz observes, draws on a tradition of melodramatic representation characterized by "rhetorical excess, extravagant representation, and intensity of moral claim."[43] Its purpose is not to deal with the monotony of existence, but rather to put an insecure and troubled mass audience in touch with an essential conflict between good and evil being played out just below the surface of daily life. As noted, filmmakers of the 1930s and 1940s believed that film, drama, and literature were appropriate and effective media for channeling morality and educating the audience, and so they took socionational issues as a framing device and the melodramatic mode as a means of emotional inspiration.

In the Chinese film tradition, family melodrama is central to the genre. "The family," Ma Ning notes, "rather than the individual or the state, was the most significant social unit in traditional China."[44] As a social institution, the family follows a hierarchical power structure, with the older generation superior to the younger and men above women. As a microcosm of society, the family becomes a stage for external and domestic crises. Drawing its tradition from Chinese theater, popular literature, and modern drama, melodrama offers representations of reality to the audience. Bipolar forces of good and evil or virtue and vice loom large as the narrative manifests ethical values and moral codes. An operative system familiar to both Chinese filmmakers and mass audiences generates the mainstream genre. In the postwar period, for instance, film production used excessive expression in making the family the locus of the social milieu. With the end of the War of Resistance against Japanese aggression, the struggle between communists and nationalists escalated. As social life became increasingly chaotic, melodramatic films brought the mass audience and its emotional world to confront socionational realities. To find the moral point in a Manichaean vision, the focus settled on the representation of woman positioned in thresholds. She appears as a multiple signifier of the urgent need to address national crises, to maintain family stability, and to sacrifice one's self to preserve ethical conventions.

The Spring River Flows East (Yijiang chunshui xiang dongliu, 1947), a two-part epic, is generally acclaimed as a classic of film melodrama. The film shows how national history and social reality come to terms through gender relations and the elaborated image of a sacrificing and suffering woman. The socionational issues embedded in melodramatic codes are essential to the film's primary narrative structure. Documentary images of historical events from the eight-year war against Japan, for instance, lend an aura of realism to the film. The tragedies that befall members of a family form the melodramatic spectacle. Viewing the film from the perspective of gender, one recognizes the male characters as active agents who participate in the discourse of nation building. The formation of the nation is represented as a masculine activity; male characters, cast as the national heroes, fight or die in the war between China and Japan. In contrast, the central female character remains a passive, suffering figure who joins in the discourse of nation narrating, thereby uncovering a feminine process where the virtuous wife and the sacrificing mother encode social reality as well as melodramatic expression.

The stark gender dichotomy appears in the division of space: men occupy the public, national realm while women inhabit the domestic sphere. The mapping of socionational space in the film contrasts rural and urban settings, occupied and unoccupied territory, front and rear lines. The spatial mise-en-scène also marks conflicts and differences between colonizer and colonized, rich and poor, men and women. The spatial politics of difference that positions the film characters casts the men as national

The Spring River Flows East, 1947

heroes while portraying women, children, and the elderly as dependent and vulnerable. For instance, the leading male protagonist leaves home, joins a first aid team, and commits himself to antiwarfare activities. His brother enlists with a group of communist soldiers to fight the invaders. The respected school principal, a guerrilla leader, saves the lives of the villagers and dies a martyr. In contrast, women remain in domestic spaces and register the private effects of national crises and social turmoil.

The primary narrative structure alternates between the Chinese-Japanese war as national discourse and the family melodrama, with the female image as its annotation. The insertion of documentary-like footage of the Marco Polo Bridge incident indicates the onset of the Japanese invasion of China and the War of Resistance. As Japanese troops take Shanghai, family members—the elderly, the women, the baby—become not only victims, but also signifying figures of the national disaster. The master shot of crowds running for their lives is immediately followed with a close-up of the distraught family. While the husband struggles at the battlefront, the family left behind suffers and endures. Inserted shots—the father-in-law hanged by the Japanese, the old and the young forced to plough the fields, the shabby house falling to pieces during a thunderstorm—illustrate the national discourse and intensify the melodramatic representation.

The family melodrama uses gender relations and moral principles to explain national issues. More specifically, the female figure is employed in the construction of national discourse and ethical-moral values. "The melodramatic imagination is profoundly moral," Robert Lang states; "it does not simply stage a battle between good and evil, but rather tries to establish that clear notions of good and evil prevail, that there are moral imperatives."[45] The moral imperatives in *The Spring River Flows East* turn out to be the restoration of patriarchal Confucianism, traditionally inscribed on the female body. The old order assigned women the roles of chaste, dutiful daughterly or maternal figures of virtue. The female protagonist, Su Fen, is the embodiment of the ideal role type. She is a loyal wife to her husband, a filial daughter to her mother-in-law, a good mother to her son, and an angel to those who need her. The idealization of feminine qualities such as suffering and sacrifice is the driving impulse behind the film's melodramatic force.

As moral value is preserved but the new order not yet envisioned, the melodrama undertakes its operative mission: bringing troubled reality to the audience. In the second part of *The Spring River Flows East*, the film reveals suffering, investigates evil, and calls for justice. With the larger national picture set in the background, the dichotomies of virtuous wife/unfaithful husband and good/bad women take center stage. The melodramatic representation places "emphasis on the domestic sphere of powerless women and children protagonists whose only possible agency derives from the virtue of their suffering."[46] Disenfranchised women and children stand in contrast to the degenerate husband, sexually seduced and morally corrupted by two evil female figures. The placement of women in both traditional and immoral positions indicates their significance to the construction of different discourses. Whereas displaying the suffering woman legitimizes the call for justice, exposing the evil woman identifies a scapegoat for male degeneration and family tragedy.

The primary editing structure of the film employs contrast through montage, making social-gender conflicts explicit to the audience. For instance, the husband's dissipated life in Chongqing and the afflictions of the women and children in Shanghai are brought side by side onto the screen. The editing first shows the sorry circumstances of the struggling family: shabby shelter, sick grandmother, hungry child, exhausted wife. The film then cuts to a striking contrast: the husband and his rich new mistress in a luxurious bedroom engaged in a sexual act. Alternating scenes reinforce the contrast and rivet attention on the tragic reality. A rainstorm soaks the whole family as leaks sprout everywhere. The grandmother holds the frightened child as the wife fights to fix the window. While the family prays for the return of their man and the dawn of a new day, the cut shifts to the bedroom scene again, where the new couple frolics in bed.

The film further underscores the contents of class difference and gender conflict in terms of melodramatic form. Montage shots divide the characters into poor and wealthy classes, visually displayed through spatial contrasts between the fallen territory of Shanghai and the unoccupied Chongqing. Class difference aggravates gender conflict, visually articulated through images of the virtuous/evil women and the corrupted man. We notice that the virtuous women and the children suffer greatly but rarely act, while the evil women actively transgress social and sexual lines. By emphasizing one woman's excessive suffering and another's forceful destructiveness, the film uses women to elaborate the discourses of ethical values and immorality. In either case, woman bears responsibility. Thus the melodramatic imagination absolves the man from responsibility and situates him as prey to female sexual entrapment. In Lang's view, "the melodramatic imagination seeks to reveal a moral universe in operation, even where it is unable to show good triumphing. The law might be paternal, familial, social, and divine but the melodrama investigates it, challenges it and in some fashion articulates how it functions."[47]

In the film's final sequence, the cinematography propels the melodramatic sentiment to an excessive conclusion and reminds the audience that bad women are the root cause of tragedy. A close-up shot of the grandmother and her grandchild, facing the camera and crying at Su Fen's death, seizes a focalized position of the victimized and the sympathized. Onlookers who surround the victims and comment on the tragic scene remind the audience how to identify with them and thereby how to judge the moral issues. While the maternal cries and the absence/death of the female body announce the tragedy to the audience, the sound of a car horn constantly interrupts the melodramatic enunciation and switches our attention to the two evil women. The interruption again alternates our attention between the heartless women and the condemned ones. The epic ends with the male protagonist ascending to the mantle of hero in the discourse of the nation-state yet taking no responsibility for his immoral acts. By contrast, women in melodrama carry the constructive discourse of the nation-state as virtuous wives and subordinate mothers, or they spawn a destructive national discourse as evil seductresses.

Films concerned with national discourses and family melodramas exemplified "progressive films" in the late 1940s. In addition to *The Spring River Flows East*, these include *Eight Thousand Li of Cloud and Moon* (Baqianli lu yun he yue, 1947), *Myriad of Lights* (Wanjia denghuo, 1948), and *Crows and Sparrows* (Wuya yu maque, 1949). Beyond these conventional early classics, some artists and works sought an alternative enunciation. Director Fei Mu and his films stand out as important examples. The significance of Fei Mu's films lies in their departure from the shadow-play concept and melodramatic effect or, more precisely, in their search for a possible realm between shadow and play. His masterpiece, *Spring in a Small Town* (Xiaocheng zhi chun, 1948), uses minimal poetic devices to depict a psychological world where ethical principles conflict with emotional desires. In a war-ravaged old house in a small town live a couple, a maid, and the husband's sister. A friend's visit interrupts their everyday boredom. The central position of the woman as wife, sister-in-law, and former lover of the visitor drives the narrative while an omniscient female voice-over carries the narration. Positioned as narrator and character, the female voice and figure are designed to control both the diegesis and nondiegesis.

The voice-over introduces the woman herself, the location, and the unspoken problems with her husband, as well as the coming of the visitor. The voice then shifts freely between the woman's inner monologue and narrative explanations, revealing a loveless husband-wife relationship and her emotional longing for her former fiancé. In addition, the dissociated voice

Spring in a Small Town, 1948

comments on other characters and explains the narrative development. The voice-over narration also acts as a distancing device to keep the audience from being interwoven into the dramatic narrative. The film does not resort to flashbacks, crosscuts, or melodramatic effects. What the audience observes is the subtle revelation of a threeway relation as the voice-over links past to present and desire to morality. Finally, sexual desire yields to moral principles and rational thinking. The film ends as the narrative began: the female protagonist seeing the visitor, her former lover, off from the ruins of the town walls. The absence of national subjects and melodrama's conventions makes the film, in official terms, an insignificant and apathetic work. Its significance becomes apparent only when film history and criticism consider films that dissent in topic and style from mainstream productions.[48]

Chapter Two

Reconstructing History

The (Im)possible Engagement between Feminism and Postmodernism in Stanley Kwan's *Center Stage*

ALLUSIONS TO EARLY FILMS AND film stars call on the memories of the audience and refer to the images housed in film archives. When memories and fragments are reconstructed, however, they enter a process of cinematic reproduction and cultural reinterpretation. In other words, a reconstructed history involves a mode of historiography where spatial/temporal and sociocultural displacement blurs the lines between past and present and between historical images and textual reconfigurations. Stanley Kwan's *Center Stage* (Ruan Lingyu, 1992) is such a film. It remakes the past for the comprehension of the present, and it recreates the semicolonial Shanghai of the 1930s for the postcolonial Hong Kong of the 1990s.[1]

To examine notions of history and its reconstruction, *Center Stage* employs an intertextual form that involves the film's (meta)narrative-cinematic structures: Maggie Cheung, a film star of the 1990s, plays Ruan Lingyu, a silent screen star of the 1930s;[2] a Hong Kong film crew reconstructs the classic film footages; documentary-like interviews with veteran actors and commentaries link past and present. The film thus presents the audience with a triply juxtaposed picture: Ruan's personal life story as primary source, her images framed in archival clips as representation, and the present remake as reconstruction. The film's metastructure has drawn critical interest from various interpretative slants. Julian Stringer discusses how *Center Stage* reconstructs the star image in a search for subjectivity in contemporary Hong Kong. The film's rewriting of the bio-pic, according to Stringer, raises questions about the use of multiple languages, the re-presentation of Ruan's on-screen image and off-screen persona, and the moment when "the city is discovering itself at the very moment of its disappearance."[3] Although the bio-pic image of Ruan Lingyu remains ultimately inaccessible to us, Kristine Harris annotates Ruan's fragmented stories with historical details. Harris tells of the engagement between film directors and the female image, the discourse of the new woman and its visual representations, and the role of woman in public spectacle and private domain. Kwan's *Center Stage,* Harris concludes, brings together "two golden ages of world-class cinema: early twentieth-century Shanghai and late twentieth-century Hong Kong."[4] To extend the analysis, I argue that the film's thematic concentration on the female subject in relation to film history invites a feminist reading of the film, while the interplay between past and present and China and Hong Kong promotes a postmodern consciousness.

This chapter participates in the debate over the compatibilities and contradictions between feminism and postmodernism through an analysis of Stanley Kwan's *Center Stage.* The premises from which my arguments extend suggest that conversations between these two theoretical groups have hardly found an agreeable ground. We generally concur that although postmodernism and feminism may have different primary "others" (modernism and patriarchy respectively), they share a concern for understanding systems of representation and for requestioning the master narratives, such as history and philosophy.[5] Yet while the vocabularies of the two critiques sound compatible, their fundamental principles appear contradictory. Postmodernism, with its fragmented narrative structure and metacoding system, allows no privileged position for an autonomous speaking subject. The feminist critique, however, has fought to seize a female subject position in history and in representation. As postmodern practices attempt to decode and disrupt foundational structures, feminism tries to insert gender difference into mainstream discourse. While concerned critics consider the possibilities for introducing sexual difference into postmodern critique, *Center Stage,* a production of postcolonial (Hong Kong) and postsocialist (China) conditions, problematizes the issue. The central question in this analysis asks how the film seeks to understand contemporary sociocultural transitions by reconstructing film history and female images from the past. The hypothesis I propose underscores the difficulty of merging feminist criticism with postmodern practice.

The film structure reflects the historical moment when Hong Kong returned to Chinese rule in 1997. Postmodernism is a slippery concept, and the multiplicity of meanings tagged "postmodern" can itself be read as a sign of postmodernism. As postsocialist (China) and postcolonialist (Hong Kong) societies become ever more involved in the arena of globalization, the notion of postmodernity suggests a consciousness and discourse that break national boundaries. Thus the contemporary sociohistorical, political, and economic transitions in China and Hong Kong call attention to the geopolitical imagination as a postmodern condition. Yet the possibility of speaking about China in terms of postmodernism remains controversial. A self-contradictory society where centralized political power and capitalist economics coexist, China shows signs of postmodern fragmentation: the transformation of popular culture, spreading commercialization, and application of postmodern ideas in literary and cinematic experimentation.[6] The return of Hong Kong to China marks a sudden transition from the island's British colonial past to its future in relation to Chinese communism.[7] Postmodern consciousness arises at the moment when one discovers that the world has no fixed center and that power relations are volatile in the face of sociopolitical change.

While the concerned public considers the future of Hong Kong since its return to China, serious film productions in Hong Kong have turned to the past, seeking notions of history and identity, questions long ignored in the discourse of Hong Kong. The mix of popular productions and auteur innovations should be the point of departure for a consideration of Hong Kong cinema.[8] As Hong Kong reverts to China and its films enter the global market, however, the general audience's perception of Hong Kong cinema primarily means action or kung fu films. The hybrid genre—Asian martial arts and Hollywood gangster thrillers—involves an "intricate cultural politics of screening Asian masculinity in the present setting of global entertainment."[9] Action films, though dominant among mainstream commercial productions, cannot speak for the diversity of Hong Kong cinema. Since the late 1970s, a group of auteur directors, including Ann Hui, Yim Ho, and Allen Fong, have sparked an avant-garde of Hong Kong new wave. Their films, transcending the popular norms, explore sociopolitical transitions, cultural identities, and personal styles. Following these pioneer auteurs, younger directors such as Stanley Kwan, Wong Kar Wai, and Clara Law have made the exploration more global and psychological. Diverse in theme and form, the auteur films may be said to share one obsession: Hong Kong itself as the subject of film production. For the first time, the subject of Hong Kong provokes complicated feelings, nostalgia for its past, and uncertainty about its future, an instance that Walter Benjamin would have described as love at last sight.[10]

Stanley Kwan, because of his female-centered films, has earned a reputation as a director of "women's pictures." The orientation of Kwan's cinema toward the feminine and its place in a moment of historical transition calls attention to the interrelations among Hong Kong, gender, and history. In seven feature films and two documentaries, Kwan takes an unusual slant in examining questions of past and present through articulations of the female image. *Rouge* (1987) traces how a courtesan of the 1930s returns as a ghost to modern Hong Kong to look for her lover. *Center Stage* (1992) resurrects a missing female star and 1930s film history through a cinematic remake. In his documentary production *Yang and Yin: Gender in Chinese Cinema* (1996), Kwan discusses the missing father in his personal life and in Chinese films, exposes his homosexual identity, and expresses his dedication to issues of transvestism and trans-sexuality. Because putting woman into discourse intersects with his reexamination of history, Stanley Kwan's films situate "women as intrinsic to the development of new postmodern modes of speaking and writing."[11]

IMAGE AND VOICE

In its pretitle sequence, *Center Stage* indicates a special concern for the disappearance and reappearance of history. Two interreflexive female images—Ruan Lingyu and Maggie Cheung—become the core visual icons of the reconstruction. With Ruan and Maggie as signifiers of China in the 1930s and Hong Kong in the 1990s respectively, woman as image and as connotation forges an intertextuality between past and present. The insertion of voice-over narration serves to bridge image with sound, history with explanation. As a cinematic motif, the voice-over entails a power of enunciation and commentary with narrator unseen and sound source unknown. Because of its detachment from any specific space and time, the voice-over—"a disembodied voice" as Doane defines it[12]—assumes different functions when seen from postmodern or feminist perspectives.

The disembodied voice acts to initiate on-screen narrative, generate off-screen interpretation, and address the audience directly. First, a sense of history emerges through archival female images. In the opening credits, tilts, pans, and dissolves introduce a series of photographs and framed film stills. Each shot heightens the silent image of a woman and her films: celluloid records of a certain past. We do not immediately know to whose past the pictures refer or in what sociocultural framework the stills were produced.

The past comes to us as texts without contexts—fragments isolated from the time and space of their cultural/cinematic production. Instead of a "flashback" that resituates the female image in history, a voice-over explains that "these are the early stills when Ruan starts her film career at 16. Some of the copies are *no longer available*. Given casual roles, Ruan often plays minor characters in folklore, romance, and even spooky action films. Only when she joins Lianhua in 1929 does she play serious characters."[13] The voice that lingers over the absence of the past—unavailable film copies and unknowable personal experience—indicates a sense of history in disappearance. The conjunction of silent images and the inserted voice, however, declares the emergence of history in reconstruction.

The narrator not only attempts to define who Ruan Lingyu was, but also introduces Maggie Cheung, who will be Ruan's reincarnation. The photographic images from 1930s China and the visual figure from modern Hong Kong, when set in the same frame, suggest a temporal and spatial transition from past to present. The voice-over then invites the on-screen female figure to comment on the silent image she enacts, while addressing the audience, which overhears their conversations. The double coding of on-screen representation and off-screen enunciation demonstrates textual strategy. Maggie first relates the past image to herself: "Isn't she a *replica* of me?" The displacement of Maggie with Lingyu—a postmodern allusion to a historical figure—transforms the past female image from memory to narrative. The identification of "me" in the present with "she" in the past indicates self-consciousness about the historiographic interrelation between woman as historical image and woman as enacting agent. The rhetorical question seems to ask, as an actress might, Where should I situate myself when associated with the actress in the past? A further inquiry can be inferred: Where should Hong Kong situate itself in a moment of sociohistorical transition?

The intertextual encounter between the past image and the present impersonator suggests that history comes into meaning when memory faces a moment marked by its emergence and disappearance. The unseen voice-over narrator raises a further question of memory and history. The voice asks Maggie, "People still *remember* Ruan Lingyu after she committed suicide almost half a century ago. Do you want people to remember you?" Maggie replies: "It's not very important whether the audience will *remember* me. Even if they do so, it will be different from the way they think of Ruan, because she is now a *legend*." This exchange between the female protagonist within the frame and the voice off-screen marks a moment when memory as legend fades out and history as re-presentation takes form. The refusal to speak about Ruan Lingyu in the framework of memory raises the possibility of setting the past as history and of situating the female self apart from yet linked to the legendary figure. Maggie's response to the director's question clearly indicates that *Center Stage* will never be a work of memory only, but a work of re-presentation different from and in relation to that memory.

The desire to understand present-day culture in relation to the past is a postmodern impulse. The search for a female subject, missing in history yet centered in representation, is a feminist tension. Feminist criticism has taken gender difference as a process of producing meaning. From this perspective, an inquiry into the female image and film history might begin by asking how woman is constructed in the history of cinematic representation. Does she have a voice or subjectivity of her own? If the response is negative, the feminist critique will reexamine and reenvision the representation. Precisely the disembodiment, which generates a postmodern vantage on history in terms of the female image, separates the female voice from the female body and allows an autonomy of female subjectivity.

The introductory voice-over projects a male voice from the present to the silent female image of the past. A process of discourse production occurs where the female body presents a narrative world and the male voice generates a discursive authority. The voice and the image, therefore, indicate a "treacherous course" between postmodern and feminist practices.[14] From a feminist perspective, the silence conceals a woman's history: Ruan's life story and her films in the 1930s. The female image, preserved in archival form and presented in silence, suggests a historical subject but not the subject of history. From a postmodern point of view, the film is not interested in locating the missing history of the female subject but in reconstructing history through re-presentation. The narrator's cinematic detachment from the image track and sociocultural distance from the past reinforce the discursive power embedded in the voice. The female image is seen but not heard; the male voice is heard while its source remains unseen. The voice promises to project its authoritative knowledge to the female body, convert female images into historical metaphors, and use the images for the discursive production of history.

When the audience discovers that the voice belongs to Stanley Kwan, the voice-over assumes directorial authority in controlling the intersection of on-screen narrative and off-screen enunciation. We witness the participation of the male voice in the creation of discourse and the use of the female body in the construction of re-presentation. The introductory narration separates voice from the female body, while the directorial authority replaces Ruan Lingyu with Maggie, thereby supplanting the silenced female image with an enacting impersonator. The conversation between the director in voice-over and the character in diegesis cleverly links the authorial voice with the figural modes. Moreover, the metastructural (dis)placement reinforces the positions of the speaking subject and the spoken figure. For instance, Ruan's film footages remain historical references in the background. Maggie appears to speak for the silenced image. As the directorial voice-over in his extradiegetic position poses questions and guides Maggie to comment on Ruan Lingyu, the voice alludes simultaneously to the temporal, spatial, and sociocultural engagement of past with present, history with explanation, and China with Hong Kong.

The distance between the male voice and the female images associates the voice-over directly with the audience. As the voice-over assumes multiple positions—introductory, directorial, and participatory—it precludes the possible insertion of a female voice or point of view. When disembodiment reinforces the voice as a mastering device over the female body, a postmodern hegemony is born in the name of decentering the subject and denouncing the masters. After the film clearly announces its postmodern intentions, the title, *Ruan Lingyu,* finally appears, its three Chinese characters (translated as Actress or Center Stage) laid over Ruan's photographic image. In terms of a cinematic remaking, the question remains how to represent history and for what purpose.

Ruan Lingyu, 1992

THE ORIGINAL AND THE REMAKE

The remake, a particular cinematic form, establishes referentiality between the "original" and itself and thus becomes intelligible in terms of the prior text that it cites, reiterates, revises, and transforms. "Unique in its facility to replay and repeat its own form," the cinematic apparatus, as Anne Friedberg indicates, can do the task of "being them and mocking them at the same time."[15] However, as Linda Hutcheon concludes, "Any return to history will bring forth not the history of ordinary reality but the world of discourse in which these texts are situated." Whatever we can grasp as "past" is ineluctably textual: "There is no directly and naturally accessible past 'real' for us today: we can only know and construct the past through its traces, its representations."[16]

Alternation between the archival segments and the corresponding remakes constitutes the primary narrative/cinematic structure of *Center Stage*. Taking the remakes as contemporary allusions to the early film sequences, *Center Stage* relies on an intertextual structure to seek to explain the referent—namely, to reconstruct a history from fragments of a vanished past. In viewing the two texts simultaneously, the audience is aware that the original already exists as a form of referential illusion (Ruan Lingyu's films as visual re-presentation). While the reconstruction can reveal and interpret the process of production, it is unable to provide access to the historical realities. The intention of the remake, therefore, is to explore the possible connections among constructed realities and a lost referent.

The first example of the remake begins with a screening of *Goddess*, the classic silent work made in Shanghai in 1934 (dir. Wu Yonggang, Lianhua Studios). A prostitute framed within the screen approaches a potential client, but a policeman interferes and the prostitute tries to escape. *Center Stage* then cuts to the present filming site, where the remake continues the scene while the old segment fades out. The intertextual crosscutting of the early text and the present reproduction self-reflexively suggests a shift in female image from Ruan to Maggie, in spatial/temporal location from Shanghai to Hong Kong, and in discursive development from historical narrative to present reconstruction.

The connection between the original and the remake raises the potential for parody. From a postmodern perspective, parody can be a gold mine of referential complexities. The concept of parody, in Hutcheon's terms, refers to the process of "incorporating textualized past into the text of the present," suggesting an emphasis on the idea of textualization or articulation.[17] The fragment from the archival film *Goddess* comes to us as a form of re-presentation detached from the historical or discursive context of the

Goddess (remake), 1992

film's production and reception. The remaking of *Goddess*, then, enacts visually the preexisting text by revealing piece by piece the filming process by which the early film gets remade. In other words, the re-presentation of *Goddess* turns into its reproduction. As the progeny of the classic film it replaces, the remake announces itself secondary, but at the same time it insists that it is more than the original, in a way prior to it, its presenter and interpreter. In sum, the remake reinscribes and transforms the re-presentation of the cultural past with a double coding of then and now. A feminist inquiry, however, looks for what is missing or suppressed in the process of remaking.

While cinematic contrasts such as silent versus talkie or black and white versus color mark the visual transition of past text to present remake, the subject of woman in history and in representation (i.e., the referent) is erased. *Goddess* concerns a loving mother who must become a prostitute to support her son. The film's title, which can be translated as either "goddess" or "prostitute," indicates a woman's polar identities in a traditional society. She is at once a virtuous mother and a lowly street woman sacrificing and selling her body in order to pay for her son's education. The directorial focus on woman's dual positions emphasizes her social and patriarchal burdens: good mother in the sense of Confucian virtue and a prostitute in terms of female sexuality. The film visually demonstrates the female protagonist's dual position in terms of private and public space. When city lights go on in the cosmopolitan city of Shanghai, the prostitute walks the streets to attract customers. Close-up shots of parts of the female body—her feet, face, and legs—transform the woman into an object of sexual fetish. When the lights fade and the sun rises, the prostitute hurries home and becomes a dutiful mother caring for her child. As the camera pans through the domestic space, her *qipao* (traditional dress) and cosmetics remind the audience of her dual identities, superimposed through the image of the mother and the dress of the prostitute. The cinematic depiction of the street and the home, the conflation of prostitute and mother, earned *Goddess* a reputation as one of the best classic films in Chinese film history and won Ruan Lingyu fame as the queen of Chinese cinema.

The ambivalent relationship between intertextual interventions and female subjectivity becomes apparent when fragments are extracted from the original and transferred into the remake. For instance, the remake inserts simultaneously a speaking subject, a within-the-screen director, and an enacting actress, Maggie as Ruan. The use of another voice to explain the female image indicates a problematic exchange between the perspectives of postmodernism and gender. When the on-screen director interprets the old text and directs the new, the voice entails a discursive power, remaking as well as annotating history. When Maggie impersonates Ruan, mimicking her every bodily gesture, however, she only duplicates an image, changing from black and white to color. In other words, the female images, either framed in the original or screened as impersonation, correspond to the directorial voice. The voice controls the discourse of enunciation, while the female images (past and present) remain silent and duplicated. Because of the film's concern about textual reconstruction rather than gender difference, the remake allows neither female voice nor female identity.

The question of why a postmodern production mutes the female voice and thereby neglects woman's subjectivity and identity can be elaborated through the notion of fragmentation. The remake presents mere fragments of a twice-told tale, first in silence and later with an interpretive gloss. The fragmentation disconnects the subject of woman as a loving mother and a prostitute from the textual entirety and the sociocultural context. After she is dislocated from the nexus of history and the language of gender identity, woman's historical and social particularities—serious concerns of feminism—disappear. To understand the erasure, one might consider the opposition of the theoretical domains of postmodernism and feminism. The postmodern remaking from fragments denies the analysis of meaning concealed in the text yet favors structural operations. Fragmented narratives, characters, and images are useful elements for a present reconstruction because unrelated pieces will confuse and deconstruct master concepts of centrality and originality. When no subject position can be assumed and no historical originality can be traced, feminist theory has great difficulty in finding a discursive position from which the feminine can articulate itself.

SELF-REFLEXIVITY AND CINEMATIC APPARATUS

Efforts to reconstruct the original through the remake end with a realization of difficulty. The film director then turns to film's own medium for a self-reflexive exposure of the filmmaking process. The concept of self-reflexivity refers to "the process by which texts foreground their own production, their authorship, their intertextual influences, their textual processes, or their reception."[18] Moreover, self-reflexivity in cinema might well include "the designation of the apparatus (cameras, monitors, switches); the disruption of narrative flow; the juxtaposition of heterogeneous slices of discourses; and the mixing of documentary and fictive modes."[19] By turning inward to its own medium of expression, *Center Stage* explores the potentials and limitations of the cinematic form toward an ever changing social world. Since the reflexive mode self-consciously draws attention to textual interventions, it reveals yet conceals women's issues in history and in re-presentation.

The following example demonstrates the different readings produced when the text is treated from either a postmodern or feminist approach. The final image of *Goddess* fades out, and the film cuts to a new interior setting where Maggie, on a hospital bed, is rehearsing a scene. Hearing the order of "Cut" from off-screen, we see another within-the-screen director (Liang Jiahui, who plays Cai Chusheng, a director in the 1930s) instructing Maggie on how to play Ruan Lingyu in a film sequence. The image track shows Maggie repeating her lines while the sound track delivers the director's orders: "Ready, camera, action." The remake brings no satisfaction, however. The acting director orders the sequence shot one more time. After a number of crosscuts between Maggie and Liang, the film surprisingly introduces the camera and the cinematographer to the screen, self-reflexively exposing the shooting apparatus to the audience. Moreover, the following high-angle master shot frames the entire film crew—the actors, the director, and the camera—in a single mise-en-scène, freezing the moment of making a film about filmmaking. As the present remake dissolves into the classic film footage, subtitles set against the original image of Ruan Lingyu finally inform us that the film crew is remaking a sequence from the classic *The New Woman*, the silent film directed by Cai Chusheng in 1935.

The remake of the film in the 1990s finds it difficult to convert the image and voice into re-presentation. Constraints on the female voice result precisely from the absence of woman's "other"—namely, the traditional suppression and media humiliation of "new women." The question of how the female subject can be re-presented when her other—the patriarchal discourse—is absent and when one can hardly define a privileged position for the female speaking subject remains problematic and debatable between postmodern practice and feminist interpretation. Keeping this contradiction in mind, we might reflect on the impossible merger between the two theoretical critiques. Maggie, the contemporary star playing a star, tries in vain to repeat the final outcry—"I want to live and I want revenge"—in all its dynamic power. In its fragmented form, the remake is unable to explain to enactor and audience why she wants to live and against whom she wants revenge. Repeating the lines but not the lost voice, Maggie fails to utter the female experience silent in history. The female voice cannot be articulated without the presence of an opposing social discourse.

Center Stage turns to its own medium of expression to explain why the female voice struggles to find expression. Maggie has indulged herself in the emotion of the character and starts to sob under the white blanket. Liang, playing the director, sits by the side of her bed. In a single long and high-angle shot, the take captures not only the two characters within the frame, but also the cameras, the monitor, the switches, and the technicians around them. Stanley Kwan, the director of *Center Stage,* enters the frame with another moving camera to remind Liang: "You forgot to lift up the blanket to have a look at Maggie." The self-reflexive apparatus constitutes a metacinematic structure of film-within-a-film, director-directing-director, and camera-exposing-camera. At the moment when one shot places the metacinematic apparatus in a single frame, a reflective audience will recognize that the entire process of revelation becomes possible only because there is one more camera off-screen.

The self-reflexive revelation foregrounds the filming process as the most fundamentally problematic aspect of re-presentation. When re-presentation and the articulation of re-presentation are exposed at once in front of the audience, the conventional notion of film production and perception—a question of cinematic apparatus—requires new explanation. In modern film theory, the concept of a cinematic apparatus stresses the interrelation between technology and ideology. Instances of the cinematic apparatus, according to Jacqueline Rose, include "the ontology of the visible" (visual images and narrative construction), "the process of production" (film as an institutional and industrial commodity), and "the process of projection" (the spectator's identification with camera and fiction).[20] The perceptual subject is positioned to recognize the concealment of the mechanical operation, which constitutes the ideological effect.

If the cinematic apparatus conceals its construction of reality, then the self-reflexivity in metacinema, and in *Center Stage* particularly, engenders "a constant *double encoding*—inscribing and subverting prevailing conventions."[21] Exposure of the filming process disrupts the narrative flow and undermines the notion of a coherent and self-sufficient subject as the source of meaning or action. The presence of cameras, monitors, and technicians erases the usual concealment of the mechanism, dissolving the line between cinematic re-presentation and the articulation of re-presentation. Film narrative and film production coexist in the same screen. This double or even multiple encoding suggests the kind of "fundamental and sustained opposition" that Patricia Waugh sees as characteristic of metafiction: "The construction of a fictional illusion and the laying bare of that illusion; to create a fiction and to make a statement about the creation of that fiction. The two processes are held together in a formal tension which breaks down the distinctions between creation and criticism and merges them into the concepts of interpretation and deconstruction."[22] But what happens to the experience of the spectator when self-reflexivity seeks to re-present not another motion picture but the filming process itself?

Postmodern spectatorship takes shape when motion pictures no longer offer a primary cinematic identification or mirror reflection. Instead, there emerges a moment of crisis and change in the consciousness of spectatorship. Initially, when the self-reflexive mode blocks the audience's desire to know the world through transparent illusions, the inability to position oneself within a cognitive viewing/showing space causes frustration. Second, metastructure denies the viewer a focal point or "window on the world" in favor of asserted multiple perspectives. The experience of viewing becomes a feeling of being lost in a world transformed into sheer images of itself (or a world processing its own mechanism as simulacrum).[23] Moreover, the disruption of narrative coherence and continuity creates further frustration. With the intrusion of off-screen revelations, the master narrative collapses: Why does the current film refuse to tell me what the film *The New Woman* is about? What is the relation of this present remake to the film history of the 1930s? Who is that female image Maggie fails to reenact? The audience sees ample signifiers yet cannot locate the signified. Furthermore, when the cinematic apparatus joins the mise-en-scène and the film crew appears as screen characters, the audience cannot fully identify with the character, the fiction, or the camera. Thus, postmodern reflexivity stresses not a single identity or subjectivity, but the fragmentation of subjectivity.

As the audience becomes aware that "meaning" is constructed primarily through an internal processing system, the new question of postmodern spectatorship is whether to reject or to participate in the creative process. As Wheeler Winston Dixon observes, "The instances of reflexive film practice incorporate the audience into the work—not as a by-product of exhibition and reception, but as an essential part of the entire apparatus of cinema."[24] The multiple encoding system, which articulates and at the same time mocks its own articulation, situates the spectator as a critical receiver as well as a participant producer. The critical receiver recognizes the process of film production and its fragmented suggestiveness and acknowledges the crisis in re-presentation. Drawn into the process of articulation, the film audience takes up spectatorship as critique. When a self-addressed filming process depends on its viewers to convert and complete its construction of meaning, the relationship between film and audience shifts from one of exhibition and perception to one of production and inscription—an interactive co-creation.

While the remade text offers neither a privileged viewing position nor an autonomous identity, feminist criticism questions the positioning of woman as mere image or, in Doane's definition, as "the focal point of an address."[25] The study of female spectatorship, therefore, takes woman's positioning as the point of departure for an examination of repressed female subjectivity. Since the postmodern remake disrupts this focal point of address with its multiplicity of re-presentations, it opens up diverse positions for female spectatorship. After close observation, we notice that the modern woman in the "original" and in the remake remains as image, already present or waiting to be re-presented. The remake is anxious about the process of reproducing the female image while controlling female subjectivity. As the director and his casting crew assume the role of commentator, the film refuses the woman the position of a speaking subject. When the cinematic apparatus invades the film screen and interferes with narrative continuity, the subverted re-presentation denies a focal point of address for female spectatorship. As a result, we have to conclude that while the postmodern remake opens up possibilities for subverting conventional representations, at the same time it frustrates feminist attempts to pursue female subjectivity. In taking history as a textual form, postmodernism emphasizes the process of textual construction and the revelation of that process. Women remain as historical images but do not assume historical subjectivity.

DOCUMENT AND DOCUMENTARY

In addition to self-reflexive exposure of the cinematic system, *Center Stage*'s structural transitions juxtapose fictive narratives with "documentary" illustrations. The insertion of archival photos and videotaped interviews—what historians would call documentation—challenges the conventional relation between history and documentary. "The document," as Hutcheon observes, "can no longer pretend to be a transparent means to a past event; it is instead the textually transformed trace of that past."[26] The photographed historical figures and recorded video images, as they participate in the reconstruction, again pose the question of how to know the past when it comes to us as texts. The director of *Center Stage* self-consciously reveals the nature of photographed images and videotaped interviews as a process of postmodern connotation.

As the following analysis demonstrates, Kwan introduces archival photos to the audience yet at the same time undermines their status as historical documents. A quick camera pan reveals two press photographs. An accompanying voice-over explains that these are photos of Zhang Damin and Tang Jishan, Ruan's male partners in the 1930s. Each figure in its photographic form indicates the presence of an absence: the emblem of a past that has long been lost to history. In its visual yet mute form, the photographed image presents a historical figure shorn of explanation. Kwan spent great effort to find these two archival photos, not so much to collect documentary evidence as to provide an "original reference" for his cinematic reproduction. In transforming the silent image into an animated character, *Center Stage* attempts not to render photographic images as history but to reveal the arbitrariness of the two visual forms—photography and cinema—as mechanical recreation and reproduction. Thus the film reinforces the idea that consciousness of history is mediated by re-presentation.

When the sequence cuts immediately from the photographed figures to the actors who play them, the film exposes the contradictory or arbitrary nature of the relation between documentary reference and re-presentation. The two actors who impersonate the past suggested by the photographs reinforce the paratextual meaning of document and re-presentation by questioning the original figures they play. Instead of a seamless restaging, we see the actor address what happens to the character from the past whom he performs; we hear the directorial voice-over providing an answer to the inquiry. The distance between the enactor and the enacted challenges the idea that documents provide a transparent window on history. Dialogue between the film characters and the director emphasizes the contemporary interpretation of historical documents, not their authenticity. As the actors express their uncertainties about the historical persons they play, the film self-reflexively educates the audience to read history and the past as multiply structured re-presentations, whether photographic or cinematic.

In addition, the film inserts taped interviews of historical eyewitnesses to legitimize as well as to subvert the meanings of history. The insertion of the videos and film actors' comments about the interviews, however, calls the documentary into question. In the first videotaped sequence, an interviewee describes in Chinese the moment of Ruan's suicidal death. The subtitle reads: "1990, Li Lili, actress of the 1930s." While the audience is ready to assume Li Lili's status as historical eyewitness, the subtitle immediately exposes a temporal and spatial displacement: the story and the character of the 1930s have been narrated and framed in the 1990s. The displacement, while simulating documentary authenticity, indicates an attempt to see the past from a postmodern perspective. Given this point of view, we can discern a discursive interplay between *taped* narrative and *projected* commentary. The former comes to expression as memories and the latter as enunciation through mechanical articulation. In other words, the film sutures the viewer to mechanically recorded memories while simultaneously revealing that suture through a voice-over narration. Such self-exposure becomes further reinforced when the sequence cuts to the film crew watching the taped interview as an audience-within-the-film. Thus the audience of the film is encouraged to identify with the audience-within-the-film, viewing and recognizing together the recorded representation we call "history."

The question raised in the following video segment concerns whether the recorded image embodies a documentary truth or a documentary effect. The video screen introduces Sun Yu, a veteran film director of the 1930s. The subtitle again reminds the audience that the segment has been recorded in 1990. Unlike Li Lili, who recounts the past from memory, Sun Yu has lost his memories to ill health and aging and remains a silent image. From a directorial voice-over, we learn that Stanley Kwan offered the veteran director an album of old photographs so as to jog his memories. Sun Yu is unable to recognize them at all, and a month later he passes away. In a moment when the silent image suggests that history and memory have faded away, the taped historical figure entails only a documentary effect, not documentary authenticity. As the historical person remains an image subject to the voice-over interpretation, the audience will not confuse documentary

evidence with the filmmaker's hypothesis. In speaking for the historical figure and tracing his lost memories, the present film director experiments with
a postmodern production where history emerges as less a matter of stories
than of images. The voice of narration does not so much explain historicity
as self-consciously pose that important postmodern question: "How exactly
is it that we come to know the past?"[27]

In the film's final video presentation, attention is given to the discursive
interactions between taped narrative and inserted commentary. The video
screen introduces Maggie, the interviewer, and Chen Yanyan, the interviewee, with the subtitle "1991, an actress of the 1930s." While Chen recalls her
relationship with Ruan Lingyu in the old days, the camera pans across each
cast member as an audience commenting on Chen Yanyan. Each comment
focuses not on Ruan Lingyu, an historical absence, but on Chen Yanyan as
historical eyewitness. A moment of confusion follows: who is telling the
story, and whose story is being told? When the historical account becomes an
open subject upon which players project their comments, the film subverts
the notion of historical totality in favor of multiple explanations. The intrusion of commentary precludes narrative continuity and filmic coherence,
while the voice-over explanation provides contemporary angles on the past.

Center Stage is not primarily interested in defining the meaning of the
documentary texts. The video insertions ultimately inscribe as well as subvert the absent history (Ruan Lingyu and her early films). The (dis)con-
nection between the female subject and the presence of multimedia
reproduction makes the possibility of talking about female subjectivity in
relation to postmodernism even more problematic. To consider the problem in terms of the cinematic signifying system, we might take the videotaped interviews of historical eyewitnesses as the signifier and the absent
female subject as the signified. The signification then suggests an arbitrary
relation where the documented texts mark the absence and the lack. Since
the film crew emphasizes the documentary effect, not the evidence, the
arbitrary relationship between signifier and signified collapses. Postmodern
practice, while scoffing at conventional signification, prevents a feminist
search for the missing female subject. In a quest for the lost voice or identity, feminist criticism must address gender difference and/in representation. Unfortunately, because of the complete erasure of the female subject
from representation, any attempt to recover the difference becomes
impossible. The erasure opens up textual space for inscription but denies
the gender spectrum in which a woman's history might be located. Taped
interviews that reinscribe Ruan Lingyu's life stories from the memory fragments of historical witnesses merely interpret or recreate history. In the

form of video images produced in spatial/temporal displacement, history becomes a set of mobile texts, continually (re)produced in different forms.

(IM)POSSIBLE ENDINGS

In her study of metafiction, Patricia Waugh notes how "metafictional texts often end with a choice of endings, or they may end with a sign of the impossibility of ending."[28] In its attempt at closure, *Center Stage* strives to reach possible endings. Ruan's suicidal death, while putting a literal end to the female protagonist's life and punctuating her filmic narrative, engenders multiple visual interpretations. Self-reflexive alternations between the end of the narrative and the cinematic process of that ending further reinforce the question of how to define history and whether history entails an ending.

In a farewell party for Mr. Skinner, who has introduced a recording facility to the Lianhua film studio, the film characters become excited about the possibility of speaking on-screen. Ruan, however, announces that she will give an upcoming presentation in Mandarin on the subject of women. The explicit message announces the coming of sound to Chinese motion pictures in the 1930s; the implicit message suggests the emergence of a female voice in the wake of gender consciousness. The paradoxical inter-textuality of cinematic sound and the female voice opens up an (im)possible communication between postmodernism and feminist criticism. As the film narrative continues, however, the audience senses Ruan's difficulty in utter-ing a female voice, even as sound comes to motion pictures. Ruan tries a couple of phrases in Mandarin yet confesses that she cannot speak the lan-guage well and has to change into Shanghai dialect or Cantonese. Simulta-neously, we hear Ruan's friend translating Ruan's words into English for the American guest, Mr. Skinner. In a metalingual moment, Ruan's inability to speak Mandarin or English—master languages—foreshadows her inability to voice her internal feelings. With a suicidal plan in mind that she cannot confess, however, Ruan instead kisses each film director and pieces together the history of her film career in relation to each director's mentorship.

A following series of crosscuts links Ruan with each film director and attempts to establish a narrative coherence, using different spatial/tempo-ral frames. After Ruan kisses each director to express her gratitude, the film crosscuts immediately to Ruan's death scene: what has been narrated in one frame becomes interpreted visually in another. As the camera switches back and forth in crosscutting, the editing strategy alternates the position of speaking subject. In one frame, Ruan will start to introduce a director; in another, the director, sitting by her deathbed, comments on Ruan's life. A subtle transition from woman as speaking subject to woman as object to be commented upon by her mentors again reflects problems in the relation of postmodernism and feminism. We see an ironic contradiction where, on the one hand, the film narrative attempts to construct an autobiographical female self by allowing her to speak of history, while, on the other hand, the crosscutting denies this possibility as it shifts from film narrative to filming process. In sum, from a postmodern point of view, the subject "must be first differentiated from a living human being [and] is always a socially and culturally constructed *position*."[29] The subject position always undergoes the process of shifting and (re)construction. Feminist criticism also emphasizes the sociocultural position or construction of subject and subjectivity. Whereas the postmodern text strives to uncover the ongoing process of (re)construction—the sociocultural in textual terms—feminist critique, in its analysis of subjectivity, clearly seeks to recover the subject that is female, often a repressed or marginalized "other."

As it ends her personal history, Ruan's death suggests the potential ending of the film. The cinematic articulation of the death mise-en-scène, however, initiates a renewed sense of filmic activity. Crosscutting continues to blur the distinction between narrative construction and cinematic deconstruction. The alternation becomes so absurd that the viewer might properly feel confused about whether to experience tragedy in Ruan's death or pleasure in seeing the filming process. The dead body of Ruan Lingyu in close-up fills the frame while the sound track's melody of lament intensifies the atmosphere of mourning. At the moment when the audience thoroughly immerses itself in the mood, we hear the director's order to cut because Maggie begins breathing. The "invasion" of the screen by camera, cast, and director radically violates the conventional definition of the film frame and mocks the audience's perceptual conventions. Framed within the screen, the director self-consciously explains that he has only one photo of Ruan's final moment. He has to concoct an ending for Ruan's life and the film through imaginative creation and arbitrary articulation.

Finally, *Center Stage* puts film narrative and the filming process into a single frame. We see the acting "director" stress his final remarks on Ruan's death while Ruan rises up from her "deathbed" to let an assistant add makeup to her face. Clearly, the cinematic vision foregrounds not so much the scene of Ruan's death as the cinematic articulation of the death mise-en-scène. After remaking numerous fragments of histories and uncovering the process of doing so, *Center Stage* ends where it began: an archival relic of Ruan Lingyu, history as image and text. The process of reconstructing that past, however, has engaged the energies of producers and viewers.

Part Two

Socialist Cinema

Chapter Three

Constructing and Consuming
the Revolutionary Narratives

THE TRANSITION TO A MARKET economy and the rise of consumer culture have turned contemporary China into a society that cannot be easily defined as either socialist or capitalist. This ambiguity, as well as the swelling multiplicity of cultural forms at the end of the twentieth century, is evident in such extraordinary phenomena as the "Red wave" and "Mao fever."[1] A "Red wave" of commercially packaged revolutionary songs, plays, and films not only floods the market, but also feeds a certain nostalgia for the totalitarian past. In 1991, China's audio-video bureau distributed and sold 5.5 million copies of an audiocassette entitled *Red Sun* within six months. In 1996, organizers from the China Institute of Art restaged a series of revolutionary plays, including the ballets *The White-Haired Girl* and *The Red Detachment of Women*, and the musical *The Long March*. In 1999, more than five hundred old films formerly concealed in archives inaccessible to the public poured into the market in VCD form.[2] To an outside observer, it is astonishing how past revolutionary artifacts and present commercial packaging have so seamlessly come together.[3]

The cult of Mao shows the unusual engagement between the old, state-controlled mass culture and the new, market-driven popular culture. At the moment when the past reemerges in commercial and entertaining forms, I am intrigued by the question of how to define these intertwined cultural phenomena in the context of postsocialist China. How does a socialist cinema under political censorship and with a state-run production system manage to pursue ideological ends to instruct a mass audience? In addition, how can a national apparatus, so different and isolated from the rest of the world, survive in its socialist forms? Taking these primary questions as points of departure, I will examine the socialist film production system in relation to the state's socialist ideology and the conditions of contemporary mass culture.

SOCIALIST CINEMA

In a chronological sense, socialist cinema refers to film production from 1949 to 1966, the period from the establishment of the People's Republic of China (PRC) to the beginning of the Cultural Revolution. Film production under the censorship of the Chinese Communist Party (CCP) changed from the cinema of social criticism to a cinema of state apparatus. The process transformed a director-centered and studio-owned popular medium for the urban audience into a state-controlled, ideologically censored institution for the masses.

Specific criteria for film production emphasized workers, peasants, and soldiers as both the filming and viewing subjects—the characters portrayed on-screen and the audience of the film. The film characters typically appeared as either oppressed proletarians to be saved or counterrevolutionaries to be defeated and were usually depicted in the easily recognized categories of proletarian/landlord and hero/villain. The central character, or narrator, takes the form of a prototypical hero or heroine who acts as a mouthpiece for the state and a social model for the audience. In order to enlarge a character's heroic stature, extensive use of close-ups places the hero in the center of the frame, distinct from and superior to everyday reality. A preference for montage editing visually reinforces the viewers' sense of the hero's dominance over events.

Neither the narrator nor the generalized characters, however, can dominate the filmic narration. Beyond them lies the agency of the discourse that relates the film narrative to "progressive" social attitudes. This sociopolitical discourse dominates the film's diegetic world and participates directly in the film's enunciation. A conventional pattern of film narrative unfolds in the following manner: a conflict between the proletariat and corrupt overlords arises, and an idealized character arrives to champion the cause of the poor and prevail against the rich. If the relationship between the hero and his working-class followers appears to reach an impasse, a background power, either the Communist Party's current policy or a political event, will issue a solution to the crisis, ensuring that the hero triumphs and the cause of the proletariat advances.

The engagement between character and spectator, between representation and perception, operates through what Louis Althusser calls interpellation:

> Ideology "acts" or "functions" in such a way that it recruits subjects among the individuals (it recruits them all), or "transforms" the individuals into subjects (it transforms them all) by that very precise operation which I have called interpellation or hailing, and which can be imagined along the lines of the most common everyday police hailing: "Hey, you there!"
>
> Assuming that the theoretical scene I have imagined takes place in the street, the hailed individual will turn round. By this mere one-hundred-and-eighty-degree physical conversion, he becomes a subject. Why? Because he has recognized that the hail was "really" addressed to him, and that "it was really him who was hailed."[4]

A question that needs further examination is how ideology and cinema as a system of representation "hail" or "interpellate" not just individuals, but also a collective subject of the mass audience.

First, socialist cinema, in terms of construction and perception, emphasizes an imaginary relationship that ties mass spectators to their social conditions of existence. Film viewing is a fresh experience for a proletarian class newly labeled the masters of the society. The moving images and unfolding narrative constitute a sociohistorical world both familiar and utopian to the eyes of the mass audience. Viewers are situated in socially and historically specific settings: class oppressions in the old society, poverty and suffering under poor living conditions, wartime combat, and political struggle with counterrevolutionary forces. The familiar world offers the viewer a subject position as either a victim of class oppression or a participant in the revolution. The audience readily identifies with this position because film constitutes its images and narratives from the perspective of the proletarian class and in the language of communist ideology.

In addition, identification with the peasants, workers, and soldiers on the screen further conceptualizes the spectator-as-subject because of shared class identities. The viewer senses becoming an integral part of the totalitarian image projected onto the screen. Under real film viewing conditions, representation and perception could become so intertwined that viewers often threw trash at alien characters or shared solidarity with class fellows on the screen. Audience involvement with the screen representation recalls Jacques Lacan's concept of a mirror image, where the child sees the image of himself in the mirror and takes it as an imaginary identity defined by self-other or absence-presence. Althusser suggests that "such recognition and misrecognition work as well in the social world at the level of the ideological; the human subject is given back through ideology an imaginary construction of his own autonomy, unity, and self-presence."[5]

What is given back to the proletarian spectator is not so much individual autonomy as a collective class status. Perception and representation engage both the collective body of the mass audience and the totalitarian authority of the state, with the former on the receiving end of the production line. Viewers do not find identities of their own; the ideology embedded in cinematic representation provides them with social identities. As the film representation typically unfolds as a melodrama of class struggle or ideological persuasion, viewers find no space for projecting personal desires onto the screen. They must choose to side with either the proletarian figure or the reactionary villain. Bonnie McDougall, in her study of popular literature and performing arts in China, explains that "the mass audience in contemporary China exercises very little choice. . . . Its choice is circumscribed by an authority that is more concerned with what the masses should have than with what they want."[6]

The engagement between representation and perception goes beyond the imaginary relation and moves into a symbolic sphere. Ideological interpolation encourages its proletarian spectator to transcend the identity of one oppressed by the old society and to ascend as a master of the new state. This attractive proposition inspires an urgent need to learn to speak the socialist language and adopt the socialist attitude. Under such sociopolitical circumstances, cinema is seen as the perfect medium to carry out such an educational mission. Cinema as a visual and ideological apparatus produces and distributes uplifting messages: the newly established socialist state promises a bright future for the masses, secures national identity against international bullies, and pursues economic power at a rapid pace. In keeping with such propagandistic claims, filmmaking offers model figures such as the revolutionary hero, the noble worker, or the stalwart party member. Identification with them, however, is unlikely because these figures are larger than life and far from ordinary. They are models for emulation and not for identification. Inspired by social supermodels yet without hope of becoming one of them, the members of the mass audience align themselves with the characters who need to be enlightened, saved, and educated by the elite models through ideological discourse. Film perception, as a result, is a process of repressing one's self-consciousness and displacing subjectivity in favor of ideology.

In addition to ideological interpellation, socialist film discourse ultimately rests on a gender structure. Since 1949, socialist China has promised women the legitimate right to enter the public realm and has represented them to the outside world as "the upholders of half the sky." The discourse of Chinese women's liberation since that time has created a myth, one that after each revolutionary movement leaves open the question of whether socialism liberates women. The national myth of women's emancipation refers to woman's double status: her signifying function for communist ideologies and the concealment of her gender difference. The official implications of emancipation indicate an ideological process toward the socialization, politicization, and masculinization of women. First, socialization mobilizes women into the workforce so as to bring them equal rights with men. Second, politicization introduces women into power structures so as to legitimize the ideology of gender equality. Finally, masculinization convinces Chinese women that they can perform all tasks as well as men. "Emancipation" thus alters a sexually distinct human being into a sexless subject of the nation-state. For decades, Chinese women have "enjoyed" the awarded liberation without having a clear sense of their sexual suppression at the hands of the ideology of consensus.

The recently awakened awareness of this denial of sexual difference has inspired a gender consciousness among many Chinese women. As Li Xiaojiang, a leading scholar in the field of women's studies in China, recalls, "In the social environment of 'Maoist equality,' it was exceedingly difficult to grasp one's own sexual status. I knew I was a woman, but I didn't recognize that this implied special characteristics, that a difference existed between me and other people, or rather between me and men."[7] And as Meng Yue, a Chinese female critic, summarizes, "There were sexes without bodies, classes without people, and desires without objects."[8] The ideological conventions that enabled the negation of sexual difference made it impossible for women to be "women."

Women's liberation, when examined beneath the mythology of the communist revolution, reveals numerous dilemmas faced by Chinese women. The socialization of women into the public domain presents them as equal with men but demands that women play social roles as workers along with traditional roles of wives, mothers, and daughters. The political acceptance of women into government organizations, while offering power to women, also uses them as mouthpieces for party ideology. The masculinization of women, while making women appear as strong as men, confers new social expectations without obviating the yearning for femininity. Moreover, as Meng Yue and Dai Jinhua observe, "Women are no longer required to be obedient to men, but women and men together equally obey the sexless collectivity or its symbol," which sits on "the throne of the past patriarchal figure."[9] The collective moral directive to sacrifice a female self in the name of a social role and to suppress one's gender identity in the name of equality compels Chinese women to shun difference as an aberration and to embrace the formless anonymity of consensus as an ideal. Beyond social and political explanations for the myth of Chinese women's emancipation lie other factors: the lack of gender consciousness by women themselves and the psychological burdens of self-sacrifice. To put everyone else's needs (husband, family, working unit, the state) above her own has been the defining value of a virtuous woman.

Thus gender again provides an illuminating perspective on these issues, one that enables me to investigate how the system of film production and the apparatus of the nation-state integrate woman into the construction of socialist discourse. The discourse, under the catchphrase of "gender equality," conceals gender difference with class categories. By "degendering" the female body and erasing sexual difference, the screen image of woman is transformed from a "ghost" of the old society to a "master" of the new state, from an unlearned individual to an enlightened heroine. Her primary visibility as the signifier of socialist ideology coincides with her unremarked status as the sign of suppressed gender difference, and this dual function lies at the heart of the myth of the socialist cinema. Overtly politicized in the past but boldly commercialized today, socialist cinema must be viewed in a framework of postsocialist conditions and the concomitant forms of popular culture if we are to understand the nature and meaning of its transformation.

GHOST OF THE OLD SOCIETY, MASTER OF THE NEW STATE

The transformation of woman from a ghost of the old society to a master of the new state has been a central theme in socialist film production, as illustrated by *The White-Haired Girl* (Baimao nü, 1950) and *Li Shuangshuang.* An understanding of socialist filmmaking starts with the question of how the discourse of class acts as a political ideology that defines all individuals according to class origin and as a conceptual apparatus that manipulates literary and cinematic creations. In his study of "class" in Mao Zedong's thought, for instance, Stuart Schram explains that class category relies on "objective-subjective" criteria, where "an individual's objective class nature could be modified as a result of subjective transformation brought about by indoctrination or by participation in revolutionary struggle."[10]

My review of socialist cinema focuses on the question of how class conflict overpowers gender relations, thereby incorporating gender difference into class struggle. Such concerns can also be found in Meng Yue's analysis of the film *The White-Haired Girl* and Roxann Prazniak's critical comments on Mao's stance toward women.[11] Both recognize that the application of Marxism in socialist China subordinated gender oppression to class struggle. Reviewing *The White-Haired Girl* with gender and class in mind, I raise two specific questions: How does the cinematic system articulate a transformation of the female image from a real woman into a white-haired ghost and vice versa, and how does the narrative shift generate a class-dominated narration where gender relations are subordinated to class oppression?

The configuration of the female protagonist, Xier, unfolds through her relations to her father, lover, and landlord. The first narrative structure, the father-daughter bond, collapses as the film strives for a discursive construction of class exploitation. Initially, the film reveals that in a class-divided society a biological father cannot protect his daughter but can lose her to repay a debt. One New Year's Eve sequence from the film presents a visual demonstration. Parallel editing simultaneously reveals class confrontation and the father-daughter bond in terms of spatial dislocations. Xier cuts paper flowers and decorates the window while she waits for her father to return home. The father, Yang Bailao, braves snow and wind to reach the

The White-Haired Girl, 1950

landlord's mansion to pay his debt. As the sequence cuts back, we see Xier making up her hair in front of the mirror and singing happily as a bride-to-be. The camera then takes us to the landlord's mansion, where the landlord forces Yang Bailao to sell Xier to settle the debt.

The crosscuts invite the audience to witness how class difference can sever the father-daughter bond. The film narrative uses parallel editing to send a dual message: gender relations initiate the narrative, but class discourse manipulates the narration. As the father-daughter relation yields to class conflict, "woman" entails a double coding: a gender other, subordinate to the paternal figure, and a class victim, signifier of socioeconomic injustice. The female image represents the sexual body and class identity. For instance, the father was prepared to marry Xier to Chun, a young peasant who grew up with her. The arrangement reflects a traditional gendered transfer, wherein a daughter becomes a wife through an arranged marriage. Socioeconomic pressures, however, threaten the potential happy marriage and subvert the father-daughter tie. After the film narrative informs the audience that repayment of the debt requires selling Xier to fulfill the landlord's sexual desire, we realize the cinematic designation of the landlord as both a class oppressor and a sexual violator. Thus the film transfers Xier from the father to the landlord and explains her impending sexual abuse as a consequence of class confrontation.

As class empowerment rips paternal protection from the daughter figure, the filmic construction repositions her in relation to a male lover, Chun. The male lover's engagement with Xier and his inability to save her from the oppressor again transforms a gender/sexual relation into a class conflict. In another sequence, the day scheduled for the wedding turns tragic when the father commits suicide and Xier is taken away by force. The death of the father ends the father-daughter relation and leaves Chun to save Xier. The film narrative has Chun attempt to rescue Xier but fail, as the landlord class crushes a single poor peasant. With Chun vanquished, the landlord "possesses" the woman. At this moment, discursive continuity is in jeopardy: who can free Xier from her living hell after her father's death and Chun's failure? The moment of rupture gives room for the insertion of political ideology: only the Communist Party can save the poor, and only the army can triumph over class oppressors. While the male hero is sent in search of the Red Army, Xier is left behind to endure class oppressions. When it leaves the love story behind, the film sets aside gender discourse. The female image is preserved for continuing duty as the embodiment of class humiliation.

The film construction, however, faces the challenge of how to explain gender oppression and sexual abuse in terms of class discourse. An establishing shot leads the audience to a hall where Xier is lighting a Buddhist lamp. The landlord, Huang, enters the room and embraces Xier from behind. When Xier screams for help, the camera tilts up to a banner inscribed with the characters for kindness and mercy. The camera then pans to another banner inscribed with the phrase, "the hall of kindness." Then a quick cut to the bedroom shows a maid finding that Xier is not in her bed. As we follow this woman and the camera back to the hall, a close-up shot reveals Xier with her mouth gagged and her hands tied behind her back, suggesting that she has been raped.

Sexual violence against the female body is an extreme form of gender oppression. The camera, however, shies away from the sexual attack and only suggests the rape through three montage cuts. The sexual assault, present in narrative but absent from representation, is recruited to serve the concept of class conflict. Consequently, rape is no longer a violent gender/sexual conflict between victim and attacker but a class confrontation between owner and servant. The female body, therefore, serves as a trope for the discursive construction of class. Moreover, assertion of class ideology through the erasure of female sexuality leaves no room for inscription from a woman's perspective. In addition to the class issues that the female body signifies, the film narrative adds an ethical burden to the female body. The film asks Xier to bear the shame of being raped and suggests her attempt at suicide. The film then invests the female image with class consciousness, allowing Xier to take the insult as class hostility and resolve to seek class revenge in the future. At this level, the signification of the female body goes beyond its function of dual coding. Woman is the sexual object violated by male force, the bearer of the humiliation requiring self-sacrifice, and the class victim calling for revolutionary emancipation.

Xier endures not only rape, but also the subsequent pregnancy. Female sexuality and class oppression reach such a contradiction that her giving birth to a dying baby becomes a strategic means for mediation. With a storm raging outside, deep inside a mountain cave, five close-up shots of Xier's face, hand, and body struggling with pain complete the process of childbirth. Off-screen sound delivers the baby's cry, yet the following image shows Xier burying the infant under stone and mud. The baby has to die because it bears a shameful class identity as the landlord's seed; its elimination maintains Xier's pure class status as an oppressed peasant woman. In addition, the disappearance of the baby allows the film to continue to render Xier as a class symbol, not a mother. In order to preserve Xier as a chaste daughter figure to the father symbol, later versions of The White-Haired Girl drastically reduce the sexual aspects of the film narrative. Each revision violates the integrity of literary or cinematic creation, as political ideology freely manipulates the narrative construction.

The rape of the woman, the death of the baby, and three years of life in a mountain cave finally turn Xier into a white-haired ghost. The implication is clear: the father cannot protect Xier and Chun cannot save her; only the Communist Party and the revolutionary army can bring salvation. The film ends in a dramatic transformation that is politically promising yet narratologically coercive. Chun finally returns to the village as an army officer, more of a revolutionary symbol than an individual. The male hero is represented as the vehicle of the party's policy and the agent of salvation. A master shot sets the stage for a class struggle where peasants denounce the landlord. Among them stands Xier, the victim and signifier of class oppression. Almost overnight, the poor are liberated, and Xier changes from the white-haired ghost to a black-haired woman thereafter happily married to Chun.

The transformation of the woman from ghost of the old society to master of the new state requires gender/sexual erasure and class rearticulation. The film narrative strives to restore the woman to her daughterly position, subordinate to two father figures: the birth father, Yang Bailao, and the symbolic father, the Communist Party. Attachment to the biological father preserves the daughter in the patriarchal tradition and proletarian class condition. Engagement to the symbolic father, however, suggests the possibility of a woman's emancipation. Yet as a poor peasant, the biological father also needs to be saved and is doomed to lose the daughter. The symbolic father can offer the daughter all fatherly promises: a happy marriage and class liberation. The daughter figure, after sexual violation and unbearable suffering, receives a long-awaited liberation at the expense of female sexuality and subjectivity. The woman's body and visual image exist throughout the film as a site for the discursive inscription of class; she never appears as an author inscribing herself. In sum, class discourse is gendered discourse, where gender/sexual relations operate in the form of class conflict and female subjectivity is concealed in class identity. After the CCP has saved the woman from the old society, a further question concerns how class ideology and cinematic apparatus construct the image of the model socialist woman.

THE MODEL SOCIALIST WOMAN

The film *Li Shuangshuang* (dir. Lu Ren, 1962) uses a comic form to depict a strong-minded female peasant undergoing socialist transformation in rural China. The film conveys how enthusiastically the peasants, especially women, embrace the party promise to lead them into a bright socialist China. In so doing, the film places its female protagonist in the locus of conflict between traditional, patriarchal practices and socialist, collective ones. The two systems, however, are different forms of patriarchy. Judith Stacey, in *Patriarchy and Socialist Revolution in China,* sees both the Confucian tradition and the socialist order as patriarchal systems.[12] The former maintains the family as the basic socioeconomic unit, with its members under the authority of the head of the household. The latter transforms the familial structure into a collective order and places the masses under the leadership of the CCP. The intertwined patriarchal ideologies and practices drive socialist filmic representation; they also problematize it. As a consequence, the female screen image assumes dual responsibilities: propagating new governmental policies while demonstrating old patriarchal confinement.

The cinematic construction of an oppositional relationship between husband and wife initiates, drives, and dramatizes the film narrative in *Li Shuangshuang.* Shuangshuang is portrayed as an outspoken character and model figure. She is known for her sharp tongue in unmasking others' selfish affairs and for her loyal devotion to government policies. By contrast,

Li Shuangshuang, 1962

the film depicts the husband as Shuangshuang's opposite and as a comic motif in the narrative. The film thus politicizes gender relations as the wife readily follows party policies while the husband stubbornly believes in patriarchal principles. The reversal of gendered divisions of power attempts to demonstrate socialist "gender equality," thereby selling socialism to the audience. To do so, a spatial division between family and commune creates a zone of conflict where contradictions unfold. The commune system mobilizes women for collective labor production and "equal" distribution, whereas family values require woman to remain in her domestic status and observe male authority. The socialist catchphrase of "equal work/equal pay" therefore becomes problematic.

The problem lies in an unequal sexual division of labor: the party's call for women to participate in collective production against patriarchy's restriction of them to the domestic sphere. In conveying this message, the film foregrounds Shuangshuang to demonstrate her duality: she proselytizes for the new policy, and she fights against the old system. The husband, the mother-in-law, and male peasants, however, collectively oppose her idealistic motives and socialist deeds. The cinematic spatial division enacts the contradiction. In the fields, for instance, a shot/reverse shot shows the husband, Xiwang, observing women working as a team. From this male vision, the camera educates the husband and the audience that women are no longer confined by their reproductive function but have joined the socialist workforce. The camera then shifts to the domestic space of the home. A close-up shot of the house door shows a chalk-written note instructing the husband to take care of the daughter and do the housework. The wife's note insults the husband's pride, and he decides to put on a show of force. Shuangshuang returns from the field to cook the family dinner. The husband waits to be served and announces that he cannot break with convention to share the housework with Shuangshuang.

While entry into the workforce allows the woman to contribute to productivity and gain a socialist gender identity, the new role conceals the double burden she shoulders. In public space, woman becomes a competent labor resource. In the domestic domain, however, she maintains her traditional position. In this sense, "the collective agriculture leveled no fundamental challenge to the traditional view that female labor was naturally different from and subordinate to that of men."[13] The film, of course, would not suggest such an explanation, since its premise is that socialism frees women from their domestic constraints. The film thus reveals the contradiction and blames the husband's unwillingness to share the housework, but the complaint is actually lodged against the traditional paradigms.

After the film establishes its female image as a socialist model, it strives to legitimate such an image with ideological underpinning. Shuangshuang becomes not only an enlightened peasant woman, but also a mouthpiece for party policies. The film encourages her expression, verbal or written, in the fashion of socialist discourses. For instance, Shuangshuang places a poster on the village board that announces women's desire to participate in field work and exposes problems in the work-pay system. The text concludes by quoting Mao Zedong's slogan: "Women are the upholders of half the sky." As she speaks in the party's voice, Shuangshuang becomes an enunciative vehicle for propagating policy. This subjected position forces the woman into a contradiction: in public she is encouraged to voice the government view, but at home she is kept silent. Thus the film narrative continues to illustrate a broader socialist picture through husband-wife conflicts.

The vigorous image of Shuangshuang shakes up life in the village. For instance, she reports to the commune authority when she finds Xiwang and his friends doing poor quality work in the fields. She stops a man from visiting his potential fiancée when she learns that it is to be an arranged marriage. Shuangshuang speaks up in public against the unfairness of giving the village cadre a pension or the cadre's wife work credit she does not deserve. Shuangshuang's unselfish socialist behavior, however, embarrasses the husband. He first sets up regulations intended to silence Shuangshuang and then threatens to leave home. In one sequence that shows the husband-wife conflict in terms of a series of shot/reverse shots, Xiwang acts as if he is going to leave Shuangshuang. To intensify the situation, shot/reverse shots separate the couple in different frames. The occasional insertion of a two-shot suggests a temporary mediation as Shuangshuang persuades the husband not to leave.

At this moment, we discover that the camera does not lead the viewing subject to notice the gender dichotomy of husband and wife but rather to see the ideological differences between progressive socialism and conservative patriarchy. Chris Berry, in his analysis of the sequence, explains that "in the case of Chinese cinema, the position of the viewing subject is not necessarily hooked up to questions of maleness in the same way as in the west."[14] The questions of why the husband is portrayed as the woman's ideological rather than sexual other and whether the female subject speaks in her own voice require more explanation. In this film, the husband-wife relation goes beyond connotations of heterosexual marriage or familial structure. Here the family serves as social territory and cinematic space, where the film indicates how the Chinese peasantry follows enlightened government leaders into collective socialism. Woman, the newly awakened peasant, walks out of the household and participates in public affairs. Woman's transition from domestic to public, however, brings her double responsibilities: good wife to her husband at home and model socialist in public. The double burden debunks the claim of gender equality in China: peasant women visibly share the field labor as they conceal their extra workload at home.

Although the husband appears to dampen the woman's zeal, he maintains his patriarchal authority at home and institutional power in public (Xiwang is a field-labor clerk and amateur veterinarian). The husband therefore can plausibly threaten to leave home whenever conflict occurs. The contrast between the progressive wife and the conservative husband is a proxy for ideological conflict. The contradiction, therefore, will not be resolved within the couple but must involve a superior authority. The village or Communist Party officials, for instance, hold the final power to judge right from wrong. Governmental policies validate the new model worker and reject the sluggish traditionalists. Given such a rigid, moralistic perspective, one understands why, when conflict occurs, the film sends Shuangshuang to party secretaries to report problems and seek support.

As the socialist cinema renders gender discourse into class categories, a primary sense of sexual difference remains. The difference, however, is politicized and erased as revolutionary model theater comes to center stage during the Cultural Revolution.

REVOLUTIONARY MODEL WORKS

In addition to the social and political devastation it brought to contemporary Chinese history, the Great Cultural Revolution left behind a "cultural heritage" represented by the revolutionary model theater (geming yangbanxi), a term that refers to a group of theatrical and musical works consisting of five reformed Peking operas, two ballets, and a symphony. From 1969 to 1972, film directors, at Jiang Qing's request, completed the adaptation of all eight model works to the film screen.[15] The reproduction of these model works followed three guidelines: positive characters had to be more prominent than other characters, heroic characters more important than the positive ones, and a main hero more grand than the other heroic figures. Cinematic clichés accordingly depicted the hero in close-up shots and bathed with high-key lighting. In contrast, the enemy appeared in low-key lighting and high-angle shots. It is surprising that the model theater did not fade away once the Cultural Revolution (1966–1976) had ended and been condemned. While those ten years of nightmare still haunt those who survived them, the restaging of the model works, along with other red classics, creates the postsocialist phenomena of marketing the past and consuming the revolution, as I have argued at the beginning of this chapter.

English-language discussions of the revolutionary art works of the Cultural Revolution have begun to attract attention in the scholarly community. Chen Xiaomei calls for "new avenues of research and new approaches" in order to demarginalize the study of the role of model theater in the Cultural Revolution.[16] A number of articles examining posters published before and during the Cultural Revolution have appeared in *Modern Chinese Literature and Culture*.[17] Art historians and cultural critics have studied how the icon of Mao Zedong became a central image in avant-garde art works, as well as in artifacts of popular culture.[18] Trevor Thomas Hay argues that the revolutionary model theater was not simply the manifestation of political struggle or propaganda. The model works retain a popular appeal to audiences drawn from the broad masses of workers and peasants because the master narrative of the Chinese revolution has been effectively integrated into China's theatrical traditions.[19] Taking the film versions as examples, I ask why the relics survived as the era that produced them vanished. Why did the model works appeal to their original audiences and also to viewers today? How does an art form, opera or cinema, integrate political ideologies to produce and reproduce meaning?

The film adaptations constantly reproduced model works to convey political ideologies to mass audiences. The significance of reproduction, however, lies not in the mechanical process but in the reconstitution of meaning with each remake. For instance, *The White-Haired Girl* has been revised numerous times since its debut in the early 1940s: from *yangge* (folk dance) play to stage drama and from art work to children's book. This popular narrative was adapted into a feature film in 1950 and then remade as a modern revolutionary ballet in 1972. In transferring the narrative from one medium to another, the remakes perpetuate a canon that presupposes a spectator already knowledgeable about the narrative and also convey political messages through a familiar story.

As the camera transforms the staged ballet into film, the reproduction recycles as well as revises the story. Reviewing the early film version and the screened ballet, the audience realizes that the theme of class struggle remains essential and the primary plot familiar. To mark the work as a revolutionary model play, however, the ballet *The White-Haired Girl* distorts the previous narrative through politicized revisions. Thus the death of Xier's father, Yang Bailao, is not a suicide but rather a murder at the hands of the landlord. Xier does not finally return to her female and peasant identity; she

The White-Haired Girl (revolutionary model ballet), 1972

enlists in the army. In addition, the rape sequence is eliminated, and the pregnancy disappears from the narrative. Few viewers would fail to miss the emphasis on class conflict and proletarian resistance. More important, the ballet production subordinates gender relations and female sexuality almost completely to class politics. The potential romantic relation between Dachun and Xier instead becomes one of savior and saved. The sexual interaction between the landlord and Xier is reinscribed as simple class oppression and resistance. Since I have already addressed these issues, my discussion now shifts to the questions of why such a politically oriented work appeals to audiences and how the filmed ballet turns an unfamiliar form (ballet) into a popular one (film) familiar to a proletarian audience.

The revolutionary model work takes the ballet art form and shapes it to fit political ends. When the prologue to the ballet *The White-Haired Girl* begins with the music of an orchestral symphony, for instance, the Western musical form with a Chinese melody clearly indicates the theme of social oppression and proletarian resistance. The pas de deux foregrounds the two leading characters not so much as intimate partners but as revolutionary companions. The ballerina's solo expresses the class oppression that

The Red Detachment of Women (revolutionary ballet), 1971

turns the woman into a white-haired ghost, while the solo of the danseur displays a political force that will save the oppressed and punish the perpetrators of injustice. The group dancers, surrounding either their hero or heroine, announce that the masses are longing for communist salvation. The moment of integration between political ideology and the language of dance seems absurd and leaves one to wonder whether the revolutionary ballet resurrects or abuses the classical art form.

In addition to *The White-Haired Girl,* one of the most memorable of the revolutionary ballets is *The Red Detachment of Women.* When viewing the ballet today in its filmed version, one is unsure whether it is an artistically crafted performance or a politically inspired ballet; the two ironically coexist. The grace of the performers is clear. Equally obvious is that every choreographed piece is designed to express a political sentiment. This multi-act narrative ballet, under the guidelines of the three principles, conveys how communism transforms a girl from slavery into the proletarian avant-garde. The stage setting is divided into areas liberated by communists and controlled by local bandits. Solos are given to the woman, a figure of the oppressed, and to the communist, a symbol of salvation. The presence of rifle-wielding women in uniform replaces dancers in tutu-style skirts, while the pas de deux represents either class conflict between abuser and abused or a political liaison between the communist savior and the woman in need of salvation.

No matter how politically charged and theatrically spectacular, the model ballets remain a staged form with little access to a mass audience. It is the cinematic transformation that popularizes the high art form and reproduces the political coding. Transferred to the screen, the model ballet reaches beyond the theater to people in factories and villages. Now the camera rather than the choreography decides which character takes center stage and what the audience is supposed to see. For instance, numerous close-up shots are used to highlight the oppressed Xier and the hero Dachun. Different camera angles are applied to magnify the hero's dominance and the enemy's insignificance. The intertextual integration of the ballet form with the filmed version lures the audience with a familiar tale as it blurs the lines between popular culture and high art, serving up ideological art for the workers.

Taken as a group, the model works exemplify a revolutionary genre, virtually the only genre created during the Cultural Revolution. And examination of such a genre would be "incomplete without attention to its relationship with gender."[20] Gender and genre are interwoven norms that work together in the construction and reception of revolutionary discourse. First, the world of the model theater is designed to establish the nature of heroism and exemplify heroes. Such exemplars are embodiments of ideals for the masses and agents of party ideology. The operatic or cinematic process ensures that these heroes are positioned to resolve conflicts and lead the masses. Hong Changqing in *The Red Detachment of Women* (Hongse niangziju, 1961), for example, transforms an oppressed girl into a Communist Party member. Li Yuhe in *The Red Lantern* sacrifices his life to fulfill his underground mission for the revolution, and in *Taking Tiger Mountain by Strategy*, Yang Zirong penetrates the enemy stronghold to carry out a secret operation. Conflicts arise and obstacles appear, but behind each hero lies the invisible collective power of communism. As Ellen R. Judd explains in her analysis of revolutionary heroism, "Each hero acts autonomously and efficaciously by virtue of access to a transcendent source of power, the power of the communist party."[21]

Second, the paradigm of heroism encompasses female as well as male heroes. The model genre presents an unusual persona, a principal female lead, at the center of the narrative and thus as the locus of revolutionary discourse. This female heroism, however, stems from political motivations rather than from an acknowledgment of sexual difference. The filmed opera *Azalea Mountain* provides a persuasive example. At the very beginning, the opera introduces its female lead, Ke Xiang, as a communist representative, a prisoner of the local armed foe, and a martyr's widow. Such positioning erases her gender identity as woman/wife and emphasizes her political status. The politicized rather than sexualized female body thus constitutes a gender discourse contrary to Western feminist assumptions, as gender relations are defined by class and party standing rather than by sexual status. Ke Xiang's revolutionary mission is to contact the local peasant resistance and lead them to overthrow their oppressors. The communist heroine is the decision maker and guide, there to instruct and enlighten the peasants.

The opera does use gender difference in portraying the conflicts that drive the narrative, but always with specific political connotations. A traitor figure, for instance, sows discord between the female communist representative and the peasant leader. He incites the physically masculine and impetuous hero by asking why a woman is allowed to lead the army force and usurp his male power. Here gender difference is evoked to agitate political rather than sexual contradictions. To reinforce the heroine's leading position, the narrative structure assures the peasants that she is one of them in terms of class orientation yet superior to them because of her communist status. With access to political theories and military strategies, she serves as the only agent. Final resolution for each conflict, however, comes only with party orders or policies. Victory requires the party's leadership of the collective revolutionary forces. In addition to images of heroines such as Ke Xiang, an older generation of viewers will remember Fang Lizhen, a party representative in the opera *On the Dock*; A Qingsao, an underground communist operative in *Shajiabang*; and Granny Li, a martyr in *The Red Lantern*.

Why should the revolutionary genre accommodate female heroism? As the example of opera demonstrates, the centrality of a female hero does not suggest a tendency to seek female subjectivity or sexuality. Female heroism is part and parcel of the revolutionary narrative. Nonetheless, the foregrounding of politicized female bodies and the predominance of women superiors suggest a desire for authorship, pursued by Jiang Qing for her personal and political ambitions. Jiang Qing, or Madame Mao, enjoyed a reputation as the standard-bearer for opera reform during the Cultural Revolution. The political theater either created or suppressed under her supervision reveals how she exploited the collective talents of many artists and the rich resources of traditional opera in the service of the revolutionary model genre. Moreover, she established personal authorship and political power through the implementation of an official form of feminism. Taking female heroism as her narrative strategy and my analytical framework as a point of departure, I see the integration of gender and genre as crucial to the rise of political theater and a personified political authorship.

The heroine portrayed in the revolutionary model genre is no longer a sexual other but a politicized image. Such an image signifies official feminism, where gender is defined through class categories and women are presented as sexless entities. By adopting official feminism and subordinating gender difference to generic conventions, the model works incorporate women into the revolutionary discourse. While woman is placed in the vanguard at center stage, however, the insertion of personal and political authorship occurs under the guise of generic norms. In such a circumstance, "Gender and genre become inextricably linked in terms of authorship, because each reflects the determinants of the other."[22]

The effort at personal authorship indicates Jiang Qing's desire for authority and her psychological reaction to loss. As an insignificant actress, Jiang Qing did not share in the aura of female film stars in the 1930s. As Mao's wife, of course, she lived in the shadow of a demigod. When she emerged as a public political figure in her own right during the Cultural Revolution, Jiang Qing seized the opportunity to advance her political authority and public reputation. By involving herself in opera reform, she was able to reengage the profession that had ignored her and to overcome the memory of her past powerlessness. The strategy of inserting female heroism in terms of official feminism strengthened Jiang Qing's political credentials while associating her name with progressive reform in the arts. Ultimately, her accomplishment put the gender identity of the individual woman completely behind the mask of collective heroism.

My final question concerns how the revolutionary model theater was able to attract mass audiences with its political orientation and simplistic narrative structure. The popularity of these works during the Cultural Revolution was almost beyond imagination; they were received in a collective state of frenzy. Professional and amateur troupes brought the plays to every corner of the country: farm fields, factory shops, military posts, school playgrounds, railway stations. The model works in various forms—radio transmissions, films, posters, comic books, picture collections, piano adaptations—filled daily life with ever-present images and sounds. Men and women, both old and young, constituted not only the audience, but also the performers of the model plays. A billion people sang one melody and spoke one language. Indeed, the era revealed a remarkable phenomenon where the model works remained virtually the only genre undergoing constant mechanical reproduction. This ceaseless activity ensured that the orientations, expectations, and conventions of the genre system kept circulating between texts and viewer and between production and distribution. "This semantic overdetermination," as Barbara Mittler points out, "was to assert and to reflect the total control over the content, purpose and mechanisms of cultural production exerted by the self-sanctioned makers of culture under Jiang Qing." These works were certainly presented as models—fixed and final systems that "don't allow for a freedom of interpretation."[23] Participants accepted the form, rehearsed it, and internalized the one allowable meaning.

As a mediator between text and viewer, the revolutionary genre shapes the production and reception of political discourse. The model works exemplify the possibility and final absurdity of integration between traditional opera and modern reform. Eliminated from the traditional opera are the painted faces and colorful costumes, along with the role types of *dan, sheng, jing,* and *chou.* Inserted are images of workers, peasants, and soldiers in their politically defined costumes, makeup, and "heroic" gestures. Such replacement allows the mass audience to identify not with emperors, princes, or beauties, but with proletarian characters like themselves. As the subject on- and off-stage, integrating representation with reception, the working class becomes the master of art. Beyond the veneer of politicized coding, however, operatic or generic aspects such as singing style, acrobatic movements, and certain stage conventions remain. The audience goes to the model opera expecting not only the familiar sounds of *xipi* and *erhuang,* but also political spectacles.[24] The spectacle that in the past energized the generation of the Cultural Revolution now entertains the consumer. When *The Red Lantern* was restaged thirty-eight years later, in 1998, with its original crew in Shanghai, those who had been patrons in the past were curious to know if their models were still familiar and meaningful. New viewers watched to see how these ancient revolutionaries performed as commercial attractions.

POSTSOCIALIST MASS AND POPULAR CULTURE

Among the concepts used recently to describe the current political and social situation in China, "postsocialism" has been proposed as a possible explanatory term. In his analysis of Huang Jianxin's films, for example, Paul G. Pickowicz proposes the idea of "popular perception" as a postsocialist phenomenon, referring to "public awareness of the failure of the traditional socialist system and the absence of a socialist identity among ordinary people."[25] Arif Dirlik, in his examination of "socialism with Chinese characteristics," also sees in China today a loss of faith in socialism, since the system has failed to sustain its promise of providing its people with a progressive present and a communist future. Dirlik concludes that China is facing an extraordinary dilemma, posed by socialist nationalism and global capitalism. The notion of postsocialism, therefore, is proposed as a hypothesis for a possible understanding of contradictions that China embodies today.[26] Based on the proposals of these two scholars, Xu Ben, in his discussion of Chinese cultural criticism, argues that the term "postsocialism" suggests the "death of the socialist vision" and the continuity of "post-totalitarian control and domination."[27]

In my view of China's postsocialist condition, both the state apparatus and the mass populace participate in cultural production and reception. The terminology of "post" as prefix and "socialism" as root helps us to understand that the phrase connotes the failure of socialist ideology in its conventional form, as well as the efforts to sustain it through alternative means. The historical moment of rupture and continuity creates an ideological vacuum and stirs psychological anxiety, which strongly affects both policymakers and the general public. The coexistence of the market economy, commercial culture, and socialist structures leads officials to revise socialist ideology, while the people experience feelings of ambiguity and uncertainty. As bureaucrats pursue methods of ideological control, citizens seek freedom of choice. The postsocialist condition thus arises out of the interplay among official discourses, the growth of markets, and a thriving popular culture.

The integration of political subjects and commercial forms endows both mass and popular culture with postsocialist characteristics. In *Understanding Popular Culture*, John Fiske distinguishes mass culture from popular culture. Mass culture, according to Fiske, refers to the dominant forces producing cultural commodities in a capitalist system, whereas popular culture signifies how people evade or resist those forces—that is, how they assert a "right to make one's own culture out of the resources provided by the commodity system."[28] Although addressed to the conditions of cultural production in the West, Fiske's distinction sheds light on the multifarious cultural phenomena in contemporary China, where state-run mass culture intersects with market-driven popular perception. In a nation-state where totalitarian politics coexists with a consumer economy, ideological censorship and market regulation intervene in the sphere of production. Moreover, the dividing line between mass culture and popular culture is not clear.

Cultural production and reception under postsocialist conditions simultaneously embody differentiation and integration. The state-run cultural bureaucracies, relying on central power and institutional measures, advocate mainstream productions (zhu xuanlu). The works of the mainstream line (visual, written, or musical) propagate political ideologies, sustain the socialist system, project heroic models, and suppress opposing voices. In return, mainstream works enjoy government funding, distribution, and reward. The culture industry as well as the mainstream, however, undergo a continual process of commercialization and consumption. As cultural consumers, viewers and readers have opportunities to choose what to see and what to read. Producers and distributors have to take audiences, sales, and profit margins into consideration. Striving to survive and succeed in an ideologically controlled mass culture and a market-driven popular culture, artists or directors struggle to find a mediating point that can accommodate official interests, audience tastes, and economic profit. As Francesca Dal Lago stresses in her study of contemporary Chinese art, "the transition of propagandistic models from ideological dissemination to mass consumption creates an unexpected correspondence between socialist and consumerist systems of mass communication."[29] Efforts to commercialize the red classics and to redefine nationalism present two examples of the confluence of ideology and consumerism.[30]

After red images and revolutionary songs faded from the cultural scene as China entered its new, postsocialist era, hardly anyone would have predicted their reappearance. It is indeed somewhat startling to again hear revolutionary songs sung throughout the nation. But today, the red melodies attract listeners by means of a disjunction, especially between content and form. The ideological lyrics, hegemonic and popular in the revolutionary past, remain the same: the sun is the reddest, Chairman Mao is the dearest, party brilliance always shines in one's heart, and so on. These words might sound ridiculous to contemporary ears, but they once were sacred words that inspired citizens to devote their lives to Chinese communism. The new versions of revolutionary songs sound lighthearted and sentimental, as pop stars, accompanied by modern instruments, use a soft and seductive female vocal treatment to mollify the radical rhetoric and turn the tunes into enchanting leisure commodities. The rhythm and the melody charm listeners into singing along and invite them to indulge in the pleasurable consumption of cultural nostalgia.

Nevertheless, the carnival of red classics is not simply a matter of nostalgia because revolutionary artifacts and the cult of Mao have become the subjects of mass production and popular consumption. For producers and distributors, the obvious reason for repackaging the red classics is to generate profit. But the question of why these particular political and cultural artifacts, buried in history and neglected by memory, have been chosen requires explanation. Members of different generations embrace the red texts for various reasons. For veterans of the Cultural Revolution, the songs recall their ideological beliefs and life principles. To sing them again evokes nostalgic feelings deeply inscribed in memory. The response might be a pessimistic pride in having been a revolutionary participant or the traumatic memory of having suffered at the hands of the revolutionaries. The familiar words, repackaged in new music, remind listeners of the disappearance of the past and the emergence of the commercial present. The encounter is ambiguous; they are not sure whether the past explains the present or mocks it. For the generation born after the socialist era, the concept of revolution belongs to the realm of myth. Literature, films, and music can either alienate or fascinate the younger generation. Artifacts that narrate the unknown era can inspire young minds eager to comprehend recent history, or they can provide targets for ridicule and mockery.

REMAPPING NATIONALISM

With the melodies of red classics lingering in the air, the call for a new nationalism in China began to appear on state-run media and through mass cultural forms. The active existence of socialist art forms and their ability to energize the promotion of nationalist pride surprised and excited audiences and critics. After the Cold War, China faced the challenge of integrating itself into the global system while maintaining its socialist identity. Moreover, the market economy and consumerism penetrated every aspect of social life. Under these circumstances, official orthodoxy, such as Marxist-Leninist and Maoist thought, could not easily exert its hold over the masses. Unofficial discussions on the subject of China turned either to traditional sources for philosophical support or to the West for theoretical inspiration. At a moment of social transformation and market transition, cultural producers like writers and filmmakers reassessed the guiding principles for thinking about contemporary China. The result has been a notion of nationalism that is politically moderate and appealing to both domestic and international audiences.

In his careful analysis of the place of third world criticism in China, Xu Ben indicates that nationalism has been the most utilitarian mechanism of state ideology.[31] At home, the concept legitimizes the government's authoritative position over the masses. Internationally, nationalism provides a fortress against issues such as human rights and democracy. Moreover, nationalism entails not only political but also commercial values. Cultural artifacts branded as inherently Chinese increase the odds of turning a profit. The nationalist sentiment, Xu observes, results from the collusion between the state apparatus and commercial form.[32] In light of Xu's arguments, I am concerned with the questions of how the cultural production system uses nationalistic inspiration and mass cultural form to reassess or reconstruct a postsocialist orthodoxy and how gender is used as a political inscription in the reconstruction of nationalism. Answers to these questions can be seen by examining mainstream filmmaking in the 1990s.

Chinese nationalism, according to Allen S. Whiting, takes affirmative, assertive, and aggressive forms: "Affirmative nationalism centers exclusively on 'us' as a positive in-group referent with pride in attributes and achievements. Assertive nationalism adds 'them' as a negative out-group referent that challenges the in-group's interests and possibly its identity. Aggressive nationalism identifies a specific foreign enemy as a serious threat that requires action to defend vital interests."[33] China tends to remap its nationalism against current world conditions. An analysis of mass media, especially filmmaking, best explains the anxiety over how to situate China in the global village.

Films about revolutionary histories, one of the mainstream genres, put revolutionary epics and leading communist figures on the screen. Choosing revolutionary historiography as the subject matter assures ideological purity in mainstream production. The benefits of producing such films include budgetary support from the government and network distribution in the market. In order to make ideological movies that appeal to today's audiences, however, filmmakers must balance a film's political implications with its commercial potential. In the film *The Great March* (Da jinjun, 1998), for example, the audience discovers that the narrative focuses not so much on the civil war or history but on the friendship between communist leaders (Deng Xiaoping and Liu Bocheng) or else the personal engagements between officials and soldiers. The humanizing and melodramatic approach tries to make the violent revolution appear benign and the enigmatic communist leaders appear beloved. In other words, the ethical reassessment of revolutionary histories softens ideological dominance so as to reinforce its historical resonance. Adding human touches to the communist figures shortens the distance between the charismatic leader and the ordinary citizen.

In addition, *The Great March* gives equal narrative weight to the opposing Nationalist Party and its military. This opens up the possibility of a contrast or comparison between the two rival powers, thereby providing the film with narrative credibility. The result of such effort turns the revolutionary history into authoritative discourse, legitimizing "affirmative nationalism," on the one hand, and inspiring faith in the Communist Party and its leaders on the other. The assertion of affirmative nationalism aims to reinforce nationalist pride in the historical achievements that occurred under communist leadership. The genre of historiography, however, ignores women and gender issues. A clear message is conveyed: history is the story of the nation-state and the father-son bonds that produced it. As representations of history have kept woman silenced and unseen, the concept of the nation-state remains patriarchal under the mask of a nationalist humanism with gender difference effaced. Films falling into this category include *The Decisive Battle* (Da juezhan, 1991), *The Ceremony of the Birth of the New Country* (Kaiguo dadian, 1989), *Conference in Chungqing* (Chongqing tanpan, 1993), *Mao Zedong's Story* (Mao Zedong de gushi, 1991), and *Zhou Enlai* (1991).

Concern about constructing China's national identity in reaction to a Western other is evident in another genre of mainstream filmmaking, one that reflects the theory and practice of Occidentalism. The notion of Occidentalism, defined by James Carrier as "stylized images of the West" and by Xiaomei Chen as "a counter-discourse to Edward Said's Orientalism," takes the Western other as a dialectical component of self-definition.[34] Chen further distinguishes the concept into official and anti-official Occidentalism. The official discourse "uses the essentialization of the west as a means for supporting a nationalism that effects the internal suppression of its own people." The anti-official discourse "uses the western other as a metaphor for a political liberation against ideological oppression within a totalitarian society."[35] Opposition occurs between Occident and Orient, as well as between official and nonofficial discourses. But "there is more to Occidentalism and Orientalism," Carrier indicates, "than the general desire to distinguish the familiar and the alien and to heighten the difference between them."[36] Recent mainstream filmmaking in China, for instance, has witnessed a tacit understanding among government officials, filmmakers, and audiences to relocate Chinese national identity in terms of constructing and perceiving a Western other. The cinematic encounter of the Orient with the Occident creates pictures of both alienation and integration.

The cinematic strategy of using a foreign other to reflect a Chinese self seeks to reawaken national patriotism against today's global conditions. *My 1919* (Wode yijiu yijiu, 1999) focuses on the historical moment in 1919 when a Chinese delegation and Western powers negotiated Shandong Province's sovereignty at the Versailles Peace Conference. Failure to preserve the sovereign rights provoked a nationwide reaction known as the May Fourth movement. The film attempts not to rechronicle historical events but to advocate today's national sentiment by depicting individual Chinese acting heroically against the collective imperialist alliance, showing how a weak country could pursue national sovereignty. At a special screening of the film for delegations participating in World Trade Organization (WTO) negotiations, for instance, a Chinese deputy cried out that we need another film like *My 1919*.[37] The mirror image of a Western other, therefore, prompts an assertive nationalism that sees Western power as a challenge to China's national identity and its position in world affairs. The patriotic mood evoked through visual reconstruction corresponds nicely with China's contemporary sociopolitical moment, when "China can say no" is a constant refrain in the media.[38] Films that serve such interests include *The National Anthem* (Guoge, 1999) and *The National Flag* (Guoqi, 1999).

While the portrait of the Western other in *My 1919* embodies imperialistic evil, the Westerner becomes an international emissary in *Lovers' Grief*

Lovers' Grief over the Yellow River, 1999

over the Yellow River (Huanghe juelian, 1999). In this film, engagement with the Western other indicates the desire to win global standing and gain the confidence needed to prevail over Western power. The film unfolds from the perspective of an American pilot who witnessed China's war resistance against Japan. The focus of the film is not so much on the war as on an American's romance with a Chinese female soldier, making the alien other into an ally. When the film wisely situates the narrative within the framework of a nationalist war and international romance, it seeks to integrate political interest with commercial viability. Simultaneously revolutionary and exotic, the image of the woman warrior symbolizes the justness of the patriotic war and provides the sexual/romantic interest for viewing pleasure.

Images of the Western other in Chinese representation, evil or angelic, pose the question of whether Occidentalism is a counter or an alternative discourse to Orientalism. As official and commercial cultural producers search for a language to speak about the national self, Occidentalist discourse allows a voice oppositional to the West when it presents a threat or an affirmative voice when the West symbolizes modernity. The voice oscillates accordingly when removed from its social, historical, and economic conditions. On the one hand, it attempts to collectivize the mass consciousness under nationalist ideology; on the other, it tries to alleviate nationalist anxiety. Like the image of the Oriental in Western representation, the image of the Occidental other in the Chinese imagination is a mirror image of the visual construction of the self. An examination of socialist production within the framework of new nationalism may add a historical explanation to today's cultural debate over Occidentalism.

Chapter Four

Gender Politics and Socialist Discourse in Xie Jin's *The Red Detachment of Women*

THE CONCEPT OF SEXUAL difference has been the fundamental premise for the construction of feminist discourse. Seeking to extend the analysis of gender, however, socialist feminist criticism has called attention to the relationship between female subjectivity and class identity.[1] Recent trends in feminism redefine differences that embody not only sexual but also racial, economic, and cultural categories of analysis.[2] This chapter participates in the discussion by posing such questions as these: What happens when gender relations are established more on concepts of class than of sex? Does gender difference persist in the absence of sexual difference? If so, how is it constructed and what are the sociocultural implications? These questions can be pursued by examining a genre of revolutionary films produced in socialist China that suggests alternative perspectives for examining feminist theories and gender relations. The following discussion explores how sociopolitical ideologies and semiotic articulations in socialist film production constitute a gender allegory in which the erasure of sexual difference masks a complicated gender suppression.

In *The Red Detachment of Women*, a classic revolutionary film, the gender allegory is a system of ideology and cinematic representation where woman is shaped as a discursive device and semiotic code for the construction of a master narrative of communist and revolutionary history. The allegorical construction involves three stages: (1) incorporating female identity into class consciousness; (2) elevating proletarian ideologies over class interests; and (3) glorifying the final image of the revolutionary heroine, politically sublime but not gender specific. Often, woman is subordinated first to the repressive tradition of patriarchy, then to the collective symbol of communism. Facing these two symbolic father figures, woman in socialist representation experiences a double bind. While patriarchy places her at the bottom of society as an other, communism replaces her gender identity with a political mask. The allegory becomes even more problematic when the female subject is willing to relinquish her gender identity without knowing the costs. Exploring this socialist gender phenomenon should broaden our discussion of gender and representation in different sociocultural contexts and film practices.

The film narrative tells the story of how a woman enslaved to a regional landlord follows the guidance of a communist leader and joins a revolutionary detachment. The female protagonist, Qiong Hua, tries to free herself from ruling-class oppression. Despite all her efforts, she fails. Qiong Hua is confined in jail until the arrival of the communists. The communist mentor (Hong Chanqing) not only saves her life, but he also initiates a process of proletarian enlightenment. Rescuing her from the hands of the oppressors and instructing her through political rhetoric, Changqing transforms Qiong Hua into a member of the proletarian vanguard. All the characters and their

The Red Detachment of Women, 1961

relations are informed by an ideological discourse that touts the party's leadership and the power of collective arms.

The female protagonist's movement from social victim to Red Army soldier occurs in a cinematic structure of spatial transition. The filmic setting is divided into two ideologically distinct spatial worlds: the revolutionary territory of Red Stone County and the Kuomintang-controlled Coconut Village. To heighten the contrast between the two spaces and opposing forces, director Xie Jin uses a number of cinematic devices.[3] Intimations of the dark force occur through extreme low-key lighting and night shooting, which places Coconut Village under layers of shadows. Woman's oppression becomes visible when the off-screen sound of a whip striking flesh yields to a close-up of the female victim being tortured, hung by her hands in a dungeon-like cell. The physical entombment of the woman deep within the prison symbolizes the reactionary social forces responsible for her torment.

As the camera cuts to Red Stone County, where the Red women's detachment resides, cinematic devices draw attention to an entirely different world. Daylight filming, in bright sunshine, signifies the hope and radiant future in the liberated "Red" land. Diegetic music in the form of revolutionary songs reflects the glory of the triumphant ideology. An open field, filled with throngs of uniformed female soldiers, shows the power of collectivity and genderless identity. As the camera crosscuts between an extreme low-angle shot of the party representative on a stage delivering his political message and a high-angle shot of the women soldiers being indoctrinated, gender difference gives way to the political relation of the leader to his followers at the dawn of a new society. The stark distinction between bright and dark worlds is made literal through a close-up shot of the stone boundary marker between them.

Beyond the cinematic mobilization of the female protagonist from "dark society" to "bright future," the film underlines gender in terms of the female body and male gaze. As we see the female body at first enslaved and under the male gaze of a communist figure, the notion of body and gaze evokes a double coding of gender and politics. The film discourse ensures that the female body presents the collective identity of an oppressed social class. The master narrative of revolution precludes woman from representing her body as individual and sexual. In her bodily repression, woman bears signs and codes that signify larger social issues. To expose the decadent nature of the nation-state through the sufferings of its people requires that woman pose for exhibition. As a displayed victim, she not only provides physical evidence and persuasive witness to social oppression, but also affirms the legitimacy of the male revolutionary political mission.

In Western feminist criticism, discussions of the female image/body and male gaze have primarily concerned the critique of sexual difference. In contrast, socialist film discourse denies sexual difference while fostering class consciousness. As a result, gender relations appear to be class-based, where the suppressed woman aligns with her communist saviors. A series of questions arises: How can we discuss gender relations in terms of a class difference theoretically and visually bound to the female image under an authoritarian male gaze? With woman depicted as an oppressed other subject to emancipation, does the viewing experience still offer voyeuristic and narcissistic pleasure? How does the cinematic system work to ensure that spectatorial instruction rather than simply pleasure is the primary effect? The most perplexing question that I intend to explore is how socialist films initiate a gender transgression—from woman into proletarian—in a framework defined by the female image/body and the male gaze.

The film's establishing shot, in a close-up, introduces the female protagonist as she runs from the scene of a local landlord's arrest. In darkness shadowed by extreme low-key lighting, two communists disguised as wealthy expatriate Chinese catch sight of the escaping woman. So initially the woman falls under the gaze of male communists. The meeting of genders, with the woman as a fearful, servile person and the men as political agents, suggests the primacy of class relations over sexual difference. Quickly apprehended, the woman is imprisoned and lashed. In a mise-en-scène of the enclosed jail, the display of the female body imprinted with lash marks, seen by the audience through the two communists' caring gaze, forms the second confrontation. As the film visually introduces and reinforces a class-bound engagement between the female protagonist and the communists, the savior's vision becomes the authoritarian viewpoint from which the narrative unfolds and enunciation proceeds.

Looking along the lines of the male gaze, however, we note the conjunction between the woman's gender identity and her class orientation, which places her in a social-gender double jeopardy. The female servant, defined by gender, bears the brunt of patriarchal oppression. The patriarchal landlord can turn her into a concubine and servant or sell her as his property. Her identity, defined politically, evokes discourses of revolution and emancipation. "The relationship between gender difference and class difference," as Christine Roulston points out, "is problematized by mutual suppression and exclusion."[4] To amend Roulston's statements, class and gender operate simultaneously in a dialogic encounter. The engagement between hero and victim conveys the enunciative message that the female protagonist will remain oppressed in her feminine identity, yet she will be emancipated, politically, only when she becomes a proletarian through the guidance of her communist mentors.

The transition in identity from a woman to a proletarian begins with the inscription of the female body. The act of painfully marking a woman's flesh serves to relate her class identity to its potential transition. When whipping leaves welts on the female body and the sounds of vigorous lashing and cries of pain elicit audience sympathy, the spectacle of punishment emphasizes the female protagonist's status as social victim rather than sexual object. At the moment when the body functions as a visual emblem of class torment, the female body's gender distinctiveness dissolves into a social icon. Thus the film situates the viewing masses and the viewed object in a salvation fantasy: a woman is being beaten and she needs to be saved.

Representing the female body as a socially abused other denies pleasure in looking and inspires class consciousness. The woman's body not only displays her pain, but also reminds spectators of their own humiliations and circumscribed social status. Thoughts of misdeeds and injustices perpetrated by the ruling class enact a shared class identification upon a specifically female body. From this social vantage, the beaten woman becomes one of our proletarian sisters. Identifying with the social position of the female image, spectators face a dilemma: they cannot save the woman, nor can they identify with the counterrevolutionary forces. The communist savior, therefore, becomes the only symbol of hope and positive identification; those who will emancipate the woman will do likewise for society as a whole. Political ideology ordains that only the Chinese communists can save the nation and liberate the oppressed, thus establishing a socialist semiotic articulation. The active voyeuristic gaze takes woman as an object, a passive social victim, while the narcissistic spectator identifies with the heroic savior.

Exposed to the communist vision, the female body legitimates a politically defined gender relationship. Further display under a collective gaze fixes the body firmly with class identity and therefore with revolutionary discourse. Before the assembled soldiers, the female leader asks Qiong Hua why she wants to join the army. The protagonist unbuttons her collar to reveal her bruises to the entire detachment. Bodily marks rather than language answer the question. Although the detachment accepts her, the silence of the female voice in the presence of the class-marked body reflects the subservience of female sexuality to a totalitarian ideology. When Changqing, now a party representative, meets Qiong Hua again, his gaze falls on her body to complete the initial stage of gender suppression: the moment of gaining proletarian status at the cost of her gender identity.

POLITICIZING GENDER

After incorporating the female identity into a collective class entity, the film narrative continues to repress gender difference by politicizing the mind while subjecting the body. The process strives to implant the notion of people-as-one: "identification of the people with the proletariat, of the proletariat with the party, of the party with the leadership, of the leadership with the Egocrat."[5] In the mobilization of woman into the totalitarian oneness, semiotic strategies reinforce the link between femininity and revolution. Whereas the patriarchal force violates the female body with a whip, communism subjects the mind to political orthodoxy. As the female subject gradually loses her self to the collective identity, she becomes a gender-neutral figure.[6]

The politically awakened woman understands that she will find her emancipation only when she subordinates personal desires to communist ideologies. Qiong Hua, now a soldier, confronts her oppressor as she carries out a military order. Personal rage and class hostility drive her to fire on the enemy. In a low-angle shot of her and a reverse high-angle take of the opponent, the film clearly demonstrates her transition from an enslaved woman to an armed soldier. Because Qiong Hua violates a military regulation, however, the communist leader punishes her with confinement. The mise-en-scène of the little hut where she is held recalls the water cage of her prior imprisonment. The dominant forces, patriarchal or communist, restrain the female body as the site for the intrusion of their competing ideologies. If corporal punishment torments the body to obey the patriarchal order, ideological instruction teaches the mind that the personal is political and the individual a part of the collective.

The appearance of individual female frailty calls for the emergence of a sublime figure, often male and communist. My use of "sublime" addresses a visual image rather than a theory of aesthetics. The sublime figure has been a dominant image in modern and contemporary Chinese literature and cinema. Larger than life and above the ordinary, the heroic image exemplifies not an individual identity but rather the sociopolitical and cinematic criteria for art production. The sublime figure functions as a carrier of political ideologies, a model for imaginary identifications, and a narrative strategy for creating revolutionary allegories.

In relation to the sublime stands the figure of the subaltern, referring to a social class—more specifically to women, subordinated to patriarchal oppression, on one hand, and positioned for revolutionary emancipation on the other. Because of her dual identities as social victim and political alien, the repressed female subaltern is a signifying subject unable to speak for herself, yet she embodies sociocultural meanings. As the sublime and the subaltern enter into a gendered relation, sexual difference is reduced to rhetorical indoctrination, for the task of the sublime is to teach the subaltern how to speak. Woman thus returns to the realm of a new hierarchy, "which is patriarchal in yet another way."[7]

The imbalance in power between the sublime figure and the subaltern is reflected in and reinforced by the language they speak. In *The Red Detachment of Women*, the rhetoric of class (at the expense of sexuality) constitutes the primary lexicon for the characters. Each film protagonist, situated as a storyteller, narrates and repeats shared experiences of class oppression. The class discourse is so dominant that it conceals fundamental separations among individuals. Three communicative encounters elaborate clearly how the rhetoric of class transforms a specific man and woman into sociopolitical entities, the sublime and the subaltern. In an early sequence where the communist savior asks the newly freed woman about her family, she responds with an outpouring of family tragedies: the death of her father and her mother's homelessness, caused by the landlord's actions. In another establishing shot of a mass scene, the female protagonist, parading an oppressor before an angry crowd, repeats her personal and family histories. Her denunciation tells how the communists have delivered her from bondage to a revolutionary mission. During a later conversation, the party representative recalls how anti-revolutionary forces drowned his father in a river and how his mother went blind. He then inspires in Qiong Hua the belief that freedom depends on the awakening of the entire proletariat.

From these sequences, we notice that when the subaltern speaks, she speaks in a given language. As Robert Con Davis and David S. Gross put it, "The subaltern in itself cannot be empowered to speak except through ventriloquism."[8] The retelling of family tragedies does not advance personal expression but rather voices a class orientation. In relating the story of class oppression, the speaking subject signifies a gender positioning that locates woman in the master discourse of revolution. To learn to speak the correct language, Qiong Hua admires the male communist as a sublime figure. In a conversation with her friend, for instance, she asks why the party representative and the female commander can see further and know better. The response is that they are members of the Communist Party. Elaborating the thesis visually, the film narrative contrasts personal impotence with collective force in a battle sequence. Through the party's leadership and collective effort, the detachment arrests the local landlord, secures the village, and liberates the peasants. Persuasion in the form of discursive reasoning and visual inscription leads the subaltern to willingly look to the sublime model as a symbol of knowledge and emancipation.

The revolutionary rhetoric that positions the sublime and the subaltern as educator and educated also creates a class/political affiliation between them. Voicing the same language, these homeless and parentless sons and daughters become revolutionary brothers and sisters in search of a communist father and proletarian truth: "The notion of class is dependent on the recognition of a group of people functioning as a politicized community and sharing the same socioeconomic interests. . . . Class is therefore a public, not a private concept."[9] In the film narrative, class bonding denies a gender relation primarily characterized by sexual difference. Caught up in the class category defined by the ideology of a totalitarian power, woman as a gendered other and private being diminishes. Shaped twice, first by patriarchal tradition, then by political orthodoxy, woman finally joins the collective-social family, liberated to embrace a new form of servitude.

The audience might wonder how a miscellany of individuals can be transformed into a chosen people under entirely unpromising conditions. In their study of Chinese revolutionary discourse, David Apter and Tony Saich explain that after the subaltern is shown explicitly how to transcend herself, the ideological apparatus will provide the individual with exceptional opportunities through collective enterprise.[10] For woman, the striking opportunity is the potential transition from subaltern to female sublime. Such a transformation comes to fruition through a cinematic articulation.

Against the setting of a dramatic battle scene, in a life-and-death moment, the party representative informs Qiong Hua that the party has accepted her membership application. A close-up with her image superimposed over her application form, accompanied by background music of the "Internationale," indicates a visual moment when sublimation of the heroine emerges. The visual motifs dynamically project the political mission over the female body, and the close-up symbolically magnifies the newly constructed identity. The "Internationale" further enhances the effect of sublimation by linking the image with the heroic chords. Qiong Hua is thereby no longer a female slave or a naive soldier, but a self-consciously fulfilled proletarian. The revolutionary woman attains legitimacy previously denied her, such as the power of leadership and the position of speaker. Yet this politically empowered and gender-repressed identity, in its abstract, signifying, and public form, suggests a complete abandonment of female subjectivity—female experience, personal voice, or sexual desire—a "dark continent" completely concealed or politicized within socialist film construction.

If a communist woman assumes a powerful and sublime position, how does the film relate gender and power? In order to insert a space of legitimacy for the heroine, the film narrative transforms the party representative, Changqing, into a revolutionary martyr. In a fight between the Red detachment of women and counterrevolutionary forces, Changqing falls into the hands of the enemy and faces execution. The film stages Changqing's martyrdom as a heroic spectacle for the instruction of Qiong Hua and therefore the audience. Compared to the earlier sequence, where she was positioned for the male gaze, the present segment has her witness the captive body. Her vision registers how a loyal communist sacrifices his life for the greater glory of the collective. Moreover, removal of the male sublime allows the advance of the female hero. This exchange, however, does not suggest a power transition between male and female heroes, for the substitute ascending to the heroic position is a woman in male masquerade. The masquerading heroine does not signify female subjectivity because her entrance into the collective sphere depends exactly on the erasure of anything that is feminine. Alternation between the two gendered images, therefore, indicates a power negotiation between political ideology and gender position. The transformation of a woman into a female sublime illustrates the ideological notion of women's emancipation, where the moment of liberation is the moment of yielding one's female subject position.

As bearer of a sociopolitical position, the heroine exists no longer as a female other but as a visual signifier or discursive mouthpiece for the master discourse. As Qiong Hua masquerades with the party representative's accessories—document case and pocket watch—she is the rebirth of Changqing. She speaks to her followers with precisely the same rhetoric that Changqing used to educate her. She successfully organizes the detachment members, just as Changqing once did, into an efficient combat unit. The cinematic mise-en-scène at the end of the film raises Qiong Hua's image and sublime position to an extreme. A low-angle camera shot enlarges the party representative as she gives a political speech on-stage. A reverse cut in high angle introduces the masses of newly emancipated women, dressed in uniform and eager to march for the revolution. The scene recalls the opening sequence, only now the speaker is not Changqing but Qiong Hua. The film's final shot, an extreme close-up in superimposition again, projects the female body against the communist red flag, while the Red detachment's song lends connotations to the image: "March on and march on. We shoulder serious responsibilities as soldiers and embody deep enmity as women. In the past Hua Mulan joined the army in the name of her father; today women of the detachment fight for the people."

Sound, image, color, and camera together constitute an apparatus for producing the allegory that subsumes gender to a strident political ideology.

The thematic music that initiates and ends the film introduces contemporary Chinese women to a legendary figure—Hua Mulan—as a model to follow. The heroine originally came from the *Song of Mulan* (Mulan shi), written and circulated during the Northern Dynasty (220–589). The narrative folk song depicts the story of a young woman who disguises herself as a man to fight in the war in her father's place. Although numerous revisions have shaped the form and content of the song, the figure of a woman warrior and female transvestite remains central. As Chinese women call into question the masqueraded identity, readers and audiences in the United States have witnessed recent revisions of the legend into transnational forms.

In *Woman Warrior* (1975), Maxine Hong Kingston devotes an entire chapter to a fictional rewriting of the story.[11] Mulan exemplifies a fantasized figure in the dream of an Asian-American girl. The young protagonist dreams that she becomes a woman warrior after fifteen years of harsh training with an old couple, and she demonstrates her filial piety to her family, the village, and the emperor. Kingston refuses to disguise completely her female character's gender identity. The heroine not only dresses like a man and fights as a general, but she is also a loving wife and caring mother. At the end of the chapter, we realize that the fantasy of becoming a woman warrior reflects a desire to fight racial discrimination against Asian Americans in the real world.

Disney's cinematic remake of the story generates a transnational encounter. In the exotic setting of ancient China yet in the familiar formula of an animated Disney feature, the film *Mulan* (dir. Barry Cook and Tony Bancroft, 1998) is a masqueraded text: a Hollywood mass-market commercial wrapped in Oriental iconography. Themes such as family values, self-exploration, and social restrictions link Eastern cultural conventions to Western expectations. The entertaining motifs—sidekicks, comic relief, and musical numbers—ensure that the audience will enjoy a Hollywood experience. As I sat in the theater, immersed in the stylistic beauty of Disney's animation, my curiosity about how faithful the representation was to the original or whether a Chinese legend could attract a Western mass audience unconsciously faded out.

Each revision or rewriting views the figure of Mulan from a different ideological perspective. The original narrative enacts a daughter's filial piety to her father and the family. The socialist representation presents collective gender-neutral action for revolutionary ends. The Asian-American sociopolitical consensus is privileged over sexual difference, gender discourse remains unquestioned under the allegorical veil.

The concept of a revolutionary heroine without sexual identity is fraught with questions of gender repression and arbitrary representation. To persuade the audience of the veracity of socialist aesthetics and thus of ideology, the film inserts a subplot: the story of Hong Lian. Her life story is parallel to yet distinct from Qiong Hua's experience. At age ten, Hong Lian was married to a male corpse, and for the ten years since then she has "slept" with a wooden sculpture representing the dead man. When the film introduces Hong Lian, she appears dressed as a man and is on her way to look for liberation from her particularly severe instance of patriarchal repression. The metaphor of cross-dressing indicates that the old system leaves women no way of surviving. The moment when Qiong Hua and Hong Lian decide to pursue revolution marks the cinematic construction of the triumph of ideology over gender: communism will free Qiong Hua to become a revolutionary soldier and allow Hong Lian to drop her masquerade and ascend to "true womanhood" in the eyes of the state. The narratives of Hong Lian and Qiong Hua contribute to revolutionary mythmaking as a mode of discourse.

Two metaphors that emphasize qualities of femininity—marriage and childbirth—seem to support yet contradict the myth of gender transition. For instance, in a conceptual montage, the camera introduces Qiong Hua as she places one after another the plaques of newly established revolutionary local governments. The following long take and close-up further reinforce the mise-en-scène of the liberated region: street theater about class struggle, training exercises for young children, and the joyful harvesting of crops. A master shot reveals a carnival festival where the detachment members celebrate their collective victories. The event at the center of the carnival is Hong Lian's wedding ceremony. The film narrative is not interested in the personal story behind Hong Lian's marriage. Setting the wedding in a festive carnival suggests that the individual's life fulfillment is part and parcel of collective empowerment. So while the old society married Hong Lian to a wooden man, communism finds her a real husband, implying that the revolution not only brings woman emancipation, but also restores her femininity.

The wedding within the carnival presents a semiotic linkage between private and public, personal and collective. The private and the personal, however, are subordinate to the visual form of revolutionary carnival. Quite different from the Rabelaisian imagery of "an undestroyable nonofficial nature," the revolutionary carnival staged by the Red women's detachment is a spectacle to show the collective dynamics of communism. Seen from a political perspective, the carnival casts "an ecstatic collectivity, the joyful affirmation of change, a dress rehearsal for utopia."[17] Seen from the perspective of gender, however, the carnival mise-en-scène is a spectrum of coded transitions. Hong Lian's earlier world, the closed form of the straw hut where she was confined, is visually contrasted with the open form of the festival field where she is freely married. The human figure of her husband replaces the wood figure in her bed. To underscore the idea that communism has not only found her a husband but also trained her as a Red woman soldier, Hong Lian still dresses in uniform while her husband wears civilian clothes. As the dress code further indicates, the double recognition of being a woman and a revolutionary becomes possible only when she submits to the collective body. The carnival scene can be seen, in Jamesonian terms, "as a master code in which competing class discourses struggle for ascendancy."[18] As the camera shifts from the newlywed couple to the party representative to Qiong Hua, the alternation suggests a remedy to the repressed sexual relationship between the latter two.

The return of Hong Lian's femininity finds further elaboration in the second visual metaphor, childbirth. A sudden, nondiegetic sound of a baby's cry announces the birth of Hong Lian's child. Her pregnancy and labor go unmentioned. In a spatial setting of the battleground and the temporal moment of the party representative's martyrdom, the birth of the child is represented not so much as bodily experience as a sign and metaphor. First, the birth of the infant symbolizes the coming of revolutionary descendants. (We learn the gender of the baby through the line: "We are going to have one more little Red woman soldier.") Second and more important, the birth validates the official discourse that revolutionary woman can fight on the battlefront as well as produce revolutionary heirs. By screening the female fighter in military uniform and as a mother but without a maternal body, the semiotic designation supports the film's ideological purpose.

Does Hong Lian simultaneously embody true femininity and revolutionary identity through the metaphors of marriage and childbirth? If not, how does the socialist cinematic coding system constitute a gender allegory in the guise of revolutionary discourse? Western feminist criticism situates childbirth metaphors in the framework of public and private spheres. The concept of the public sphere as man's domain and the private sphere as woman's place provides a point of departure to explore gender inequalities as well as female creativity. The structure of patriarchy assigns women to a domestic space and to a reproductive function. Women produce babies as acts of nature but not ideas as acts of culture. Feminist revisionists, however, see in the childbirth metaphor an attempt to "validate women's artistic effort by unifying their mental and physical labor into (pro-)creativity."[19] Such critical comments become problematic when childbirth in this specific socialist film is introduced as a public spectacle rather than a private experience.

We see an ambivalent gender phenomenon, patriarchy, yet in different forms. Typically in the West confinement of women to a domestic space has defined gender difference as a matter of bodily difference. In socialist representation, public spectacle merges the female body into the revolution, thereby erasing the fundamental difference. The erasure suggests not a lack of difference between the two sexes but rather the dominance of an unsexed public facade. Ideology and semiotic manipulation render women as signifying codes, thus denying the Chinese woman a vantage point from which to search for her female identity and subjectivity. As a spoken subject and represented image, she looms on the screen largely oblivious to the loss of her gender identity. For the revolutionary heroine, sexual difference has no bearing on self-knowledge.

Two female images, one heroic and another feminine, finally complete the construction of a socialist version of gendered meanings: communism emancipates Chinese women politically so that their reproductive function can serve the greater glory of the state. Qiong Hua's claim to the status of female sublime, however, comes at a price: she is stripped of her gender identity and given a body without sexual connotations. Hong Lian's moment of engagement in femininity comes when she dons the symbols of marriage and childbirth rather than from personal experience. She is a wife in a soldier's uniform and a mother who does not embody the womb and breast.

"Why, with all the desexualization and disembodiment," Wang Ban asks in *The Sublime Figure of History*, can "communist literature or any repressive hegemonic discourse exert an emotional impact and have a hold on our imagination?"[20] Wang's inquiry points to the need for a critical look at the interplay of perception and representation under socialist conditions. To begin with, we need to consider the theory expounded in Mao Zedong's "Talks at the Yenan Forum on Literature and Art," which has dominated artistic and literary creation since its dissemination in the 1940s. According to Mao's doctrine, the production and distribution of art (including film) should address a mass audience "of workers, peasants, soldiers and revolutionary cadres." Representation and reception highlight notions of class struggle or social repression. Viewing position and audience identification, therefore, depend on one's class status and sociopolitical interests. Because of the shared social experiences projected onto the screen and received by the mass audiences, socialist film production is able to link filmic representation and viewing position through class ideology.

The concept of ideology as defined by Louis Althusser requires a system of representation that elaborates how the individual is related to the social formation. As discussed in chapter 3, Althusser's central premise advances the notion of "interpellation," where individuals are compelled to identify with representations that are historically and culturally specific.[21] In imagining Althusser's ideological state apparatuses as cinematic ones, Kaja Silverman extends the notion of interpellation as the "insertion" of the subject into a preexisting discourse: "The individual who is culturally 'hailed' or 'called' simultaneously identifies with the subject of the speech and takes his or her place in the syntax which defines that subjective position. The first of these operations is imaginary, the second symbolic."[22]

In the process of representation and reception, interpellated viewers recognize themselves in model heroes who provide each individual with an imaginary identity. The imaginary inscribed in *The Red Detachment of Women* goes beyond gender and psychological conventions. First, the female protagonist's political enrichment at the price of gender denial sets an imaginary model for the viewing subject, defined as a collective proletarian class. Because of the shared social-class positions, the representation of woman as the oppressed awakens the viewing subject to her own class orientation. The hero's transformation from repressed to emancipated inspires fantasies of salvation in the viewing subject. Identification with the imaginary collapses, however, when the viewing subject realizes that the figure of the symbolic power and the dominance of collective force function as the authoritarian agent of woman's gender transformation and social emancipation. Identification with the imaginary is therefore a misidentification.

Second, from the perspective of gender, the process of identification addresses a collective male spectatorship that is politically autonomous and sexually masculine. In realizing that the heroine is subject to sociopolitical force and constructed for interpellation, the male spectatorship shifts its identification to the symbolic power, the Communist Party. The oscillation indicates a gender-class contradiction: identification with the imaginary empowers one's social commitment to women's emancipation, and identification with the symbolic intimidates masculine desire and social confidence because of one's inferior class orientation. Misidentification with the imaginary and subordination to the symbolic creates an unusual socialist spectatorship—politicized and gendered at the same time.

The portrayal of class sisters moving from enslavement to heroic stature certainly appeals to a female spectatorship, especially in a socialist era that calls for and produces heroes. The envisioned female spectator identifies with the imaginary transparently without any consciousness that the images and narratives are socioculturally defined. As the female protagonist goes through her gender transformation by means of the communist enlightenment, the viewing subject is taught that access to collective power depends on one's denial of feminine identity. Only after one adopts the military uniform, learns to speak the political orthodoxy, and erases sexual/personal marks can the repressed female become the daughter of the symbolic father—the party. One cannot pursue revolutionary identity without negating one's gender subjectivity. In a half century of Chinese communist history, the image of the female heroine hailed an entire body of women to devote themselves willingly and unquestioningly to the discourse and mission of revolution.

Part Three

The New Wave

Chapter Five

Screening China

National Allegories
and International Receptions

A WIDELY REMARKED achievement of China's fifth-generation directors is how their new wave films have taken a national cinema to international screens. By turning national identity and cultural history into visual images, this small, radical group of newcomers to world cinema initiated a transnational engagement in which Chinese productions for the first time drew serious attention from the West. The identifying label—fifth-generation directors—refers to more than a chronological convenience in grouping directors in China. It indicates the creation of the new cinema, characterized by national allegories; an aesthetic experiment in the visual language system, distinct from the films of the past; and an elite status with access to foreign capital and international distribution.

This chapter investigates a series of questions: What has made the fifth-generation directors internationally known and their films iconographic representations of China? How does the new cinema enunciate national experience in terms of a visual language system? How does gender become central to the discourse and visual construction of national allegories? How do production and perception cooperatively turn the new cinema into a subject of academic or theoretical discourse? With these questions in mind, I propose that the "naming" of a few directors as a generation serves to express historical memory and national trauma as shared, collective experiences. The skillful use of a film language system as a means of enunciation allows a rewriting of history as national allegory. At the same time, the tactic of gendering the nation and sexualizing representation exoticizes national images and seduces the international audience. Moreover, a cross-cultural analysis of non-Western cultural texts within the framework of Western theories poses again the unsettled negotiation between third world cinema and cultural imperialism.

NAMING

Beginning in the 1980s, the emergence of the fifth generation of film directors subverted Chinese film tradition with innovative films known as the Chinese new wave. "Fifth generation" refers chronologically and aesthetically to young filmmakers who graduated from the Beijing Film Academy in 1982.[1] As a group of mavericks, they radically reassessed the Chinese film tradition. As individuals, each marked his or her films with a personal signature. While grouping the directors under a collective identity, the label "fifth generation" is misleading. Under the banner of the fifth generation, for instance, individual subjectivity and diverse perspectives are obscured for the convenience of conceptualizing a new cinema and its directors.

In fact, the directors grouped under "fifth generation" are few. Nonetheless, the privileged few stand for a whole because their autobiographical accounts are shared by an entire generation. The common experiences and identities are rife with ironies, where ideological ideals contradict bitter realities. Born with the advent of a socialist China after 1949, this group of filmmakers grew up with a naive dream and a dogmatic education: the Communist Party was China's salvation, and only socialism could lead the country forward. They spent their childhood as Young Pioneers with red scarves and their adolescence as Red Guards in red armbands. Belief in a wonderful socialist society and the dream of China's perfect future under the leadership of the Communist Party were then crushed by political and economic realities during the Cultural Revolution. "The Cultural Revolution," as Wang Ban suggests in his study of trauma and history in Chinese film, "is the indispensable framework, both psychic and historical, that is crucial to understanding the works of the fifth-generation filmmakers, whether in their earlier or 'post' phase."[2] During the chaotic years, they were sent to China's most backward regions as peasants or farm workers.[3] Relegated to the bottom rung of social life, they became first-hand observers of the real lives of ordinary people, and their rough experience in the rural areas made them question what they had been taught. Exposure to the hard life of the peasants provided them with a fresh perspective on human values and China's cultural heritage. Most important, the conflict between ideological

orthodoxy and social realities fostered a cinematic and psychological tendency toward investigation.

In addition, the characteristics that distinguish them as a new generation of directors derive from their departure from films in the melodramatic
tradition and their rebellion against the revolutionary models of socialist
production. The impetus to defy convention sprang from their conscious
and persistent pursuit of the meaning of cinema and its language system. Each of their films directs the audience to the existence of the camera
and the mise-en-scène, and thereby to a subjective self constructing
the scene. Indeed, prominent aspects of a semiotic approach and subjective
cinematography mark the new wave films as a visual revolution. When
cinematic codes, image and sound, carry the burden of the construction
of meaning, the visual force enables directors not only to resituate Chinese cinema in the category of visual arts, but also to represent China
through a sign system heretofore politically manipulated and aesthetically
ignored.

While audiences and critics respond enthusiastically to the visual
beauty of new wave films, they remain aware of embodied ideological tendencies. In the introduction to his study of the Chinese new wave, Ma
Ning describes this cinematic movement "noted for its artistic inventive-
ness, its re-appropriation of the rich cultural heritage of the nation, and an
eagerness to deal with social issues."[4] Thus the passion of new wave directors for cinematic language suggests not mere aesthetic innovation but
rather ideological reconstruction. The visual system has provided them
with the discursive and cinematic means to subvert mainstream ideologies
and reinterpret the experiences that constitute national history.

To challenge ideology within an ideological system is, however, fraught
with dilemmas. The directors faced the question of whether new wave films
could depart from the mainstream and the cinematic apparatus of the state
merely by means of aesthetic reform. Under the sociocultural conditions of
the 1980s, when modern reforms coincided with political control, the creation of a new cinema in terms of visual subversion enabled re-presentation
but not a countercinema. The subtle position of the new cinema, as Chinese film critic Yao Xiaomeng realizes, "subverts and submits to the cinematic tradition."[5] In response to the same question, Zhang Xudong
describes the new cinema as a "substitute" for the socialist and theatrical
tradition, as well as "a supplement to an ongoing national cinematic discourse."[6] Zhang further confirms that "the fifth-generation and the new
cinema as a whole are inconceivable without their relationship to the
nation and its effort at constructing a new image and mythology."[7]

In the process of representing a nation through myth and image, the fifth-generation directors choose allegorical structure for their interpretations of sociocultural history. Frequently mentioned yet less often explained, the use of allegory in Chinese new cinema is dialectical in nature because the allegorical mode involves interactive engagement, where one set of agents "allegorizes" another. As one discourse consistently encounters the other, the interplay creates a double vision, inviting the audience to observe not only what but also how meaning is constructed in a given text. The dialectical discourse permits a simultaneous treatment of sociopolitical issues as well as psychological expression.[8] For the fifth-generation filmmakers, the dialectical relation appears especially in their infusing of visual signs into the reinterpretation of hegemonic discourses, political or historical.

Chen Kaige's unusual framing in *Yellow Earth* (Huang tudi, 1984)—heaven above, earth below, and human beings between—visually illustrates the philosophical engagement between man and nature. By inserting a communist figure into the frame and the discourse, however, the director invites the audience to witness an allegorical confrontation between ancient conceptions and communist ideology. The allegorical relation questions whether revolution can ever modernize traditions and enlighten the masses. Tian Zhuangzhuang's stunning cinematography in *The Horse Thief* (Daoma zei, 1986) unveils a marginal culture exotic to the eyes of Han Chinese. The mise-en-scène, which is so alien yet striking, enables the director to declare that his film is made for the audience of the twenty-first century.[9] In a ritual sequence, for instance, when the Tibetan horseman collects holy water from the temple roof, the use of an extreme low- and Dutch-angle shot subverts a possible reunion between the Tibetan god and the horse thief. In the process of prostration, multiple superimpositions reinforce the power of the religion and the dependence of its adherent. The embodiment of religious discourse within the cinematic form again appears allegorical, as the suggested meaning emphasizes how a horse thief is marginalized and rejected by the very god he venerates. The politics of adhering to, as well as rebelling from, tradition indicates the fifth-generation directors' conflicted relation with the mainstream: radical departure and necessary return are equally important.

Huang Jianxin's urban setting and expressionist mise-en-scène in *Dislocation* (Cuo wei, 1986) create a modernist art that satirizes the absurdity of socialist bureaucracy. The film demands an allegorical reading. In the opening sequence, for instance, the use of an unusual sound track and extreme red color establishes an unbearable condition in which an isolated speaker struggles with the torture of giving a meaningless speech. The creation of a

Yellow Earth, 1984

robot to replace the protagonist to attend endless meetings designates a futuristic modern condition where human and machine reflect the concepts of control and obedience. "By mocking the future," Paul Pickowicz points out, "*[Dislocation]* mocks and subverts the present order of things."[10]

Persistence in using visual signs to allegorize sociocultural history gave the fifth-generation directors access to radical reconstruction but created problems in perception. While the new wave films attracted international interest, domestic audiences and censoring authorities saw them as either incomprehensible or countermainstream. Political pressure at home coupled with warm recognition abroad put the fifth-generation directors in an awkward position. International viewers acknowledged them as image makers bringing the icon of China to the world screen. Chinese viewers, by contrast, saw a national betrayal in disclosing domestic dirty laundry to foreigners. The fifth-generation film directors were caught between the need to win domestic audiences with a form familiar to them while attracting

The Horse Thief, 1986

foreign capital by producing more national allegories. Such pressures drove the directors to return to the film tradition of dramatic stories rather than avant-garde experiments.

Zhang Yimou's *Red Sorghum* (Hong gaoliang, 1987) brought a closure to the new wave trend by returning to a tradition of narrative films. Directors looked for an engagement between fiction and film different from Lu Xun's account, where visual representation inspires the author's consciousness of writing, while writing in turn ignores the form of "shadow-plays." Contemporary directors assumed an authoritative position over literary writings. They made almost all the major literary trends in the 1980s and 1990s serve their cinematic needs. Zhang Yimou, for instance, turned Mo Yan's *Red Sorghum,* Liu Heng's "Ju Dou," Su Tong's "Wives and Concubines," and Yu Hua's "To Live" into cinematic spectacles. Chen Kaige transferred A Cheng's "King of Children" and Lee Pihua's *Farewell My*

Red Sorghum, 1987

Concubine into screen images.[11] A film director often assigns a literary figure or crew to write a script specifically for a film. The process of filming the
fictions, however, is less a mechanical adaptation than a visual recreation.
The cinematic treatment of the red lanterns, the dye mills, the Peking
operas, and the puppet shows employs the written form in service of the
spectacle. For the first time in the tradition of Chinese literature and cinema, visual language and motion pictures attained an autonomy from and
a popularity over literary writing.

HISTORY AS NARRATION

Writing about contemporary Chinese films, Rey Chow employs the concept of "primitive passion" to explain the response of filmmakers to the transformation of the dominant sign system from written literature to technologized visual images. By "primitive" she means to suggest a nostalgic visualization of the past as a way to conceive the present or future. The impelling force behind the interest in the primitive, according to Chow, results from a moment of cultural crisis—a time when the written work, the predominant sign of traditional culture, faces the challenge of a newly emerged visual system of signification.[12] The primitive, as it is imagined in the present, stands as a point of common knowledge and reference that exists prior to the present crisis. As a mode of representation, the primitive is a process of rewriting history not only between cultures, as in the practices of Orientalism, but also within a culture. For a culture positioned between Western capitalism and home-grown nationalism, the primitive expresses a paradox: primitive as in the backwardness of a third world nation, but also primitive as in primordial—the strength of an ancient civilization rudely emergent in modern form. "This paradox of a primitivism that sees China as simultaneously victim and empire," Chow argues, "is what leads modern Chinese intellectuals to their so-called obsession with China."[13]

Chow uses the concept of primitivism loosely as a kind of "othering" engaged in by writers, artists, and filmmakers. Educated elites worldwide, she finds, discover the "underprivileged" masses to be a fascinating resource for self-renewal and artistic innovation (e.g., modernism). In the third world, intellectuals turn to "socially oppressed classes—women, in particular"—as "primitive materials."[14] Aside from the question of whether "primitivist" is an apt categorization of Chinese directors, an insistent concern or even an obsession with the subject of history creates a new framework for a number of male-directed films. Chen Kaige's *Farewell My Concubine* (Bawang bie ji, 1993), Tian Zhuangzhuang's *The Blue Kite* (Lang fengzheng, 1993), and Zhang Yimou's *To Live* (Huozhe, 1994) explicitly thematize and dramatically visualize China's modern history. The use of history as the substance and form of narration reinforces the directors' subjective implications. Images and sounds of the past evoke memories among those who lived through the era depicted and arouse fantasies among those who perceive the recreated historical events as viewing experiences only. This "passion" to transform the historical past into cinematic signs requires further elucidation, especially the question of how gender difference figures into the cinematic representation of history.

When history serves as primary reference for the construction of film narrative, the past becomes a myth, a cinematic system of signs on the screen, and a critical discourse for analysis. In transforming silent memory into audiovisual pictures, film directors undertake the burden of history and cultural tradition. They resist official versions of history and reinterpret the past from a subjective perspective. As a generation who grew up with the version of Chinese history promulgated by official discourse but who witnessed a different version through personal experience, the fifth-generation directors clearly understand that the personal is political and that history is first and foremost the histories of individuals confined within the history of the nation-state. They affirm that the inquiry into how to represent history creates a new space and time through which a personal voice and point of view can find expression.

Representing the past begins with a child's perspective, which enables the director/narrator to access national as well as individual memory. As the camera angle turns to the past and the film directors cast their characters as children of certain historical moments, memories silenced deeply in the subconscious come to bear. When an adult memory is seen through a child's perspective, a subversive discourse of displacement occurs as the survivors of today have a dialogue with the dead of yesterday. The central subject of history filmed through the viewpoint of the child concerns the "death of the fathers." Tian Zhuangzhuang's *The Blue Kite,* for instance, relates the death of a child's three fathers by a first-person child narrator in voice-over. Each father's death punctuates a certain historical moment and in so doing constitutes the film's temporal structure. The death of the little boy's first father recalls a time during China's anti-rightist movement. The death of the second father enacts the absurdities of the Great Leap Forward. The boy's mother then remarries again, this time to a high party official who cannot escape the violence of the Cultural Revolution and dies of a heart attack when assaulted by a mob of Red Guards.

In revisions of the past, we find that fathers are the central characters writing the history and that their victimization constitutes the major subject of historical discourse. With all fathers portrayed as the victims of a particular form of sociopolitical turmoil, their deaths signify either a break from or the continuity of the historical past. Nostalgic memory about the past and an obligation to unravel the reason for the "death of the father" drive the filmmakers to expose a subjective consciousness through the filter of a child's viewpoint. *The Blue Kite* reveals a political struggle between two types of fathers: a collective father of the state apparatus and the individual fathers of the children. The positioning of the child as witness and narrator of the fathers' story, while intensifying the burden of historical memory, reinforces the interactions between national turmoil and personal suffering. The striking contrasts between the harshness of social reality and the innocent vision of the child, or between the complexities of political struggles and the limited mind of the child, make our perceptions of the historical past psychologically burdensome. With fathers producing history as children narrate it, history as a subversive discourse and narration as a cinematic system become a male-defined channel. A voice echoes through that channel: if even innocent children must share the burden of social repression, history condemns the state as oppressive. Yet a question systematically arises when fathers write China's history through their suffering and death while sons narrate the fathers' tragic stories through cinematic representation: where are the women and the mothers?

In the temporal order, when a father's death marks the cataclysm of a historical moment, the surviving woman or mother carries the charge of the continuity of history. In *The Blue Kite,* the female protagonist marries three times in order to carry on and bring good fortune to her son. She experiences and reexperiences the deaths of her three husbands. Each time, the woman is left behind to clear up the past and start a new life. Woman as a survivor and a reservoir of suffering is conceived as the female ideal, the moral model. Commenting on *The Blue Kite,* Tian Zhuangzhuang says, "The mother in the film seems a very strong character to me. She is a survivor. That's where the strength of Chinese women lies. Chinese women are like the sea. Throw anything in, and they can accommodate it. There will be very little explosion."[15] From the director's perspective, gender relations do not appear as the product of a patriarchal structure of domination and subordination because both men and women take up the position of social victims. From another perspective, gender difference in representation depends on who writes history and on who endures the historical suffering for men and women together.

A search for self-identity, embedded in historical retrospection, examines how the self becomes confused with and dominated by China's ever-changing history. Again, adult memories of childhood and adolescence leave the present "I" restlessly pondering the questions of self/society and history/reality. Today's film directors were children of the Cultural Revolution. Having grown up amid endless social chaos, they can hardly walk away from memories of being Red Guards revolting against their "parents" or educated youth laboring in farms, factories, or military units. The pull of personal nostalgia about China's past and an ongoing ambivalence about China's present lead the filmmakers to search for a self in the shadows of

The positioning of the woman in the closed form of the mise-en-scène contributes to the allegorical construction of traditional and national oppressions. Exposure of her social status through visual representation, however, captures her in a cinematic confinement. The image-as-spectacle shows the woman as extraordinary as well as incomplete. Centered and unattainable, the extraordinary image contains sociocultural meanings. Fragmented and incomplete, the image depends on cinema for its completion. The interdependence of the image and its construction unveils discursive and psychological anxiety, where the problem of how to articulate one's star image becomes a central concern. Image creation is therefore the process of inscribing possible narratives, identities, or meanings on a visual template.

Central to this process is the question of how to create a female image that is socially repressed yet sexually seductive. From Zhang Yimou's first film, *Red Sorghum,* to his last one with Gong Li as his lead, *Shanghai Triad* (Yao a yao, yao dao waipo qiao, 1995), no one would deny the evocative power of Gong Li's face. That face, in close-up or in fragments, invites and returns a gaze filled with all possible desires. When applied to the reading of new cinema, the concept of the gaze implies not just sexual pleasure in looking, but also a transnational engagement in perception.[20] For international audiences, the female image, focused in close-up and framed in detail, signifies either Oriental myth or erotic ritual. First, as a social sign and national emblem, the image presents to the international gaze her socially violated body or culturally wronged identity. Thematic issues such as the arranged marriage, the concubine system, and sexual abuse would inspire audience imagination toward a primitive and oppressive non-Western culture. In this manner, the engagement in looking prompts a sense of colonial imagination—sympathy for the poor Oriental woman in need. The screen image meets the international gaze with her bruised body and her screaming voice reinforcing her repressed position and reassuring the concerned gaze.

As a visual icon of stunning beauty and sexual appeal, however, the female image redirects the gaze to voyeuristic pleasure. The female body typically stars in seductive spectacles: jolted in the wedding sedan in the sorghum field, lighting the red lantern to select the concubine, pounding her feet to prepare her to serve the man in bed, kneading dough with her feet. These sexual and erotic exhibitions present Chinese women for the viewing modes of fantasy and possession. Seeing the woman as a double other reinforces ethnographical vision, regulated not only by gender, but also by national and racial differences. The socially violated yet visually eroticized image ensures the viewer a taste of cultural otherness and sexual satisfaction.

In contrast to the extraordinary female image are her less than stellar male companions. They are either marginal in the mise-en-scène or unattractive in appearance. Moreover, sexual impotence is frequently a traumatic, dramatic mark of the male character. In Zhang Yimou's *Ju Dou,* for instance, the husband treats his woman like an animal because he enjoys a powerful social position yet is sexually impotent. In Zhou Xiaowen's *Ermo,* the husband's impotence implies not so much a sexual dysfunction as a fall from a position of political power as the village head. Zhang Yimou's *The Story of Qiuju* (Qiuju da guansi, 1992) situates sexual politics in the arena of male conflict. The village head kicks Qiuju's husband between his legs when he comments that the village head cannot produce a male heir. The films, however, cast men's social, sexual, and psychological burdens onto the female body in order to transcend them. As a social emblem and visual spectacle, woman is designed to bear and signify male oppression. Ju Dou's body, for instance, becomes the object of her husband's display of power and the nephew's sexual desire. Qiuju drags her pregnant body on endless trips to the city to seek justice for her husband. Ermo sells her labor in the market in exchange for a television set, while her stay-at-home husband continues to order her around. All these instances point to the fact that the negotiation of male suppression in terms of the female body presents the most disguised yet powerful strategy in gendered representation.

The anxiety about male sexual problems and thereby social positions is not incidental in these films. The phenomenon raises the question of how to read Chinese films in terms of gender differences in a way that is socioculturally specific. A number of points should be kept in mind when considering gender issues in China. First, men and women alike fall victim to the social system and state ideology. The question of gender thus recedes before the state's dominance over the individual's life and becomes less a matter of male dominance and female subordination. To represent women as social victims indicates a humanistic concern for women's issues while expressing the suffering of both sexes. Second, the direct expression of one's desire or suffering in China is still wishful thinking for the most part because of the lack of uncontrolled public space and the centralized authority of the social system. Setting woman as a visual image in the foreground with man as an "impotent" partner in the background creates a gendered space where woman can enact through her body, sexuality, and emotional release—"hysterical" screaming, for instance—what would otherwise go unmentioned and unseen.

In addition to gender issues, another aspect of cooperative Orientalism remains caught in a contradiction between cultural artifact and market commodity. Recent Chinese cinema shares this situation with German cinema. As Thomas Elsaesser observes, German cinema was "created around the very contradictions of culture and commodity, of (self-)expression value and self-exhibition value, in a modern capitalist economy that depends on export to sustain internal growth."[21] In this era of accelerating globalization, self-exhibition depends on a public screening space and cross-national capital. We can take public space to mean a concrete space such as a movie theater, as well as a metaphoric space for freedom of expression. According to Wang Hui and Leo Ou-Fan Lee, "public space" could be a space temporarily outside the surveillance or manipulation of the state and might be an emergent space for cultural critique.[22] Whether concrete or metaphoric, however, public space in China has been a politically and ideologically sensitive sphere. If willing to reproduce the official discourse, one is assured of financing for production and distribution upon release. To counter the official discourse, however, film directors have managed to find a way of their own, usually by attracting foreign capital and winning international recognition. Of course not everyone has an entry into the international market. Zhang Yimou, Chen Kaige, and Tian Zhuangzhuang are among the few directors who have been able to project a national identity on international screens.

Zhou Xiaowen, a representative of the talented directors who have not received the international recognition bestowed on figures such as Zhang Yimou and Chen Kaige, did not attract much critical attention until his ninth film, *Ermo,* screened in the West. Zhou's earlier films, such as *In Their Prime* (1986), *The Price of Frenzy,* and *The Black Mountain Road,* were either banned by the censors or sat on the shelf for years. Unlike Zhang and Chen, Zhou failed to find foreign financial backing for his projects. *Ermo* only became possible with support from Pacific LTD.

THEORIZING A CINEMA OF THE OTHER

With the combination of national discourse, cross-national capital, and international distribution, Chinese cinema can be considered a transnational cinema. The transnational encounter that attracts international attention creates a desire to read and conceptualize non-Western cultural texts. Since its appearance on international screens, Chinese new cinema has become a subject of study and research in the West. Thus begins the transformation of a national cinema from a distributed commodity into academic discourse. In the engagement between non-Western cultural texts and Western theoretical readings, scholars and film critics face the problem of how to conduct the task transculturally. Important questions remain: Can one legitimately apply Western film theories to non-Western texts? What happens when Western theoretical assumptions are used to interpret non-Western sociocultural codes? How can a cross-cultural reading be made more constructive than treacherous?

Placing national exhibition in the context of theories of reading creates an opportunity to examine some disciplinary assumptions, such as the concept of a third world or national cinema. An oft-cited statement by Fredric Jameson seems to convey a psychological mindset characteristic of Western critics:

> All third-world texts are necessarily, I want to argue, allegorical, and in a very specific way: they are to be read as what I will call "national allegories." . . . Third-world texts—even those which are seemingly private and invested with a properly libidinal dynamic—necessarily project a political dimension in the form of national allegory: the story of the private individual destiny is always an allegory of the embattled situation of the public third-world culture and society. Need I add that it is precisely this very different ratio of the political to the personal which makes such texts alien to us at first approach, and consequently resistant to our conventional western habits of reading?[23]

For Jameson, the task of the reading self is to look behind personal experience for the inevitable political implications responsible for the text's meaning. A feeling of hesitation and difficulty arises because the allegorical texts resist conventional Western habits of reading. By his mapping of the third world and his loose use of "all third-world texts," however, Jameson is in danger of dividing the world into categories of self and other (of "othering" an alien cinema). Jameson's statement provides a reference for considering the cross-cultural exchange between Chinese national cinema and Western theoretical assumptions. The reading process treats national allegories in terms of Western political, theoretical, and textual interpretations. While Chinese filmmakers have translated historical memory and national identity from written language into visual images, Western scholars have returned the visual representation to a written language system—namely, various critical discourses. As the former relies on a visual language system for self-exhibition and the latter on theoretical discourses for interpretation, the final product must be a national cinema appropriated and theorized as the object of knowledge production.

As Jameson, many critics are predisposed to see films produced in a so-called third world nation as artifacts animated by ideology. Newspaper and journal reviews of Chinese films often start from a political perspective, with a discussion of how the film fared with state censorship. The issue of political restrictions imposed on filmmakers seems to serve as the primary condition for the reading of national allegories. The reviewers' political consciousness makes a distinction between a humanistic viewing self and a repressed viewed other and employs ideological criteria for understanding the meaning and importance of a film.

Beyond the circumstances of production, film critics seek to find the political implications behind the visual images or between the narrative lines. Readings of Zhang's *Ju Dou* as allegory, for instance, conflate the old Confucian society with the contemporary regime. The master shot of the old village leaders in dark lighting and symmetrical composition is likened to the aged ruling figures of the Chinese government. A reviewer adds: "The tale also can be viewed as a metaphor reflecting on the fate of China itself, which today is ultimately controlled by a tiny clique of old men, headed by Deng Xiaoping."[24] That the personal is political in film narrative has become dogmatic in film reviewing.

While journalistic writing takes Chinese international film as a political barometer, academic writing also appropriates Chinese cinema. Western theoretical discourses have gradually constructed Chinese national cinema as a newly emerged academic topic. This process involves a position distinction, the analyst as research subject and national cinema as researched object; a power relation, the production of Western knowledge through examination of the non-West; and, finally, a discourse concealment that covers the problems raised from the engagement between theory and allegory. In a framework of current theoretical assumptions drawn from disciplines such as psychoanalysis and linguistics and from popular fields such as gender studies and cultural studies, Chinese cinema puts on the emperor's new clothes and enters the postcolonial, interdisciplinary age. Movies emerging from Chinese studios are discussed in terms of melodrama and spectacle, desire and discourse, signifier and signified, gender and sexual difference, semiotics and cinematic apparatus, subjectivity and postmodernity. We have a theoretical preoccupation with the practice of the national cinema, as Homi Bhabha forcefully asserts in his comments on third world cinema:

> The other is cited, quoted, framed, illuminated, encased in the shot/reverse shot strategy of a serial enlightenment. Narrative and the cultural politics of difference become the closed circle of interpretation. The other loses its power to

signify, to negate, to initiate its "desire," to split its "sign" of identity, to establish its own institutional and oppositional discourse. However impeccably the
content of an "other" culture may be known, however anti-ethnocentrically it
is represented, it is its location as the "closure" of grand theories, the demand
that, in analytic terms, it be always the "good" object of knowledge, the docile
body of difference, that reproduces a relation of domination and is the most
serious indictment of the institutional powers of critical theory.[25]

"Cross-cultural analysis is difficult: it is fraught with danger," declares
E. Ann Kaplan. The danger, as she sees it, comes when "we are *forced* to
read works produced by the Other through the constraints of our own
frameworks/theories/ideologies."[26] Reading from the outside, however, has
its benefits. Kaplan suggests that "theorists outside the producing culture
might uncover different strands of the multiple meanings than critics of the
originating culture *just because* they bring different frameworks/theo-
ries/ideologies to the texts."[27] Torn between the peril of "danger" and the
promise of "illumination" that cross-cultural reading might involve, Kaplan
places her "tentative" reading of women and representation in recent Chinese films within the framework of Western feminist film theories. The
given perspective, Kaplan emphasizes repeatedly, leads the Western feminist into a reading task filled with problems and possibilities.

Readings of non-Western film texts from Western feminist perspectives indeed open up possibilities for different interpretations. The interpreter, nonetheless, in striving to apply a theory to a cinematic other, may
fail to fully consider the sociocultural context of the other. Through readings of a few Chinese films, for instance, Kaplan discovers that sexual
desire/difference operates not so much between woman and man but
between woman and the state. "A nation," she explains, "that does not evidence preoccupation with sexual difference must then be repressing this
difference."[28] The entangled relationship between Chinese women and the
socialist state poses an important question in the studies of gender issues
specific to China. Failure to put the question in the context of Chinese
sociopolitical conditions while relying on Western feminist assumptions
inevitably makes Kaplan's reading problematic.

Films about Chinese women or films directed by women, as Kaplan
indicates, begin to show a consciousness of constructing a new self or
female subjectivity. This awareness, Kaplan explains, originates not from
sociocultural transitions in China but from "exposure to western cultural
products." Moreover, Kaplan does not see the woman-state conflict stemming from historical causes but from the lack of female-female bonding and

the missing representation of a mother figure. Chinese films as the study *texts* and Western theories as the defining *discourse* create possibilities as well as problems for transnational engagement. When the text is lifted from its constitutive culture, how can one generate cross-cultural analysis? While Kaplan's cross-cultural encounter self-consciously indicates a Western concern in approaching Chinese texts, native Chinese scholars and students working in the language and theories of the Western other are aware of the same issues. Zhang Yingjin demonstrates the problems by rereading the cross-cultural works of two film scholars. "Dangers in cross-cultural analysis," he says, "arise every time a theoretically informed Western critic proceeds to subject the 'raw material' of a film from another culture to an interpretive 'processing' exclusively in Western analytic technology."[29]

Rereading Chris Berry's psychoanalytic study of the silent film *Big Road,* Zhang points out Berry's mistake in likening a close relationship between two females in the Chinese film to lesbian scenes in Western pornographic movies. The inappropriate frame of reference results from Berry's ignorance of a culture-specific phenomenon of female bonding in China. In his rereading of Esther Yau's analysis of *Yellow Earth,* Zhang shows how a critic's psychological eagerness leads her to use a non-Western text to demonstrate the power of Western theory. "Once outside its frame of reference," Zhang concludes, "a critical practice is likely to find its target completely unaffected by its presumed power."[30] In responding to Kaplan's view of the pitfalls in cross-cultural analysis, Zhang further emphasizes the risk by observing the critic's dilemma—that is, how one can be aware of the dangers in cross-cultural analysis yet remain engaged by Western critical paradigms. An alternative approach suggested by Zhang posits that there is no pure discursive space in cross-cultural study, only a "dialogic mode of cross-cultural analysis."[31] The dialogic mode means to dislodge the dominant theoretical paradigms and call for dialogues, negotiations, and interactions among critics, texts, and various discourses.

In addition to sharing a concern for the blind spots in cross-cultural analysis, I wish to address questions involving the perspectives, positions, and languages we employ to confront the challenge of how to read Chinese cultural texts in an environment of Western discourses. With a Western reader in mind and theories from other disciplines in hand, scholars in the West at least promote cross-cultural exchange from the motive of self-interest. In consequence, the engagement between the emerging Chinese cinema and "mainstream" critical theories too easily leads to a hierarchical relationship where the overlay of theory and interpretation can obscure underlying cultural meanings embedded in the film. To select an Asian text as an object of research and theorize it in terms of Western discourse may indicate more of a concern with an authentic *qualification* to address non-Western cultural issues than with the sociocultural issues themselves. It is as if only through scholarly mediation and interpretation can films of a national cinema become accessible to Western readers and appear theoretically interesting enough to warrant study. It is also supposed that an analysis of Chinese films from Western perspectives offers others the possibility of understanding their own works through the illuminating lenses of these methodologies. When cross-cultural analysis becomes mostly a matter of theorizing difference, some of a film's references to native cultural realities may escape notice.

Films produced within a given social and economic system signify in ways that are culturally and ideologically specific. Notions and concepts that seem fully justified in one context might become problematic when transferred to another with distinct sociocultural, historical, and political codes. Thus consciousness toward difference, readiness for intersections, and multiple perspectives for interpretations are pivotal for cross-cultural readings. The argument stressed here is not that we should not apply Western criticism to the reading of non-Western cultural products but that neither critical methodology nor cultural tradition suffices as a controlling discourse.

To investigate what happens when we read a Chinese text through Western theoretical assumptions is to enhance our understanding of both cultural difference and critical concepts. For instance, in *Farewell My Concubine,* the scene in which the mother chops off her son's supernumerary finger to render him suitable for the opera training school presents a richly symbolic Lacanian term, castration, whereby the human subject enters the social realm of language. Beyond the apparent coherence of this cinematic representation and psychoanalytical reference, however, we notice that entry into the opera world promises not a male subjectivity but a female impersonation through gender castration and reconstruction. In Zhang Yimou's *Ju Dou,* the male protagonist's constant peering at the female character through a peephole reminds us immediately of Laura Mulvey's concept of the gaze: pleasure in looking as an essential cinematic structure in which the pattern of active/male and passive/female replicates the imbalance of power in gender relations. When Ju Dou returns the male gaze with her bruised body, however, she denies pleasure to the voyeur and leaves him with a tremendous psychological disturbance.

What scholars and critics encounter is a cinematic representation of a non-Western cultural norm. The filmic signifiers of Chinese social and his-

generates ideology and profits. In a time of few responses to the political interpellation of the nation-state, the media manipulate social behavior and psychological norms.

The intertwined controlling forces, money and media, figure in a relationship between country and city, where the rural is cast as the primitive reverse of the city. The unfortunate and the needy call for knowledge and assistance. The city, however, displays its modern superiority and either rejects the penniless or saves them with leftovers. Nonetheless, the distance between the rural and the urban is narrowed when the editing of dissolves links them and as the functions of money and mass media draw them together. While media and technology bring the rural and the urban closer to one another, an essential human connection comes apart. In the eyes of city dwellers, country people are to be ignored. In the enterprise of sociocultural production, the rural continues to provide the industry with primitive narratives to be transformed into cultural artifacts. Producers and consumers of such products—television stations and their viewers, for instance—benefit from the "content" provided by rural narratives: broadcasting profits for the former, a sense of salvation for the latter.

The return to rural geography and culture and a cinematic realism provides the director with a strategic getaway from the crisis of film production in China. Distance from history and allegory enables a point of departure for the director's efforts to retain cultural position and cinematic authorship. Preferring a documentary mode to visual magnificence draws the audience, especially domestic viewers, directly to China's current condition. The mimetic and revelatory representation of rural reality, however, never appears simple and unproblematic. In the history of Italian new realism, filmmaker and theorist Cesare Zavattini called for the annihilation of the distance between art and life. This conflation, however, did not mean "to invent stories which resembled reality, but rather turn reality into a story."[33] The process of story making, therefore, can never reproduce reality purely. Elements of fiction and ideology always enter the mix.

Linking the rural to the urban connects the primitive to modernity in a spectacle of commodification. The film's specific positioning of country children against commercial and material conditions reflects precisely the situation faced by film production today. As the national trauma begins to vanish from memory, global commercialism fills the vacuum. The inserted shot of how the village pupils take turns for a sip of Coca-Cola displays a ubiquitous sign of the transnational economy. Yet the Cannes film festival rejected the film for being so "propagandist." *Entertainment Weekly* called it a "sugary morsel of a fable . . . as wispy as it is touching" and wondered if government funding had something to do with the sentimental, happy ending.[34] Reading the cinema of an other in terms of political implications remains active, unless the reader is willing and able to consider the given text in the framework of its own sociocultural context.

Zhang Yimou's return, Chen Kaige's departure, and Tian Zhuangzhuang's withdrawal exemplify the fading of a collective identity and the emergence of a commercial era. Under such economic and global conditions, national production and international perception continue to attract and to repel. On this occasion, however, directors of the fifth generation participate as individuals, making films that constitute one key part of a burgeoning cultural production in China.

Chapter Six

The Search for Male Masculinity and Sexuality in Zhang Yimou's *Ju Dou*

ZHANG YIMOU'S *JU DOU* RENDERS repressed male masculinity and sexuality in the form of visual allegories. The mesh of semiotic coding, mise-en-scène, color, and sound track constitutes a world of parable where a sealed dye mill conceals a drama of sexual transgression and psychological conflict. The two male protagonists are in a paradoxical condition wherein masculinity is either suppressed or lost. The masculinity they seek is tantalizingly near yet elusive. One man, a socially empowered yet sexually impotent husband, indicates tradition or the state. Although his mandate is eroding, he still rules the mind and the body of the people. The other, a lustful yet socially constrained nephew, represents a masculine vitality frustrated by social forces, particularly those embodied in the more powerful male.

To set the course of narration, the film designates a female figure trapped in an incestuous relationship with the "patriarchal father" and the "suppressed son." More precisely, she is the very embodiment of an allegorical element through which men attempt to verify their own identities. As wife to the husband, the female body upholds patriarchal authority while enduring sexual abuse. As "aunt" to the "nephew," female sexuality evokes male desire and subsequent punishment for the transgression. As the father-son rivalry signifies an Oedipal complex between the individual and the collective authority of tradition or the state, the deployment of woman as spectacle allows the filmic representation and psychological exploration to proceed from a male perspective.

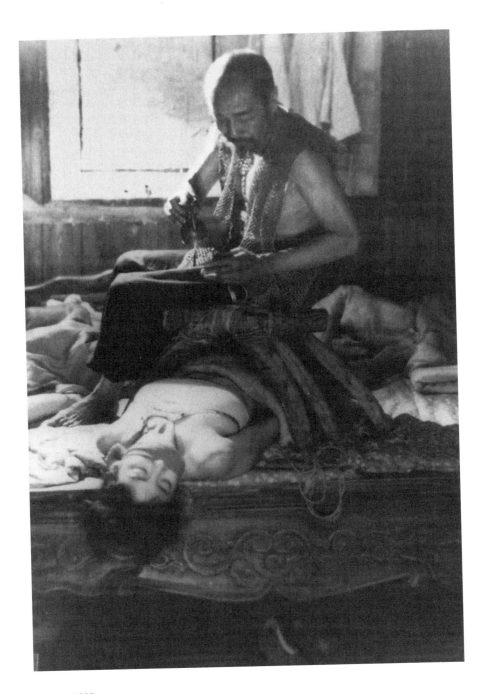

Ju Dou, 1989

Since its release in 1989, *Ju Dou* has drawn intense interest from film critics, academic scholars, and general audiences. Reading *Ju Dou* against the difficulties and errors that often occur in cross-cultural interpretations of non-Western texts, Jenny Lau finds qualities of "Chineseness" fundamental to the film's textual and conceptual meanings, especially as inherent in the cultural notions of *yin* (excessive eroticism) and *xiao* (filial piety).[1] W. A. Callahan, by contrast, reads *Ju Dou* as a political allegory invoking both communism and Confucianism. These systems of patriarchal domination, he argues, define the film narrative as a "woman's struggle against her social placement" and as a father-son embodiment of Confucian ideology.[2] The image of Ju Dou has become iconographic in Chinese film criticism; a still of an impassioned Gong Li dominates the cover of Rey Chow's *Primitive Passions*. Chow describes *Ju Dou* as "the sign of a cross-cultural commodity fetishism," and, indeed, the appetite for viewing—and writing about—Chinese new cinema is strong. One can, as Chow does, see the director in the role of exhibitionist, displaying his "exotic" female protagonist and thus engaging in the "Oriental's orientalism."[3]

Here I will supplement the growing body of broadly cultural and political analyses of *Ju Dou* by concentrating on cinematic analysis to show how the film produces meaning—more specifically, gendered meaning. As the central image in the film, the figure of Ju Dou exposes the oppressions that issue from social traditions. But behind her entrancing visibility lies the shadow of a patriarchal unconscious. In other words, a hidden male subjectivity is projected onto the sexualized heroine of the film that throws open the question of whose subjectivity and sexuality are being represented. To address this question, I rely, first, on a textual analysis of the meanings embedded in cinematic language and, second, on how the representation of woman occurs through gendered perspectives. Finally, I argue that representations of woman can convey a desire to reassert a repressed male subjectivity and sexuality. While placing women in the foreground of a film may display a humane concern for exposing social oppression, the gendered perspective that relates women to men may reveal a longing for a lost masculinity.

Cinematic representation involves the construction of gendered meanings. In this film narrative, the female figure is entangled in three character triangles. The first triangle of relations (hereafter the first narrative order) comprises the husband Jinshan, the wife Ju Dou, and the nephew Tianqing. A struggle to possess the woman and thus restore a masculinity threatened or suppressed defines the first narrative order. Elements of off-screen sound effects render the husband's social ownership of the wife, while a structure of point-of-view shots unfolds the nephew's sexual engagement with the aunt. As Ju Dou shifts her role from Jinshan's wife to Tianqing's lover and initiates a second set of relations, or narrative order, a sense of entrapment emerges. A closed film form and a subjective mise-en-scène rich in symbolic meaning place the forbidden love affair under an aura of confinement. Relations among the mother, the two fathers, and the son constitute a third narrative order, which ends the film with an unresolved questioning of the interplay between social structure and human nature.

THE STORY OF JU DOU

Set in a small northern village in the 1920s, *Ju Dou* is a film about a social system that produces repressed human beings. The dye house owner, Yang Jinshan, an old and cruel man, purchases a beautiful young woman, Ju Dou, in expectation of her bearing him a male heir. Impotent and hostile, however, he treats his new wife as a slave laborer during the day and abuses her at night for failing to bear him a child. Her tormented nightly cries arouse the sympathy and affection of Tianqing, the owner's adopted nephew, who has eyes for her the moment he sees her. The old man's mistreatment and the young man's secret passion lead Ju Dou and Tianqing to long for the death of the sadistic Jinshan. The "aunt" and the "nephew" consummate their love affair and soon after produce a son, Yang Tianbai, whom the old man initially believes to be his own.

Under the roof of the dye house and within the walls of the courtyard, secret lives and unlawful relations take place. The old victimizer, now paralyzed by a stroke, becomes the victim as he watches his wife and nephew openly having an affair. The passionate lovers, in turn, suffer psychologically and physically from their transgressions. The angry son, raised in confusion as to which man is his father, accidentally drowns his putative father and willfully kills his actual father, whose love relation with Ju Dou the boy deeply resents. With no way out from the blanketing power of the feudal system, Ju Dou sets a fire that sends the dye factory and her years of longing for liberation up in smoke.

OFF-SCREEN SOUND EFFECTS

Ju Dou is a subjective film in that off-screen sounds and point-of-view structures powerfully carry the process of narration. The sound track is beautifully constructed, yet the sound itself is shrill and striking. Functioning as a cinematic and narrative apparatus, the off-screen sound effects in *Ju Dou* not only invest the drama with meaning, but also help control the way in which meaning is produced. The narration can be viewed as a mode of representation rich with implicit meaning, with the relations between sound and space, sound and image, and sound and the viewer's imagination as primary elements. Each element conditions and is conditioned by the others; the analysis of the sound effects is a dialectical process focusing first on the nature of the sound and then its intermingling with space, image, and the reader's imagination.

Ju Dou employs a number of moments when off-screen sound effects bring the viewer's imagination into play by suggesting off-screen space before revealing images. We hear Ju Dou before we see her. Consider, for instance, sound cut one: a static medium shot of Tianqing lying in his bed is accompanied by an off-screen sound track of a woman screaming and a man shouting. As Tianqing sits up to listen, the screams grow louder and the man's words become decipherable: "You'll never bring the Yang family a male heir. You are not good for anything." Sound cut two: after two close-up shots of Ju Dou with her mouth gagged and her hands tied behind her back and a medium shot of the husband sitting on a saddle astride Ju Dou's body, the scene cuts to a closely framed exterior setting where Tianqing enters screen right as the off-screen screaming and whipping roars in. Sorrowful music accompanies the woman's cries. Sound cut three: suddenly the same screaming again emanates from off-screen. Tianqing enters frame right, picks up a knife, and runs toward the staircase. A dialogue between Tianqing and the man off-screen ensues.

As off-screen sound effects function to create off-screen space, the film image expands beyond the confines of the frame in the viewer's imagination. In its volume and distance, the sound source acts as a narrator directing the drama. However, since what is suggested by the sound source is audible but invisible, viewers are forced to imagine what is happening in the off-screen area. For instance, the first application of the off-screen sound track in *Ju Dou* (the verbal commotion) evokes suspense—something terrible is taking place beyond the screen—and creates viewer anticipation through the mystery of what compels the altercation. The audience conjures visual images of the sound's source.

The discomfort of hearing without seeing is mediated in terms of diegetic transmission—the sound passes from film to spectator, filtered through character.[4] In other words, the presence of an on-screen figure forms a character narration or point of view, connecting the off-screen space and the viewer's imagination, as we watch the face of a listener while we hear voices, sound, or music whose source is hidden. Among the three sound cuts, Tianqing is the primary channel through whom off-screen sound passes to the audience and through whom the viewer's involvement is connected to the off-screen space. Since the off-screen sound can be approached only from the on-screen character's point of view, the character narration becomes subjective. The transmission through Tianqing actively interrelates the audience with the fictional world within the frame. One listens tentatively as Tianqing listens, and one worries intensely as Tianqing worries.

Unlike visual images, the off-screen images are not rendered directly or concretely. The significance of this distancing and fluidity, which requires imagination and involvement, resides in its power to arouse curiosity in the viewers, who tend to be especially alert to what they can imagine but cannot see. The images concealed in off-screen space are often revealed with the use of shot/reverse shot editing: a retrospective and self-reflexive style. By converting an off-screen space that was imaginary in the initial shot into concrete space, the reverse shot mediates between an invisible world and the audience's concern for knowing that world. For instance, the enigma of Ju Dou's screams and the husband's tirade remains unsolved until the camera translates the off-screen sound into on-screen images. In shot one, the mise-en-scène, which reveals Ju Dou's condition (mouth gagged, hands tied), discloses the reason for her distress. Shot two, the composition of "horse riding" with Jinshan mounted on a saddle across the almost naked Ju Dou, highlights the violence inflicted by husband on wife. A return to the close-up of Ju Dou struggling to avoid hot tea poured from off–upper frame to her shoulder indicates continuing abuse.

With just enough revelation of the image to satisfy the viewer's curiosity and expectations, a cut from the interior shot to the exterior mise-en-scène, again to the backdrop of off-screen whipping and screaming, uses closed framing to suggest a sense of confinement. By allowing the audience to witness the action and then hear the off-screen sound track again, the film elicits the viewer's involvement so that fictional world and audience space are commingled. To further provoke audience interest, the anticipatory camera introduces Tianqing as he enters frame right toward the staircase. The direction of Tianqing's movement suggests a subjective narration: we want to follow Tianqing upstairs and intervene forcefully. However, Tianqing appears trapped within the tightly framed columns, the image emphasizing his impotence to act. When the shot of Tianqing shifts to a medium shot of the husband ready to disrobe, we hear the sound of lash on flesh and the cries of pain, while the image of abuse disappears from us again. In sum, the off-screen sound effects in *Ju Dou* constitute a process of narration by creating off-screen space and image.

In the marital relation, Jinshan, as head of the household and owner of the dye mill, symbolizes an ultimate economic and sociocultural authority. His position permits him to possess Ju Dou as if she were an animal purchased at market, to violate her body as if she were a reproductive machine, and to practice his power like a master riding a horse. The socially assigned relation between Jinshan and Ju Dou is simply but powerfully presented in the cinematic composition of horse riding. Sitting on the saddle, Jinshan rides the female animal and ploughs the woman's body so as to plant the seed for a male heir. The sounds from Ju Dou's gagged mouth and the bruises on her abused body utter a painful yet powerless cry. A Chinese woman's chief function in life was to further her husband's lineage. Attempts to swerve from that path were dealt with harshly.[5] Thus, social position provides Jinshan the authoritarian right to pursue lineal continuity by abusing Ju Dou. But *why* does Jinshan brutalize Ju Dou in his hunger for a male heir?

While social position offers Jinshan the right to purchase and possess Ju Dou, his sexual impotence haunts him with the psychological fear of not having heirs. To mediate the conflict between his need for social power and his sexual inadequacy, he engages in violence toward the woman's body. The contradiction between social power and sexual anxiety sets male violence against female sexuality. The fear of impotence drives Jinshan to find an object against which he might transform and reduce his anxiety. Ju Dou is represented as an agent within the text of the film whereby Jinshan's fear and sadism are brought to light. It is in Ju Dou that Jinshan is faced with the recognition of his inadequacy; it is in Ju Dou that his fear of impotence might be transformed; and it is in Ju Dou that his desire to restore his patriarchal power might be fulfilled. For Jinshan, therefore, violence is a way of covering his lack of sexual prowess, reducing his fear, and asserting his power by destroying the body of the other. In tormenting Ju Dou, he enjoys neither pleasure nor her pain, but transmits his fear and proves his power at her expense.

POINT-OF-VIEW STRUCTURE

In examining the relationship between Ju Dou and Tianqing, we encounter the cinematic point-of-view structure and the concept of the male gaze in a Chinese sociocultural context. In a cinematic point-of-view shot, the camera assumes the spatial position of a character. The camera eye becomes the eye of the character and of the audience. The significance of point-of-view structure in *Ju Dou* is to show us not only what we would see from the viewpoint of the character, but also how we would see it. A point-of-view shot, for instance, introduces an unstable relation between Tianqing as the subject and Ju Dou as the object of the look. First, a close-up of the eye of a donkey leads our vision to Tianqing, who is looking through a peephole: the establishment of the man as the viewing subject. Second, a subjective view occurs through a medium shot of the female figure with her back toward Tianqing and the audience: the revelation of the object being looked at from Tianqing's point of view. The donkey's sudden braying, however, interrupts Tianqing's furtive peeping and desire, shattering the mood and the chance to steal visual pleasure. Moreover, low-key lighting and the enclosed framing that confines the back of the female figure behind bars and in shadow suggest a spatial limit that makes seeing difficult.

The second point-of-view structure conveys the imbalanced relation between the subject and the object of the look by alternating the distance through different shots, camera angles, and high-key lighting effects. The shots that alternate from extreme long shot to medium shot and then to close-up suggest a distance between the two characters. While low camera angles distort the distance, high-key lighting makes the female character seem remote and unreachable. In a close-up, Tianqing, positioned at the corner of the foreground and blocked behind the lines of the wooden wheel, looks up. He sees Ju Dou, who is presented in a series of subjective point-of-view shots. The first is a long and low-angle shot combined with extreme high-key lighting. The long shot distances Ju Dou at the far background, framed by lines of hanging pieces of cloth. The high-key lighting places Ju Dou in a halo, and the overexposed space suggests her distance. Then, the long, low-angle shot is replaced by a low-angle medium shot where Ju Dou is bathed in the golden rays of the sun and the color of the fabric: a sense of closeness yet still out of reach. Finally, when Ju Dou looks back, Tianqing fails to control the notch of the wheel, and the collapse of the machine interrupts the looking.

The third point-of-view shot develops a gender shift between viewing subject and viewed object. Ju Dou finds the peephole. In the same position Tianqing used to spy on her, Ju Dou composes the look through the peephole. What the reverse shot reveals is her private bathing space. However, she sees no female body: an erasure or denial of the male look. Hence, by alternating the trajectory of the look, Ju Dou does not allow herself to be observed unaware. The shift from object under scrutiny into subject possessing the look establishes a female subjectivity in relation to and with emphasis on vision. Ju Dou finally stops up the hole with straw, hoping to eliminate the possibility of being looked at.

The final point-of-view shot is a silent yet powerful answering vision to the male gaze, and it erases the thrill of secret looking. The destruction of pleasure in looking is effected through the sound track, the turning of the body, and Ju Dou's confrontational gaze. Ju Dou attracts Tianqing to the peephole by closing the door and beginning to wash. Responding to the sounds, Tianqing peers through the peephole again. The return of his gaze is completed with three takes highlighting the moment of "turning." The first take is a long shot with Ju Dou's back toward the camera. The contrast between light and shadow highlights the bruises on her body. The long shot shifts to a medium shot as Ju Dou slowly turns her naked body toward the camera. Finally, a close, deeply focused, and high-key shot of Ju Dou directly confronts the eyes of Tianqing, the camera, and the audience. She turns to look over her shoulder toward the camera, seizing and fixing the viewer. Ju Dou thus reverses the visual dynamic back on the male look yet leaves the viewing situation unaltered. The wordless expression on her face and the powerful visual image of her body change Tianqing's pleasure into discomfort and the audience's as well.

THE MALE GAZE AND FEMALE SEXUALITY

The cinematic representation of looking and being looked at, of course, typically raises the issues of the male gaze and female sexuality. Although a Chinese film text may be interpreted in terms of Western film theories, notions of feminism self-evident in one context may become problematic in another owing to different cultural, social, historical, and political codes. The concept of the gaze and the structure of the look have been among the most important elements in Western feminist film criticism. Relying on Freud's theories of voyeurism and fetishism, Laura Mulvey defined the system of the look as a basic cinematic structure of active/male as bearer and passive/female as object of the look.[6] As the active male gaze dominates the narrative and the woman, the male figure occupies a position through which a sadistic voyeurism or fetishistic scopophilia is satisfied. With the passive female image associated with spectacle and space, the female character is represented as the erotic fulfillment of male sexual desire. Thus, pleasure in looking arises when point of view and shot/reverse shots direct the voyeurism of the male character to the female body and the spectator identifies with that character. Indeed, gender difference functions as a central force driving the narrative forms of Hollywood cinema. Visual pleasure is structured according to a patriarchal ideology whereby the female image signifies sexual difference while the male gaze controls the representation.

Ju Dou raises issues familiar to Western feminist film criticism but implies the concept of the gaze with a different cultural definition. If, as in Mulvey's scheme, the relation between man and woman is one of looking and being looked at, Ju Dou's confrontation of Tianqing represents a contradiction between an individual's sexual desire and social position. The female body, as before, is the site on which the ambivalence of male desire and fear is mediated. Woman plays a double role: she signifies male castration at the hands of society while reflecting male desire and frustration. In this context, one might ask: What happens when a woman returns the gaze? To what extent is the active-male/passive-female dichotomy reversible? Can a woman gain a masculine authority by returning the gaze?

The protagonists in *Ju Dou* live in a world created by circles of individual desire and fear stemming from social and narrative dislocations. As placement in the cinematic narrative conflicts with location in the social system, pleasure in looking is aggravated by fear of perversion. Seer and seen form entanglements vexed by the unresolvable binaries of pleasure/pain, self/other, masculine/feminine, and subject/object. For instance, Ju Dou and Tianqing are represented in a cinematic field of vision in which seeing is associated with male sexual desire. If we follow Mulvey, Tianqing's voyeurism should produce scopophilia arising "from pleasure in using another person as an object of sexual stimulation through sight" and also through identification with the image seen.[7] The protagonists' social positions, however, prevent the establishment of pleasure in looking and identification with the female image.

The social structure assigns Ju Dou and Tianqing to legitimate positions of aunt and nephew while the cinematic narrative transforms their social roles into a perverse relationship. The vision of the nephew toward the aunt moves swiftly from pleasure in looking to fear of being caught. Moreover, their low social status mutes the possibility of an active male gaze coopting a passive female sexuality. Under Jinshan's control, they are relatively powerless, and the lineal relation of aunt to nephew bars the seer from the seen. Therefore, pleasure in looking becomes embarrassment in peeping. Desire to love is fraught with guilt.

The fourth point-of-view shot is a powerful scene that explains how looking can extinguish pleasure. The peephole finally becomes the point where a male sexual fantasy is confronted with an abused female body. Communication through the peephole from both sides creates a frightening moment of intense sensuality. For Ju Dou, the turning of her naked body is a gesture that asserts control over and adds meaning to the representation of her body. This is a moment of liberation for Ju Dou. "When Ju

Framing not only separates but also brings elements together. As Tian-qing and Ju Dou are finally placed in one frame, the two human figures appear in parallel positions owing to the tightly framed compositions. Characters and objects are all pushed into the foreground. In the center of the frame are the two embracing bodies. Directly behind them are symmetrical columns, pressing the characters from both sides. Across the vertical lines of columns are the horizontal lines of the structure, forming a spider's web. Another layer of crossed lines fills the upper frame, and the huge wheel blocks the left corner. The enclosure seems suffocating.

A RESTRAINED SOCIAL FORM

In addition to the metaphorical entrapment constructed in a closed film form, moral and ethical values also restrain the characters from transgressive action. In other words, as Ju Dou and Tianqing taste the pleasure of the love affair, they are haunted by the fear of violating ritual principles—especially the principles of filial piety for men and chastity for women. Filial piety forms the essential value in the Confucian tradition. Elaborated in terms of the father-son relation, the elements of filial piety emphasize the obedience of the son to the father, the suppression of the son's desire in order to anticipate the father's wishes, and the repression of the son's rebelliousness toward the father. While filial piety has constituted the core of Chinese familial and social structure for generation after generation, the idea of fidelity also occurs in the form of chastity—the highest feminine virtue in Confucian tradition. However, while the representation of the seduction seeks to place Tianqing in the position of filial son, Ju Dou remains the transgressor. The difficulty of indulging in immoral acts while maintaining a moral reputation drives the protagonists only toward repression.

Mapping power relations alongside desire shows woman as the carrier of the burdens of cultural negation and physical/psychological pains while man is cast as apologist. Sexual transgression within an ethical hierarchy provides no solution for the contradiction between human desire and social institutions. Therefore, the insistence on and drive for transgression brings only social opprobrium and suffering. The inquiry into why it is woman who will bear the burdens reveals, first, a divided male self and, second, a cinematic strategy for representation. After Ju Dou is realigned from her husband to her nephew, she experiences an ironic repetition in her life history. The abuse of her body at the hands of her husband for not giving birth to a male heir is paralleled by her self-abuse with chili powder as a means of preventing pregnancy. The momentary joy of sexual pleasure is paid for with prolonged pain. The desire to escape and to love ends with destruction and death. Each time, when life meets death or piety confronts sin, Ju Dou is the figure of evil. The strategy of representing gender difference and the female character's confusion over her pain and punishment are expressed in two conversations:

(Ju Dou takes out a bottle of arsenic.)

JU DOU: Listen to me; it's either him or me.

TIANQING: Who?

JU DOU: Who else should it be?

TIANQING: How dare you? After all, he is my uncle.

JU DOU: He is your uncle; then what am I to you?

(Ju Dou and Tianqing are at the old man's deathbed.)

TIANQING: Killing one's husband cries out for punishment.

JU DOU: Didn't he deserve to die? What a loyal son you are.

(Tianqing slaps Ju Dou's face.)

JU DOU: You, too, are beating me. Revive the old man, and you can both beat me. I don't want to live anymore.

From these conversations, we recognize a divided male self, with internal desire masked by an external filial identity. The transgression evokes a conflict between private psychological need and public ethical restriction, where the individual expresses personal desire in the name of ritual values. As a split self who presents alternating personalities so as to facilitate different consequences, Tianqing struggles to express male desire—a socially and politically repressed desire. The male protagonist needs an object upon which he can impose his meaning. To represent desire, the male director requires an image through which his camera can convey meaning. In order to meet the needs of both men, the woman character is produced, standing front and center.

One should not assume that Ju Dou and Tianqing represent either heroes or rebels against the sociocultural system. Instead, they are conflicted figures who consciously enact perverse desires while defying ethical prohibitions. Jonathan Dollimore refers to this type of situation as "transgressive reinscription," where transgression performed as inversion or perversion seeks not an escape from existing structures, but rather a subversive reinscription within them and in the process a dislocation of them.[10] For instance, after Jinshan is immobilized, Ju Dou and Tianqing change their relation from aunt and nephew to that of a self-defined "couple" and thus violate the ethic of filial piety. Conflict between the force of desire and the power of filial piety drives them to search for a space where they can sustain their affair. Thus, an opposition of private/public space is constructed and alternated. On the one hand, they live like animals, hiding in a private world where the wild woods, abandoned cave, and the house cellar become places for them to make love. On the other hand, they present themselves as filial son and daughter in a public sphere where they feed, bathe, and carry around the paralyzed husband. The young couple's alternating patterns of behavior imply a contradictory psychic disturbance— submission to patriarchal authority and ethical principles while exercising individual desire.

In sum, the representation of female seduction assigns woman the role of transgressor while denying her real agency. In order to seduce man, she has to pose herself as the object of his desire by means of her sexuality. However, instead of transforming herself into a desiring subject, Ju Dou fantasizes Tianqing to be a figure of salvation, saving her from another man's oppression. The price she pays is her body, declaring that "I have saved my body for you." Thus Ju Dou retains her object position as she delivers herself from one man's sexual abuse into another's sexual desire. In the male representation of female seduction, a woman cannot consciously assert herself as a subject but only as an object of desire. In the confrontation between the seducer and the seduced, she fulfills her desire through her sexual autonomy, while man can be mirrored and affirmed by being temporarily the object of female seduction. In passing from one man to another, Ju Dou's body proves one more time the value of usefulness for her husband and the value of exchange for her nephew.

THIRD ORDER OF NARRATIVE

The birth of a son to the aunt and nephew proclaims the beginning of the third order of narrative: an Oedipal triangle of son-father-mother. The narration starts from the boy's identification with Jinshan as his father and Tianqing as his "brother." It ends with an Oedipal tragedy in which the boy drowns both his acknowledged and biological fathers in the dye vat. When we place the son-father-mother relationship in the framework of the Oedipus complex, the film's meanings take metaphorical and literary forms.

As the narrative order is transformed because of the birth of a male heir in the Yang family, a ritual of naming the baby sets an ironic tone to the relations between the child and his parents. Loud cries of the baby from off-screen proclaim the birth of the patrilineal inheritor, since he is born with "a watering spout between his legs." The camera tilts from the upper level of the house—the birthplace—down to where the village elders are gathering together to name the newborn. The composition of the mise-en-scène gives prominence to the idea of power transfer from a gerontocracy to the male heir. A group of old men sits in an ordered arrangement along the table—a social hierarchy. A soft spotlight on an old man in the center, in contrast with dark shadows on the others, highlights the symbolic position of the ancestor. After the men search the family book of names and argue over the proper choice, a writing brush in close-up finally makes its circle around the character *bai* (purity). On account of its connection to his "brother's" name, Tianqing, the boy's name is rendered as Tianbai. When *qing* and *bai* join together, the phrase carries a meaning of "purity" or "innocent from any guilt." Ironically, this son of purity is actually the son of his mother and "brother." Thus the relationship between Ju Dou and Tianqing not only violates social prohibitions in the second order of the narrative, but also manifests its transgression in the person of their biological son—the patrilineal heir.

IDENTIFICATION WITH THE "FATHER"

According to Lacanian notions, a child's acceptance of the law of the father and discovery of sexual difference occur at about the time that he enters the symbolic order of language. If so, Tianbai's identification with the father by his single utterance of "daddy" might be a persuasive instance. More important, the sudden identification with Jinshan as his father and Tianqing as his "brother" reverses the character relations (Jinshan = husband; Ju Dou and Tianqing = lovers) back to the original pattern (Jinshan = husband; Ju Dou = wife; Tianqing = nephew). In so doing, the film representation maintains the patriarchal structure by means of father-son relations while putting Ju Dou and Tianqing in the position of being punished. This cause-effect pattern of identification and inversion makes the third narrative a realm of psychological turmoil. In Tianbai's premirror phase, he lives with his mother and two fathers—his mother's legitimate husband and nephew. As the product of an incestuous relationship, Tianbai has been denied by Jinshan and twice almost killed by him. Because of the child's continued dependency on the imaginary, no real subject is constituted. After the transition to the mirror stage, however, the *absence* of his mother and the *presence* of the father initiates the child into a discovery of difference and threeness.

The absence of the mother always conveys a sense of secret incest taboo, while the presence of the father symbolizes prohibition and separation. For instance, a series of sequences reveals the maternal absence and the boy's psychological reactions toward that absence. In an external setting, the three-year-old Tianbai watches his incestuous parents disappearing into the deep woods. He stares off-screen with an expression of pain and hate in his eyes. Again, Mother leaves her bedroom to enter her nephew's room. The off-screen sound of her voice laughing or shouting resonates in the wide courtyard. As Ju Dou emerges from Tianqing's room, we see Tianbai, in a low-angle shot, standing on top of the stairs, staring at his mother from a distance. The little boy's white undergarment (symbolizing his name, pure heaven) contrasts with his mother's black coat (an ironic reference to Tianqing's name, black heaven). The boy's half-naked body (the presence of his penis) alludes to his mother's sufferings from sexual abuse. The low-angle shot of the boy and the high-angle shot of the mother indicate a position and power difference. More striking is Tianbai's stare, which aims sharply toward Ju Dou, asserting a patrilineal authority over a sinful mother. The representation reinforces a psychological contest between son and mother and thus between sexual desire and ethical prohibition.

In another sequence, an argument between Ju Dou and Tianqing on the topic of pregnancy is interrupted by the off-screen sound of something striking the window. Ju Dou comes out partially dressed and sees the child throwing stones against the house. A shot and reverse shot reveal yet another moment of psychological conflict. While alternation between shots brings the mother and the boy closer together, the psychological distance between them widens. Tianbai refuses to acknowledge his mother's presence and continues to throw stones at Tianqing's window. When Ju Dou slaps the boy's face, he answers with silence and a cold expression in his eyes. The torment between a mother's love for her son and her anguish over his behavior evokes a soundless crying from a deep, inner world. The camera then pans and tilts up toward Jinshan, sitting in his wooden bucket at the top of the stairs, singing delightedly.

The absence of the mother disturbs Tianbai's identification with the imaginary and moves him toward an acceptance of the function and power of the symbolic—the name of the father. The presence of Jinshan, the symbol of the father, signifies a social and patriarchal law. The law of the father, in Terry Eagleton's account, "is in the first place the social taboo on incest. . . . The father's real or imagined prohibition of incest is symbolic of all the higher authority to be later encountered."[11] Therefore, the moment of recognition of the figure of the father brings the child into awareness of wider familial and social relations of authority and obedience. In becoming properly socialized and assuming a place in the symbolic system, the child replaces his loss of desire for the imaginary with the gain of symbolic power through his identification with the father.

Moreover, the possibility and opportunity for this identification occur in the child's ability to code and uncode messages in language. Tianbai's Oedipal realization of the father and accession to language are constituted in terms of a psychological representation. Tianbai is dyeing his straws in the vat. Jinshan dozes in his wooden bucket. Mother is absent. The absence of the biological parents disappoints the boy but offers the old man an opportunity for revenge. Jinshan, a betrayed husband, attempts to kill the child after he finds out that Tianbai is not his son. In a silent yet tense atmosphere, a series of shot/reverse shots shortens the distance between the old man and the child with every alternation. When the old man's stick is just ready to push the child into the water, Tianbai suddenly turns around and calls him "daddy" for the first time.

Thus, language is identified with mother-loss and the admission of difference. Seconds of dead silence stir up years of suppressed emotion. The sound track of the striking of the drum awakens the old man's consciousness to identify the little boy as his son. As the parents desperately search for their *lost* son in the outside world, the acknowledged father gains a son in his inner psychological world. Thereafter, a third displacement is established: Tianqing, the biological father of Tianbai, becomes his "brother," and Jinshan, Tianqing's uncle, turns into the boy's father. Mother Ju Dou faces the psychological struggle between the two "fathers" and the son.

DEATH OF THE FATHER

Recognition by the boy, however, does not preserve the father's ultimate power; instead, it brings about the father's death. Jinshan is portrayed as a figure of social power, as well as a sexually castrated victim. In other words, the symbolic father has had his phallus removed. The Lacanian phallus signifies the necessarily absent object of desire. With the father possessing it while the mother suffers its "lacking," the phallus indicates a sexual difference. Confronting this sexual division, the male child identifies with the phallus and imagines that it will complete the mother and him. An irony occurs in the representation of the father figure, Jinshan, for within the patriarchal frame lies an impotent masculinity. As Tianbai takes the place of a castrated masculine power (that of the gerontocracy), he inherits patriarchal authority through the death of the father.

The metaphor of the dead father is visualized as such: Tianbai pulls his acknowledged father (sitting in his wheeled wooden bucket) through the door and then toward a dyeing vat full of red water. The shot of Tianbai cuts to a reverse shot of his inverted image in the water (mirror image). The same pattern is repeated for the shots of Jinshan. Then, a freeze frame and close-up shot of the rope that connects father and son appears on the screen for a second before it is broken. What follows immediately is a splash of red water and the old man's thrashing in the vat. Tianbai stands by and watches the scene without any sign of emotion. As the father's final struggle subsides and he floats on the water, the son starts to laugh: the first laugh in the child's life and the symbolic laugh pronouncing the transition from patriarchal father to patrilineal son.

The establishment of Tianbai's dominance in the third order of the narrative is visualized and formalized with montage editing. Montage and juxtaposition of shots in the funeral scene declare Tianbai's patrilineal position and the subordination of the living to the dead. Montage editing, as pioneered by Soviet filmmakers like Lev Kuleshov, Eisenstein, and V. I. Pudovkin, stresses that meanings are constructed through the juxtaposition of shots, not by one shot alone. When each shot employs one perspective of meaning, the association of separate shots could produce a unified effect. As Louis Giannetti observes, "Only by juxtaposing close-ups of objects, texture, symbols, and other selected details can a filmmaker convey expressively the idea underlying the undifferentiated jumble of real life."[12] In *Ju Dou's* funeral scene, for instance, the establishing shot introduces the funeral procession and the ritual of blocking the coffin. A close-up and extreme low-angle shot of the boy sitting on top of the coffin with the dead man's memorial plaque in his hands confirms his lineal ascension. A worm's eye view shot of the coffin and two figures prostrating themselves and rolling under declares the authority of the dead and the subordination of the living. The cumulative effect of the repeated shots, reinforced by slow motion, confirms the exaltation of the boy's social position and the degradation of his biological parents' social status.

DEATH OF THE "BROTHER"

Because of Tianbai's identification with the dead father and his position of true inheritor, his relation to Tianqing becomes one of "brothers" in which "there is nothing but the violent mutual exclusivity of rivalry."[13] The congruence between the psychological factors in the film and Freud's comments on the incest taboo further explains this Chinese Oedipal complex in psychoanalytic terms. In the film narrative, both Tianqing and Tianbai are linked to the death of the father figure, Jinshan, the former in an aborted attempt and the latter by accident. After the death of the father, they struggle against each other in regard to the mother figure, Ju Dou. Tianbai tries to prevent his mother from violating the incest taboo, and Tianqing wishes to be Ju Dou's secret husband one more time.

The rivalry between "brothers" (actually between father and son) focuses not only on the father's death, but also on the question of who rightfully possesses the woman. Tianbai's bonding with the mother and consequent hostility to the "brother" causes the final termination: Tianqing's death.

Ju Dou and Tianqing, it seems, can never be husband and wife. Years pass and still they cannot break through the social prohibitions. Throughout the film, up till Tianqing's death, they are often presented in two frames. With the heavy horizontal lines of the mill's structure blocking the characters frontally and vertical lines of cloth wrapping two sides, the closed form of the mise-en-scène produces an image of living people already entrapped in a tight coffin. Tianqing invites Ju Dou to make another attempt at reunion as husband and wife. They end up with a suicide attempt in the family's cellar. After the son finds his mother and "brother" embracing together and dying, he rescues Ju Dou but carries Tianqing to the vat. An inverted image of the two in the red water verifies again Tianbai's identification with Tianqing as "brother"—not as son. Tianbai throws his "brother" into the vat without any hesitation and kills him with a thick stick. Ju Dou's screams and the collapse of the bolts of red fabric announce another Oedipal tragedy.

The correspondence between the concept of an Oedipus complex and textual practice in *Ju Dou* uncovers a general myth about father-son relations. To try to reach an explanation on the basis of an Oedipus complex, however, a number of distinctions in the Chinese cultural context must be recognized. The first distinction concerns the prohibition of incest in light of cultural convention and the concept of filial piety. For instance, Tianbai's acceptance of Jinshan as his father comes from comprehending Jinshan's symbolic patriarchal authority. Thus, backed by tradition, Tianbai attempts to prevent his mother's incestuous sexuality. For the Chinese, according to Francis L. K. Hsu, "sex, like everything else, has its place, time, and partners with whom it can be resorted to. In the wrong place, at the wrong time and with wrong partners it is absolutely forbidden."[14] Jinshan's eager acceptance of Tianbai as his son after being called "daddy" is also motivated by ethical conventions because, as Mencius said, the lack of an heir is the worst among all the unfilial acts.[15] Bound by the concept of filial piety and a desire to take revenge on the renegade couple, father and son are able to repress their natural relation in recognition of social dictates.

A second distinction involves the imagined castration of woman and the symbolic castration of men. In relation to his mother, Tianbai does not present himself as the object of his mother's desire who will complete everything lacking in her. Instead, he keeps her in an imagined castrated stage by disrupting her sexual affair with Tianqing. In other words, saving his mother's reputation is worth the frustration of her sexual desire. The virtues and positions so specific to certain relationships are fixed: Ju Dou cannot meddle with her role as mother. In addition to the castration of woman, the film representation ironically presents two symbolically castrated *male* figures, one sexually impotent, another socially impotent. In confronting the two, Tianbai kills the old in order to end gerontocracy and kills the young to punish transgression. In sum, the truth or knowledge of this Chinese Oedipal triangle is not simply an individual's desire to reunite with the mother and to kill the father as a rival. Set against a social and cultural context, this power struggle can be read as a search for lost male subjectivity and masculinity.

Chapter Seven

Subjected Body and Gendered Identity

Female Impersonation in Chen Kaige's *Farewell My Concubine*

A DEPARTURE FROM HIS EARLY films, which were highbrow excursions into philosophical subjects and allegorical forms, Chen Kaige's *Farewell My Concubine* has attracted both critical and popular interest. The film's self-reflexive form of opera-within-the-film and visual mise-en-scène have prompted several readings. *Farewell* has been taken to exemplify a range of issues: film as history, gender and homosexuality, transnational film production, nationalistic expression, and international audiences. Pauline Chen cites the failure of film critics to see the importance of sociohistorical context to narrative construction in *Farewell*. According to Chen, the film "clothes the fresh bitterness of China's recent struggles in the dimmer tragedy of its ancient history."[1] Jenny Lau sees *Farewell* as a product of three Chinas, where mainland China's culture and cinematic resources combine with the capital and commercial enterprise of Hong Kong and Taiwan to create a transnational film. In Lau's view, the film uses a blend of melodrama and Orientalism to satisfy both national and international audiences.[2]

I will also address issues of history and art, but from the perspective of the construction of gender, especially as played out in the phenomenon of female impersonation. A central premise of *Farewell* holds that one's gender—or sexual identity—is neither a natural given nor a matter of free choice, but that institutional and social forces interact with the self to shape identity. This process operates on a subjected body: the body-self formed under the pressure of severe training to carry out assigned tasks. In the case of *Farewell*, three metaphors—symbolic castration, corporal punishment, and costuming—mark the transformation of a biological male, Dieyi, into a cultural female, the opera figure Yuji. Each of these narrative elements situates the body as the pivotal site upon which power produces knowledge and force transforms identity. This constructed self, a female impersonator, enforced through physical canings and sexual humiliations, ironically enables Dieyi to fully immerse himself in the art of opera. In addition to the question of how sociocultural norms rely on bodily practices to mold gendered identities, I want to address the significance of the feminized male— the elaborate attention the film gives to the masking of male subjectivity.

The melodrama *Farewell My Concubine* represents the life sagas of three characters in relation to the opera during a period of national upheavals. The movie spans more than fifty years in China's history: from the feudalist ruthlessness of the warlord reign to the imperialist invasion by Japan, and subsequently from the transition to a national government to the triumph of the communist regime. The Cultural Revolution brings the

Farewell My Concubine, 1993

most shocking episodes. In spatial terms the drama unfolds on and off the opera stage: in the form of the classic opera *Farewell My Concubine* and in the off-stage lives of the characters.[3]

The story begins when a prostitute, unable to raise her nine-year-old son, Xiao Douzi, in a brothel, takes him to an opera school. When the schoolmaster rejects Xiao Douzi because the boy has six fingers on his left hand, the mother chops off the extra digit with a meat cleaver. His traumatic entry into the school inspires the sympathy of another schoolboy, Xiao Shitou. From that moment, they become lifelong brothers. Everyday life and training in the opera school includes acrobatics, martial arts, and singing. Master Guan enforces the rule of discipline; he and the trainers resort to the cane. Teachers and students accept corporal punishment because they believe that to rise above others, one must learn to suffer. Years pass in the school, and Xiao Shitou, the stronger and more masculine-looking of the two friends, assumes the role of *sheng* (male lead), playing the King of Chu. Xiao Douzi, slighter and delicate-featured, is groomed to become a *dan* (female lead), playing the king's concubine, Yuji. From then on, the opera *Farewell My Concubine* comes to dominate their lives.

By the time they become stars, the powerful Xiao Shitou has become known as Duan Xiaolou and the delicate Xiao Douzi as Cheng Dieyi. The film dramatizes their complicated bond through the contrast between their on-stage roles as inseparable lovers and their off-stage lives as companions pulled increasingly apart. Xiaolou knows that theater differs from life, but he is never able to clearly separate the two. In Dieyi's vision, nothing but opera matters. Although he yearns to be subsumed by opera, he can never fully merge real life and opera. Against radical social changes, both men adjust their lives, but in different directions. While Xiaolou marries a prostitute named Juxian, Dieyi struggles to keep their stage partnership intact and unchanging. When the Japanese imprison Xiaolou, Dieyi entertains the enemy in order to release his beloved brother. Later, when Xiaolou tries to attest to Dieyi's innocence in singing for the Japanese, Dieyi refuses to lie and speaks the truth.

At the height of the Cultural Revolution in the 1960s, a time when husband betrayed wife and son fought father, Xiaolou denounces Dieyi as a traitor, and Dieyi exposes Juxian as a prostitute. The contrast between years of loyalty and the moment of betrayal is brought to a shocking climax when Juxian commits suicide by hanging herself in her wedding dress. Eleven years pass; Xiaolou and Dieyi, now two survivors of the Cultural Revolution, reappear together on-stage for a rehearsal of *Farewell My Concubine*. At the climactic point in the scene for which they have become famous—where the loyal concubine takes her life in fealty to her soon-to-be-defeated king—Dieyi *really* kills himself with the king's sword and transforms opera into a real-life tragedy. This moment of high melodrama prompted critic Terrence Rafferty to identify the ostensible theme of the film as "whether it's possible, under the pressure of terrible, soul-battering circumstances, to remain true to anything or anyone: an art, an ideal, a friend, a wife, oneself."[4]

Traditional Beijing opera is an exclusively male preserve. Since all female roles are played by men, sexual ambiguities and identity confusion can occur. The role of *dan*—akin to the English female impersonator—has been a significant tradition in Chinese opera. The purpose of *dan*, not simply the verisimilitude of woman, involves strict adherence to artistic conventions in the creation of an idealized woman. The spectator draws pleasure from the display of the high aesthetics of femininity. In order to achieve stylized artistry and great skills in female impersonation, a male actor trains for years to learn to discursively mask his gender identity by both stagecraft and the artifices of costume and makeup. Once the male actor takes the role of *dan*, he enters a gendered position and plays the female role exclusively. The depiction of female impersonation in *Farewell My Concubine* therefore raises complex questions regarding gender construction. Gender definition in the film goes beyond sexual differences and their sociocultural construction to encompass the element of psychological transvestism.

SYMBOLIC CASTRATION

When the camera focuses on the mother as she brutally amputates her son's finger, the scene suggests the Freudian concept of a castration complex. In psychoanalytic terms, castration signifies the imaginary operation through which the desiring subject learns that the only way to approach a socially accepted gender identity is to separate oneself from a presumed state of nature. One's biological and familial condition does not guarantee one's social identity within the culture. The priority of culture over biological nature and the desire for insertion into the order of the symbolic world finally articulate one's gender identity. Therefore, in order to remove her son from her whorehouse and place him in a man's world, the mother attempts to "normalize" him. Thus, a "castration" out of desire for cultural acceptance initiates the construction of social identity. Separation from the mother brings about recognition of the symbolic father (school trainer). The act of castration sends Xiao Douzi on a path not to normal manhood, however, but toward a female role. As a feminized male, Xiao Douzi faces a vexed identity. Ironically, the assigned institutional role brings Xiao Douzi in later life to what his mother had feared—"a male prostitute."

From a psychoanalytic perspective, male castration results from the threat of loss, and this mirrors how "historical trauma . . . interferes with one's imaginary relation to the symbolic order."[5] Chen Kaige's films consistently show a generational and personal inquiry into how male subjectivity is either lost or repressed in the shadow of sociocultural castration. *The Big Parade*, set in an exclusively male world, questions individual subordination to national ideology. *The King of Children* deals with the loss of generational ideals and the awakening of self-consciousness amid a primal natural landscape. *Life on a String* ponders the meaning of illusion and reality through an allegorical portrait of blind musicians who long to see the world. Chen's insistent attempt to understand diminished masculinity in terms of a subjective cinematic form, however, has often remained obscure to viewers.

The violence inflicted on young Xiao Douzi is another instance of a self-conscious exhibit of male loss in relation to historical trauma. The display of male castration indicates a sense of crisis not only of vision, but also of representation—a question of how to see and to represent male subjectivity in a chronicle of historical upheavals. The distance between representation and perception has not escaped critical notice. Commenting on Chen's early film, *The King of Children*, for example, Rey Chow shows that when women are absent and the physical body ignored, a world of male narcissism intervenes between culture and nature.[6] Zhang Xudong sees the film as an autobiographical work cast in an allegorical form.[7] Zha Jianying cites the director's personal background to explain his highbrow film style.[8] These discussions, however, fail to explain the displacement of the troubled male subjectivity. The focus on the castrated male body and later on the female mask in *Farewell My Concubine* enables the director to situate male subjectivity in the margins and in female disguise. Male castration becomes a spectacle for director and audience. For the former, the spectacle of castration evokes nostalgia for what has been lost or left unsatisfied. For the latter, the spectacle invites an acknowledgment of the male lack in representation. *Farewell* diverges from Chen Kaige's prevailing style and opposes conventional models of masculinity.

CORPORAL PUNISHMENT

After castration, the "female" man endures further humiliations in the acquisition of language as he enters the symbolic system. Here the speaking subject never gets the line right when asked to recite the lyrics in the role of a young maiden. Instead of saying, "I am by nature a maiden, not a boy," Douzi again and again repeats, "I am by nature a boy, not a girl." To dramatize how corporal punishment will train Douzi to speak correctly and transform his gender identity, the film intensifies the contradiction between Xiao Douzi's biological maleness and its social denial. The subject's resistance to the assigned gender role and the consequent force of discipline projected onto the body reveal a power relation defined by male anxiety and patriarchal authority. The representation of punishment as spectacle demonstrates the presence of power. "Public torture must be spectacular," says Michel Foucault. "It is an organized ritual for the marking of victims and the expression of the power that punishes."[9] Connecting Foucault's concept to a gender perspective, we see that the transvestite becomes the central figure of the spectacle, projecting the cinematic gaze onto the castrated male subject. The opera lyrics and the severe physical training indicate the symbolic power that subjects the body of the actor in a spectacle of submission and transformation.

Teaching and training under the discipline of the lash have held a place in Chinese tradition as a way of mastering knowledge. The Chinese character "teaching" (jiao) consists of two components. One component (pu) indicates a hand holding a stick. The phonetic part (xiao) literally means a filial relation, as father to son. The complete definition of the character "jiao" thus emphasizes a power relation between teacher and pupil and its association with corporal correction. In Farewell, Mr. Guan and the other old trainers are patriarchal father figures. Lash and cane become symbols of their authority. The belief in punishment as a way to exercise power and impart knowledge casts the relation between trainer and trainee as one of father to son. As a consequence, the father's application of discipline and the son's subordination become ritualized, producing subjected and practiced bodies. The power of corporal punishment not only physically pounds the theatrical skills into the body, but also psychologically transforms an identity from what one is to what one should be. Gender identity is part of what is being inculcated, masculine or feminine, regardless of biology.

It is the body, or more precisely the hand, upon which punishment is inscribed and into which power is inserted. The camera focuses repeatedly on Xiao Douzi's hand as the target of repression. In a close-up, his mother slices off his extra finger. Behind the window, the trainer lashes the hand nonstop. The image of the hand becomes so dominant that after the bathing scene Xiao Douzi's bloody hand fills the frame of the screen. The images of physical punishment employ the body as a sign in a signifying system. As a visual element, the body produces cinematic spectacles through the exhibition of its suffering. As a cultural object, however, it absorbs the hard training imposed by dominant powers. For the opera trainers, discipline performed on the body imparts knowledge and affirms their authority. For their pupils, bodily pain is the price paid for a social position and professional skill. Therefore, when beaten, the students respond accordingly: "It is good to be punished."

The students have internalized the ideology of corporal punishment. To give a positive meaning to harsh discipline, the film narrative adds its own footnotes to the contradictions. In one training scene, the opera teacher checks how well the students can recite their lines. Xiao Shitou receives a rap on the hand even though he gets every word correct. To explain this apparently undeserved response, the film has a character justify his actions. After each corporal punishment, the trainer or the master will comment on his motivation: "To beat you is to help your memory." "One has to swallow bitterness before one can be superior to others." Explanation of these actions attempts to mediate between punishment and pain, between body and soul. The narrative strategy of adding an interpretive gloss to the spectacle manipulates the perception of the audience. While visual motifs of violence may provoke viewer discomfort, comments by the character attempt to ameliorate our confusion by explaining the purpose behind the opera's disciplinary system.

The narrative comments point to how the ritual beatings produce a self-consciousness in the students that accepts punishment as a means of self-improvement. Opera training assumes the importance of psychological confession. For instance, the young students line up to listen to master Guan's explanation of the opera *Farewell My Concubine*. Inside the hall, Xiao Douzi, being punished again, kneels in front of a statue of a god. Master Guan describes how the concubine Yuji kills herself to show her loyalty to the king. He concludes that to learn the opera is to learn to become a human being: "A person should help himself to achieve the goals." The master's words evoke feelings of shame in Xiao Douzi. He slaps himself till his hands and face are covered with blood. Only when the idea of punishment becomes internalized as self-discipline does it produce subjected and practiced bodies—the body as the product of patriarchal discipline. Underneath the produced body, trained to carry out the tasks assigned by opera conventions, the biological creature gradually dies away.

The right to punish rests on social position. The master can strike the students since teaching and learning constitute a ritual task between father and son. An elder can punish the young because social order is hierarchical. Over time, of course, one may move from being a recipient to an administrator of physical discipline. As the young boys rehearse for a theater manager, Xiao Douzi continues to muff his lines. This time, his stage brother, Xiao Shitou, in king's costume, thrusts their master's copper pipe into Xiao Douzi's mouth and jerks it back and forth till his mouth fills with blood. After Xiao Douzi becomes an opera star, he too beats his adopted pupil Xiaosi just as the master had punished him.

In the film *Farewell My Concubine,* the boys must either accede to an authorized law and language or bear physical correction. Yet Xiao Douzi's repeated mistakes indicate that his resistance has been gradually subdued. The trainer's hand symbolizes an authorized power. It is through the power of punishment that gender meanings are imposed. It is through Xiao Douzi's self-denial of biological essence and reception of subjugation that the created gender identity becomes possible. The identity of Dieyi as Yuji thus is born after years of physical correction and psychological tribulations.

COSTUME/MAKEUP AS MASK

The apparent femininity of the impersonator comes from the actor's skills and his use of costume and makeup. In the opera tradition, strict rules specifying appropriate costume and makeup have been tightly integrated into each role. While the power of punishment produces an inner identity, costume and makeup provide its outward signs and codes. The actor displays a feminine ideal for the audience, which reads the codes to discern the characteristics of the role. This gendered cultural type represents a symbolic womanhood both conceptualized and embodied by men. Actual sexual transvestism through cross-dressing is neither the intention of the opera nor the desire of the actor. But in order to create an impression of a woman on-stage, the female impersonator draws upon what are regarded as the essential elements of the feminine character in a highly stylized imitation. The *dan* role is an artifact originating in the patriarchal mind, portrayed by male actors, and perceived by an opera audience.

Dieyi, however, fails to acknowledge a boundary between the self and the role he plays. Throughout his life he tries to lose himself in the world of opera, fixated on the image of Dieyi as Yuji. The stage relationship of king and concubine sets the basis on which he seeks the loyalty and love of his friend. A female mask conceals Dieyi's male identity. When costume becomes self and self is defined by costume, the distinction between player and role disappears; outer appearance symbolizes inner desire. In the ambiguity of self and sexual definition, Dieyi mixes stage opera with personal drama and illusion with reality. Why does Dieyi so obsessively indulge himself in the female role he portrays? And how do theatrical costume and makeup disguise and then strengthen Dieyi's gendered identity?

The concept of disguise goes beyond appearance to define a change in Dieyi's personality. In the repetition of his role, Dieyi begins to think and act as a woman. Eventually, he no longer recognizes his original identity; mask and face fuse in a self-image. His immersion in the female role receives impetus from the realization that, in disguise, a male failure can become a female success. At the beginning of the film narrative, a lack of masculinity prevents Dieyi from standing up to oppose his oppressors. Always a victim in a subordinate position, he either hides behind Xiao Shi-tou for protection or suffers homosexual abuse at the hands of men in positions of authority. With the created identity of Dieyi as Yuji, however, the mask of female impersonator sweeps away Dieyi's fear of social humiliation. In a woman's costume and makeup, Dieyi is able to place himself in a position of virtue, a model of loyalty to opera and to his friends. Through the impersonation of woman, he becomes an opera star and gains the power to seduce others. This success teaches him how to find in femininity a refuge from the harsh realities of the outer world. Thus, costume and makeup, with their potent cultural meanings, become so important to Dieyi that he seldom removes his mask.

When the male player dons the identity of the costume, audiences willingly suspend their disbelief during the performance and refuse to see past the impersonation. Audiences of traditional opera do not question the discrepancy between actual sex and apparent gender embodied in the figure of the male heroine. To see a male character playing a female role is normal; a real woman appearing on-stage would be abnormal. The theater offers perfect symbols, such as that of woman designed, impersonated, and perceived by men. The spectators' knowledge that a skilled male actor performs the female role makes plain the gap between sex and gender. On-stage, the female impersonator appeals to the audience with his highly stylized feminine performance. Off-stage, he may suffer the unwanted sexual advances of opera patrons. Thus the strength of opera convention, the absence of a woman player, and the artifice of costume and makeup erect a wall of gender ambiguity between actor and audience.

The transvestite entails a sexual ambiguity: the on-stage persona, deeply ingrained through years of rigorous training, runs up against the off-stage gender expectations. On-stage, Dieyi devotes his entire subjectivity to an idealized female identity; off-stage he becomes a sexual object violated by social force. Two scenes in the film highlight how Dieyi's cultivation of femininity fuels the fantasies of powerful men. In the first, Xiao Douzi and

frames Xiaolou, Dieyi, and their teacher together in the foreground. The reverse shot reveals Juxian at a distance, watching as the master whips her husband. Repeated depiction of men and woman in separate frames fixes Juxian as a distant observer unable to enter the men's world or to interfere with their affairs. The cumulative effect of the shot/reverse shot pattern creates a sense of separate spheres that prefigures the break between Xiaolou and Juxian.

The shot/reverse shot technique yields to the use of a long take, however, when Xiaolou punishes Juxian for her attempt to interfere with the men. When Juxian persists in trying to stop the old man from beating her husband, Xiaolou comes up to Juxian and slaps her face. A long shot with a depth of field reestablishes the scene with everyone in the same frame. As Xiaolou hits Juxian, the other men watch, and the subordination of woman to man is demonstrated and affirmed. Xiaolou's shouts of "This is men's business, so shut up" spell out the insularity of the male sphere. In short, whenever Juxian tries to intervene in men's affairs, the pattern of shot/reverse shot pushes her away. When she becomes subjected to men's will, however, the long take gathers all the men together to participate in the repression as perpetrators or witnesses.

To establish her identity as a virtuous woman, Juxian plans to bear the man's male heir. For her, the dream of being a mother means more than having a child; it is a way to strengthen her heterosexual relation to Xiaolou and her gender position in society. But because her acceptance of the conventional roles of wife and mother stems not from self-will but from repression, she becomes man's absolute other. Juxian approaches these roles with such determination that she comes across as a one-dimensional character. Only childbearing gives her some ability to negotiate with men and to balance gender relations. For instance, in the scene where Xiaolou hits Juxian for trying to stop the old teacher from whipping him, Xiaolou threatens to strike her with a long board. Juxian responds by laying her hand on her belly: "If you beat me to death, you will kill two lives. Duan's family will no longer have a male heir." Revealing her pregnancy curtails Xiaolou's violence. There is negotiation here, but the film also calls attention to the sexual division of labor.

The separate spheres of public performance and private life are gendered spaces. Men occupy the public domain and own the stage profession (the opera); women have the home and the responsibility for reproduction. Each time Juxian crosses the line of sexual division, she is punished. In the middle of a performance by Dieyi and Xiaolou, soldiers storm the stage. Juxian, heavily pregnant, rushes to aid her husband. One of the soldiers delivers a blow to her belly with his rifle butt, causing a miscarriage. At the moment of her miscarriage, one camera shot frames Juxian off-stage as she suffers the loss of her baby. Juxian apologizes to Xiaolou and deeply grieves the failure to bear him a son. The reverse shot, however, freezes Xiaolou on-stage as he looks helplessly off-screen.

After the loss of the child, the cinematic representation continues to keep Xiaolou and Juxian in separate frames. As Juxian lies in bed talking to Xiaolou, he remains off-screen, his image reflected in the mirror by the bed. The mise-en-scène suggests that Juxian will never fulfill her longing to become a beloved wife and mother. Her transition from prostitute to virtuous woman remains a dream because she cannot transcend the rigid boundary between "bad" and "good" woman imposed by patriarchal conventions. Juxian remains blind to her predicament; she fails to see how the patriarchal system frustrates her idea of a satisfying life: "We have lost our child for helping your stage brother. I have only you now. Please resign from the opera after you get your brother out of prison. As long as we live a peaceful life, I will be satisfied even if we have to beg for food."

Juxian lacks individualizing characteristics, and her self-consciousness remains at the level of domestic desire. Since the film narrative subordinates female consciousness to the norms of prevailing gender ideology and limits the representation of woman to her search for a place within the gendered social world, the woman character signifies neither female agency nor psychological complexity. She exists in the narrative for the purpose of setting off the two male protagonists. Chen Kaige explains this representation of Juxian as follows: "My understanding of a woman's life and fate is that a female comes into this world only for love."[15] Thus Juxian is auxiliary to the significant actions occurring in the social sphere, and her rivalry with Dieyi makes her more of an outsider.

While represented as Xiaolou's subordinate, Juxian stands in relation to Dieyi as his bitter rival. Whether in subordination or opposition, the female character remains man's other. In competition with Dieyi, Juxian distinguishes her identity as woman from the discursive female impersonations. When the film representation stages a direct confrontation between "natural woman" and "woman in mask," Juxian and Dieyi fight for their privileged identities as wife and stage concubine. The conflict between "natural woman" and "woman in mask" thus puts gender relations in a framework of power struggles. Important questions to consider include the following: By what means do Juxian and Dieyi struggle to establish their gender positions? How is their conflict represented in terms of cinematic structures? And what meanings are produced from these representations?

The cinematic composition introduces and then interprets the confrontation between the female and the "femaled" characters. Juxian, shoeless and bearing a parcel, comes to the theater to see Xiaolou. Dieyi, in full costume and makeup as the concubine Yuji, has just stepped off the stage. Crosscutting between the close-up shot of Juxian and the reverse shot of Dieyi immediately suggests the conflict between them. When an over-the-shoulder shot finally brings Juxian, Dieyi, and Xiaolou together, the composition makes a visual statement on their entangled relationships. Xiaolou, framed in the center, faces the camera, while Juxian on his left and Dieyi on his right face each other. The compositional weight reveals that Juxian and Dieyi will compete for the possession of Xiaolou.

In fighting for Xiaolou, Juxian and Dieyi resort to gender-specific strategies. The film narrative assigns knowledge to the man and domesticity to the woman, thus establishing the ground upon which gender meanings are constituted. For instance, the conversations between Juxian and Xiaolou and then between Juxian and Dieyi indicate how the filmic narration inserts gender meanings into its characters. Of her desire to marry Xiaolou, Juxian says, "Juxian has a cruel fate. If you take her, she will serve you like a horse and cow. If you dislike her, she just needs to jump off the floor one more time." She refers to her leap from a balcony in the brothel, an occasion when Xiaolou saved her. Juxian sees her choices as either servitude in prostitution or in marriage or death. Dieyi, however, derides Juxian for having no proper measure of herself. As the camera tracks with Dieyi as he walks between Juxian and Xiaolou, he drops off a pair of shoes for Juxian. An inserted close-up of Juxian's bare feet and the shoes that Dieyi has given her symbolizes her status as a prostitute.[16] The following conversation ensues:

DIEYI: Where did you learn the opera?

JUXIAN: How could I have the opportunity of learning the opera?

DIEYI: Since you don't have the skills to perform the opera, then don't just come here and spill dog's blood![17]

Dieyi and Juxian speak in different voices. Juxian uses the terms of social convention, while Dieyi challenges the woman with questions in his independent tones. Dieyi's dual identities—a man playing a female role—produce distinct attitudes. His obsession with the female role discloses a homosexual longing for Xiaolou. Moreover, the concealed masculine tendency damaged by social castration yet inherent in his psychological unconscious provokes a jealousy and impulse for revenge against his female rival.

The irony is that while the male character expresses his desire for truth and loyalty by assuming a submissive feminine identity, he humiliates a woman to heal his traumatized psyche and experience "maleness" through the power of domination. Female impersonation, as Joan Riviere indicates, "is a way of promoting the notion of masculine power while masking it."[18]

The male protagonist's feminine disguise—his skill at playing a woman—and his hidden masculine power produce the precise strategies that structure the relations between Dieyi and Juxian. By virtue of Dieyi's association with the signifying power of opera artifacts and Juxian's with only her biological essence, the social positions of male domination and female subordination have, in this sense, long been waiting for them. The female impersonator's apparent femininity and covert masculinity provide him with double potentials—to deal with homosexual desire on the one hand and with his female rival on the other. Therefore, as Juxian competes with him for Xiaolou, Dieyi is able to insult her by asking whether she has learned the skills of performing opera. If not, then she should stop putting her feet into the men's world.

Throughout the film, the struggle between Dieyi and Juxian is mapped onto the issue of whether Xiaolou continues in opera or abandons it. As Dieyi comes to represent both femininity and opera, the film leaves little room for the woman. In order to contest Dieyi, Juxian has to place herself in a position "that is sanctioned by and guarantees masculinist structures of representation."[19] Domesticity prohibits female subjectivity while guaranteeing male subjectivity. In other words, as she assumes responsibility for childbearing and sexuality, Juxian can only be Xiaolou's half-wife. Each confrontation with Dieyi brings Juxian much pain. In order to convince Dieyi to help gain Xiaolou's release from Japanese arrest, Juxian has to agree to go back to her brothel. In helping both Dieyi and Xiaolou fend off the soldiers' attack, she loses her unborn child. At the end of the film, both Xiaolou and Dieyi betray her.

The female protagonist is not only a signifier of male desires, but also an erotic object displayed for the audience's voyeuristic pleasure. The system of point-of-view shots presents woman for visual delectation. In one scene, when Dieyi visits Xiaolou's family on a rainy night, a series of point-of-view shots accommodates the male gaze. Dieyi (dressed for the first time as a man, in a revolutionary suit) stops to peer through the window when he arrives at Xiaolou's house. From Dieyi's perspective the viewer follows the action inside the room, and a private space is violated. Inside, Xiaolou and Juxian are making love. Outside, the voyeur takes in the scene. As the

position when applied to non-Western sociocultural conditions? What other possible assumptions should be considered if gender difference fails to explain women's problems in China?

With these questions in mind, I first listen to the voices of Chinese women in order to understand why they reject the theory of feminism. In 1989, scholars and readers witnessed the appearance of the first series of women's studies' publications in China. The series aims to promote this field of research and advocate consciousness on gender issues. Li Xiaojiang, the editor in chief, declares in her introduction that the series defines feminism with "Chinese characteristics" that emphasize "the nation as a point of departure, woman the object of research, a comparison between East and West, and men and women as a means of approach."[6] Since its inception, the series has made a monumental mark in the initiation of women's studies in China. Its call for female consciousness and theoretical research urges scholars and critics to take up various subject studies that concentrate on women's issues. In 1998, Li Xiaojiang published a collection of essays. One of the pieces, "On Feminism," is striking for its controversial statements and outspoken manner. But the surprise lies in her change in tone on the subject of gender and feminism. "I've always denied that I'm a feminist," she declares. Li then explains from different perspectives why she rejects the notion of feminism and the identity of feminist. The contrast between her early publications and her more recent ones invites an exploration of a troubled identity and the idea of "feminism with Chinese characteristics."[7]

Li Xiaojiang sees gender as an ontological construction, where language and terminology define one's sociocultural and gender identity. She explains: "The [Chinese] prefixes 'nü' (female) and 'nan' (male) are attached to the root, 'human being' (ren), whereas the English word 'woman' is attached to the word 'man.'" From this linguistic specificity, she concludes that no matter how far women's liberation is carried out in China, "there is no need to launch another revolution in our conceptual scheme because in our language the term 'woman' (nüren) is not predicated on man."[8] Theoretically, Li suggests that the concept of women's liberation originates in Marxism, not feminism. It focuses primarily on class rather than gender difference. These two theoretical assumptions, embodying their own unique systems as well as problems, should not be interchangeable, and one should never be used to attack the other. "Marxist perspective offers me a broad angle of view," Li asserts, "that enables me to transcend the limitation of woman herself and embrace the mission of emancipating humankind."[9]

Seen from a Marxist perspective, gender relations are more a matter of unity than difference. Li explains that women's emancipation in China results from the efforts of both men and women. Men's contribution, comparatively speaking, is superior to women's. Male intellectuals have for a long time clearly realized the significant connection between women's emancipation and national salvation. They provoked ideas of gender equality and put them into practice. For instance, the campaign to abolish footbinding, the creation of women's schools, and the call for women to uphold half the sky attest to the fact that male counterparts have always supported and participated in women's emancipation. To be engaged in such a relationship, Li asks in retrospect, "How can we break the arms of 'sedan carriers' who 'carried' us from tradition into emancipation?" and "How can women take men as their opponents when someday women achieve independence?"[10]

Li Xiaojiang goes on from a historical perspective to explain the irrelevance of feminism to gender conditions in China. Women's liberation in China, she argues, is the outcome of socialist revolution rather than of feminist movements. No matter how many problems are embedded within the revolution, its achievements are more obvious than its errors. It is the social revolution that legitimizes the concept of gender equality through state ideology and social discourse. This constitutional equality, Li believes, has put Chinese women in a social position superior to that of women in many other countries, even the Western nations. Since the early twentieth century, for instance, women and their emancipation have been subjects of consideration for the nation-state. Policies and practices on matters of birth control, employment, political participation, and social welfare demonstrate a difference between the social condition of women in China and in the West. Given this background, Li Xiaojiang asks again rhetorically, "What's the implication of proposing feminism in China?"[11]

Clearly, in her opinion of women's studies in China, Li Xiaojiang denies a feminist identity, a feminist discipline, and, more critically, *difference* as the primary marker of gender relations. In listening carefully to the opposing voice, either individual or collective, one hears the message that gender politics in China appear to concern women and nation more than the opposition between men and women. The women-nation polarity cannot be oppositional but must be interdependent, where one evaluates nationalism in relation to its feminist practices and woman's status according to the extent of national salvation. I argue that problems occur precisely with the embodiment of women in the discourse of nationalism. In the guise of nationalism, woman serves as a figure of the oppressed, bearing external invasions and domestic problems, a trope of resistance in the struggle for national independence, and a symbol of a component in the building of the new nation-state. What is left unexamined is whether woman occupies a subject position in the narrative and narration of nationalism.

Theoretically, Marxism sees gender in terms of class and women's emancipation as part of the proletarian revolution. As a universal category, the proletariat ignores not only gender differences between men and women, but also differences among women of various classes—for instance, between urban elites and peasants or between enlightened modern women and unawakened subalterns. The unified proletarian body with a homogeneous class consciousness conceals an uneven distribution of roles, where men are leaders of the revolution, mentors to women, and speakers for the subalterns. In the process of infusing woman as a class into its emancipation ideology, Marxism denies her a subject position and theoretical orientation. Woman is foremost a subordinated class and gendered body to the totalitarian revolutionary cause. Ignorance of her economic condition further conceals the problems that women face.

The notion of feminism is not new in the process of China's modern nation building. But since its introduction, the concept has been carried out as both discourse and practice to deal with national issues rather than a female subject. In the early twentieth century, for instance, the call for female consciousness and identity creation encouraged women to resist a patriarchal tradition. Under the socialist system, the nation-state offered woman liberation and the possibility of participation in the social, political, and economic spheres. Her presence, however, is significant only when needed to exhibit the policy or ideology of the nation-state. After many "liberations," the question remains: Does the transition from patriarchal family to collective nation-state (from *jia* to *guojia*) really bring woman emancipation? Her escape from the family and to the state freed her from the father figure of the patriarchal household only to subordinate her to the collective father of communism. From familial daughter to socialist model, she has no name of her own, no subject position.

Gender relations shadowed by nationalism are thus positioned between the enlightened and the subaltern. True, in moments of social-national transition, male pioneers, either intellectuals or politicians, have called for women to walk away from traditional confinement or commit themselves to revolutionary causes. As they speak for and write about their female counterparts, however, male saviors turn to the female body as either an emblem of national politics or a narrative site upon which to project their own problems. Written and rewritten according to various national and political discourses, the voice of the subaltern is either erased or altered. The promise of emancipation and the bestowed identity have created the illusion that an autonomous female self can be obtained only in relation to the well-being of the nation-state.

The central idea of difference that is denied by Chinese women and universalized by Western feminists is problematic because of differing interpretations. To consider nationalism and feminism simultaneously, one realizes that women critics in China and in the West have trapped themselves in discourses equally hegemonic: women's emancipation for the former and feminism for the latter. "Women's emancipation," Harriet Evans argues, "has been established as the only language in which gender issues could be publicly discussed." The terminology "*jiefang*," Evans further explains, "produced fixed and hierarchically arranged meanings, which consistently denied identification of women as agents of gender transformation . . . [and] subordinated the women's movement to the goals of social and national revolution as a whole."[12] Interactions of gender with nation as well as narration become important problems to ponder. As we are highly aware of the interrelationship between woman and nation, can we then ask whether it is possible for Chinese women to search for female subjectivity beyond nationalism and express a personal voice freed from the hierarchical notion of *jiefang*? Can woman and gender serve not only as implications of nation construction, but also as a mode of counterdiscourse?

Just as the notions of "nation" and "class" deny gender as a crucial category of analysis, a feminist focus on the male/female opposition can obscure differences among women of different nations. From an exclusive position, a limited vision allows one to believe that feminism is speaking for all women. As voices of disagreement become louder, ideas of gender and difference central to feminism demand reconsideration. The call for and practice of taking feminism *beyond* gender and difference have been well considered. In her study of feminism and the cultural geographies of encounter, Susan Stanford Friedman cites six discourses of gender identity that demonstrate recent transitions of feminism. Among the multifaceted assumptions, multiple oppression stresses the differences among women. Multiple subject positions situate the female self not as singular but as interactive with different cultural formations. A contradictory subject position emphasizes how oppression under one condition can be changed into privilege in another. Relational and situational subjectivity places gender identity in a fluid site or among geographical divides rather than as a fixed essence. Finally, the concept of hybridity focuses on geographical migration and examines how identity construction shifts through space from one part of the world to another.[13]

It is reasonable to suggest that beyond sexual difference lie differences of race, class, religion, history, nation, and experience. Questions then arise:

Should women of different geopolitical spaces, races, or nations claim their own territory and oppose each other? Can women of different nations or cultural worlds engage in conversation? If so, what languages can they speak, and what voices will be heard? Recent criticism has shared the view that Chinese cinema has been transnational since its origin when one considers its production and perception against global conditions.[14] If this is the case, I suggest transnational feminism in the analysis of a transnational cinema. In a time when cultural products and global capital, as well as theories, move fluidly across national borders, the positioning of feminism in a transnational framework is constructive and necessary. "The task for transnational feminist cultural studies," as Spivak defines it, "is to negotiate between the national, the global, and the historical as well as the contemporary diasporic." Its theoretical approaches must emphasize connection "rather than maintaining and reproducing the divides between marxism, post-structuralism, and feminism."[15] Specifically, the transnational feminist approach "problematizes the relationship between feminism and nationalism, asking how feminist practices can exist outside certain master narratives."[16] In light of these assumptions, I hope to reopen discussions between critics in the West and in China and bridge Western feminism with Chinese nationalism. These interactive engagements must follow a transnational flow rather than be one-way traffic.

Before Chinese films achieved their position in world cinema in the 1980s, the nation did not lack female directors, only women's cinema. The film industry in China witnessed one woman director in the 1920s, four in the socialist era, and over fifty since the late 1970s.[17] Given these increasing numbers, I am interested in the question of how women directors participated in socialist film production with their gender identities consciously concealed yet with feminine tendencies unconsciously exposed in their films. After 1949, the new socialist nation-state mobilized women into the public sphere. A few female directors had the opportunity to enter the film industry, then seen as men's terrain. Their presence and participation demonstrated the gender-political ideology that what men can do, women can do. The legitimacy of maintaining such a position therefore depended on the ability to produce mainstream films and observe party policies. Gender identity or female subjectivity remained invisible or subordinated to nationalistic concerns.

Although relatively few, women directors in socialist China cannot be defined as a marginal minority, nor their films as a cinema of counterdiscourse. In a nation-state where one sees class before gender difference, woman remains a screen image articulated in accordance with socialist discourses. The gender identity of a female director might be apparent only in the film credits. The guise of nondifference enables female directors to share "half of the sky" with their male counterparts. For instance, the popularity of Wang Ping, the first important woman director in the socialist film industry, comes not from any gender markers attached to her works but from her successful production of mainstream films. She is the executive director of *The East Is Red* (1965), an epic musical describing the history of the revolution under the leadership of the Communist Party. In addition, a number of sociopolitical productions reinforce her position as a mainstream rather than a female director. While contradictions between gender and revolution may trouble her film narratives, an allegiance to ideology rather than gender ensures that female characters appear as revolutionary rather than gender images. The film *Locust Tree Village*, (Huaishu zhuang, 1962), for instance, focuses on a model heroine and loyal communist, Granny Guo. To emphasize the character's heroic quality, the film positions her in the center of a class struggle and political campaign for land reform. The gender connotation of being a woman and mother is inscribed in the name of revolution when the audience shares her pain at losing her son at the battlefront. Another film, *Sentinels under the Neon Lights* (1964), indicates how a revolutionary army officer, after entering the metropolis of Shanghai, faces the urban seduction of female sexuality and materialism. The film clearly conveys the political message to never forget the class struggle and the continuing revolution. The narrative, however, relies on the officer's wife, a conventional, virtuous woman, to illustrate the contradictions between rural/urban and desire/seduction.

From the examples cited above, we can see that Wang Ping's films encounter and depict the conflicts between political subjects and female concerns. Her acclaimed film, *The Story of Liubao Village* (Liubao de gushi, 1957), further exemplifies the dilemma: the subordination as well as the insertion of feminine characteristics in mainstream film productions. The narrative is set in the late 1940s, when ordinary Chinese were still suffering from years of Japanese invasion and abuse from local oppressors. When a company from the communist army is stationed temporarily in the village of Liubao, one of the young officers falls in love with a peasant girl, as the themes of war and romance collide. A film of socialist conventions, the narrative unmistakably takes the portrayal of revolutionary heroes as its primary subject. In stressing the notion of heroism, the film reveals how its male hero represses his personal emotions toward the woman to preserve army discipline and the heroic temperament. The film casts its female protagonist as both a desirable, virtuous woman in the eyes of the army officer

Sentinels under the Neon Lights, 1964

and a sexual commodity to be sold to the local ruler. The political doctrine of woman's emancipation through communist salvation and guidance from a male hero marks the film as similar to socialist classics such as *The Red Detachment of Women* or *The White-Haired Girl.*

Even though the film conspicuously emphasizes how the male hero overcomes his emotions to commit himself unconditionally to the task of revolution, certain feminine modes surface. First, the reality of war is kept in the background and not allowed to completely overshadow the romantic narrative. Second, the love relationship constantly tests revolutionary regulations. Although leaders and peers never cease to criticize and educate the soldier, he transgresses the code of acceptable behavior. The configuration of the male hero finally coalesces after he agrees to sacrifice personal happiness for the salvation of the entire proletariat. The camera nonetheless inserts various shots that sustain the love relationship: a close-up shows embroidered works that the woman sewed for the man. The reverse shot reveals the woman seeing him off. More important, the film insists on a reunification of the two lovers at the end, albeit by means of transforming the heroine into a revolutionary woman. In addition, the use of love songs as a diegetic motif to enhance narrative transitions is consistent. The female protagonist, as someone needing rescue and love, does not have a voice or point of view of her own. Nevertheless, the melodies express, to a certain degree, an unspeakable desire.

As the example indicates, it is hardly possible to expect a woman's cinema to emerge under the system of a socialist nation-state. The master discourse of art in the service of politics and for a mass audience prevents any individual or diverse voices. Within the given framework, woman appears as a popular screen image signifying either the promise of socialist China or the oppressions of the old society. Woman as herself, however, is invisible on-screen. The emergence of female directors does not signal the possibility of a woman's cinema when their entry into the mainstream requires an erasure of one's gender identity. To gain a position in the film industry means subordination to the well-regulated discourses. Women directors therefore take the given identity as honorable rather than repressive because they finally have the privilege of sharing the camera with their male comrades and making films that reflect the master discourses. They fail to realize, however, that by identifying with the male gender and submitting to the nation-state they acquire sociopolitical recognition but sacrifice gender identity and subject position. In her analysis of women and films in China, Dai Jinhua notes the invisibility of the female gender. She explains that "while women in contemporary China are allowed to allocate the discursive authority, their gender identity in culture and in language is lost. As they truly immerse themselves into history, [their] subject position disappears or is masked behind a male masquerade."[18]

AWAKENING AND CONFUSION

The emergence of films by women directors in relatively large numbers dates from the mid- to late 1980s, when the search for a female self and a gender discourse formed a social and literary trend. In contrast to the works of their prominent male colleagues, the practices of female directors often depart from historical memory and national allegory to take women and female experience as their subjects. The gender marker, woman, is attached to almost every film title: *The Women's Story; The Women's World; The First Woman in the Forest; A Single Woman; The Death of a Female Student; Woman, Taxi, Woman;* the list can go on. The surge in such films creates an illusion that women directors are so consciously engaged in women's issues that a women's cinema is emerging in China. Yet attention given to woman as subject and to female experience as narrative does not guarantee a cinema that is gender specific. For instance, there is neither a breakthrough in narrative structure nor any experimentation in the language system, both of which are essential for a possible self-representation. The lack of female voice and point of view, as well as male possession of the camera, put the women directors in a dilemma: the possibility yet confusion of how to construct filmic representations.

A number of films elucidate the problem. As the title suggests, *Who Is the Third Party?* (Shei shi di san zhe, 1987; dir. Dong Kena) deals with the subject of extramarital relationships, a fatal violation of Chinese social norms and a tradition that often punishes the woman for such "immoral transgression." Leaving the question of the real third party open to the audience, the film attempts to subvert the convention by situating the third party as a figure of resistance and a true lover. To legitimate the lover's position, the narrative assures the audience that the couple's marriage has been moribund for over twenty years and that the wife is frigid. At the same time, the male protagonist is portrayed as a victim of his wife's daily abuse while he appears as a loving image in the eyes of his favorite female student.

Who Is the Third Party? 1987

Instead of situating the male protagonist as the nexus of the triangular relationship, the film shifts the psychological burden and narrative weight to the two women rivals. The wife, citing her "legal status," accuses the young woman of being the third party. Her rival then challenges the wife's power with an open expression of love toward the husband. One might expect the contest between the two female protagonists to generate a critical exploration of the issue of gender differences between women. Unfortunately, the narrative fails to unravel either female character's inner state and leaves them as stereotyped identities: the wife, a mean bitch, and the lover, an infatuated self-sacrificer. The lack of exploration from a woman's perspective limits the narrative to a sociopolitical discourse about judging right from wrong. Thus the lover is punished by being sent down to a remote place and denied any chance of promotion. Female consciousness appears only at the end of the film, when the lover returns a house key to the man as he confesses to the court that he should not have fallen in love with the "third party."

Peng Xiaolian's *The Women's Story* (Nüren de gushi, 1987) introduces three peasant women who take the opportunity afforded by economic reforms to go to town to sell yarn. Each of them is portrayed as a figure who transgresses traditional social norms. For Jin Xiang, the trip to town is an escape from an arranged marriage; for Xiao Feng, it is to prove to the villagers what a family without a male heir can accomplish; and for Laizi's mother, it is to make enough money to help her three brothers-in-law each find a wife. As the female body is coded to signify these sociocultural meanings, the subject of a female self can hardly take form. For instance, there is a possible sexual encounter between Xiao Feng and a construction worker. The sequence suggests to the audience that they have spent almost the whole night talking, walking, and finally engaging in sexual relations. The camera, however, shuns the sexual scene and leaves the characters disappearing into the woods. The audience finds out only on the second day, when Laizi's mother accuses Xiao Feng of doing something inappropriate. The film does give Xiao Feng a moment to explain herself; nevertheless, her emotional account claims that she acted as she did because of the discrimination faced by a family with no male heir.

The sense of ambiguity in narrative and the shunning of sexuality in representation indicate once again the dilemma of desire as well as confusion in how to pursue a women's cinema. The two examples demonstrate that the directors' gender consciousness brings about female characters of resistance and difference. Narrative structure and representation modes, however, remain conventional, where woman bears the weight of social,

The Women's Story, 1987

cultural, and political meanings rather than the subject of herself. In other words, the rise of gender consciousness yet the lack of feminine aesthetics is the problem central to women's film production. The problem prevents directors from moving beyond the macrocriticism of either social realism or cultural traditions. In addition to the discourse and voice of hegemony, what language can woman speak and what perspective can the camera assume? No alternatives have yet been found. In changing the female image but not the language, both film directors and characters remain caught in the master's house. The limited progress lies only in the fact that while woman as self was previously invisible on screen, now she is visible but not heard.

Unlike many Western women filmmakers, few female directors in China would want to be tagged with the label of "feminist." Even though their films are signed with striking female signatures, few directors would view their films as counter- or feminist cinema. Having "enjoyed" equal opportunity with men in directing films, female directors accept without question their ability to make films as fine as those of male directors. "Why should I make women's films?" declares a Chinese female director. "Men and women are all alike. I want to make war movies and epic films."[19] While it proclaims gender equality, the belief that women can perform as well as men conceals a fear of being moved from the center to the margins. To be a feminist means to be marginalized by mainstream film production in China, and to be different invites the danger of being blacklisted. As a result, the female director either holds the pen as an auteur or masculinizes herself into a "superwoman." Suppression of one's gender difference to attain social and professional status is precisely the tragedy yet unrecognized by some female directors. The denial of gender difference, however, does not disprove the existence of a female consciousness and cinematic authorship.

Nonetheless, exploration in transforming female experience into cinematic discourse continues. The search for a female voice and perspective marks the point of departure. In *Army Nurse*, for instance, Hu Mei attempts to find sound tracks to insert a female voice. The disjunction between diegetic sound in the narrative and the first-person voice-over in the sound track produces two concurrent effects: the former describes woman as a social model while the latter speaks for her inner state. In *Human, Woman, Demon*, Huang Shuqin's heroine relies on her performance in a male opera role to evoke her subjective world. As Sally Robinson indicates, the representation of woman, of a female voice, is a question of the relation between language and experience. "Gender difference is a difference in language and experience conceived as a subject's relation to discourse and social system."[20]

The creation of a female point of view in cinema poses another problem in crafting a poetics of female representation. In *Army Nurse*, for example, from the woman's point of view, man is desired but absent, one through whom the female character exposes her repressed love from under the disguise of her social model. In Huang Shuqin's *Human, Woman, Demon*, however, male characters appear through the woman's point of view as objects of female despair. The burden of securing a self-identity in relation to men moves the female character to seek a voice and a vision of herself through the opera role of a male ghost. A masked and mirrored image, the heroine asks continuously, "Who am I?" A situation in which men either vanish or remain distant while women look either off-screen or into a mirror suggests the obstacles to a female vision but also the possibility of woman realizing a strong sense of self-identity. The position as a viewer who sees nothing—or nothing beyond herself—implies a cinematic representation and production of female experience.

What has emerged from the work of Chinese female directors attests to a narrative and psychological dilemma where personal desires conflict with dominant ideologies. Diverted from direct engagement with sociopolitical and historical issues, women's films shift the exploration toward women's private worlds. Working within rather than against the cinematic institutions, female directors attempt to insert personal voice and point of view into the discourse. The expression of personal and private sensibilities within the constraints of social and public domains marks women's films as an alternative form, yet one situated within the mainstream canon. Conflict between the desire to bring a female mode into discourse and the need to not disrupt dominant institutions thus signals an anxiety of female authorship. Nevertheless, the difficulty of establishing female authorship and rendering a female subjectivity in cinema does not negate but rather attests to the vitality of Chinese women's desires.

The film *Sacrificed Youth* (Qingchun ji, 1985; dir. Zhang Nuanxin) is one of a few works that suggest the conscious pursuit of a feminine poetics. Like many movies made in the 1980s, the film offers a cultural perspective on China's political history (the Cultural Revolution) and nostalgic memories of sacrificed youth (the sent-down generation). Unlike those films, however, *Sacrificed Youth* presents history and memory as a personal and female introspection. The possibility of making history personal and the narration feminine relies primarily on geopolitical border crossing and interracial engagement. The film uses the encounter between a sent-down Han youth and a non-Han Dai minority to subvert mainstream narratives and insert female voice and perspective. *Sacrificed Youth* does not simply contrast differences between Han and non-Han cultures; it intersects them. The conventional division of the dominant and the dominated yields to negotiations between serious polarities: Han culture and Dai nature, Han knowledge and Dai experience. The most important confrontation occurs between the Han female body, concealed under a shapeless uniform, and the Dai body, adorned by exotic/erotic dress. The dress code contrasts the Han self with the Dai other and prompts the search for self-identity.

Audiences cannot fail to notice these feminine nuances. Unfortunately, as critics focus primarily on issues of minority discourse and Han representation, few have considered how the director consciously uses a female voice to address the identity crisis in the film.[21] The voice-over narration, for instance, is a perfect cinematic motif for engendering personal and psychological expression. Li Chun, the Han protagonist in *Sacrificed Youth*, like so many of her peers during the Cultural Revolution, is sent down from the urban capital of Beijing to the rural border in Yunnan. As a result of the geopolitical relocation, she is immediately confronted with an unfamiliar minority culture. As an outsider, she is at first rejected by the

Sacrificed Youth, 1985

group of Dai girls. To exemplify her marginal position, the camera often frames Li Chun in an observer's position as she watches the Dai girls' activities from a distance. To express her frustrations, the film reveals her thoughts in a voice-over narration. What the audience sees from the female protagonist's point of view is a series of visual representations of Dai femininity and sexuality. What the viewer hears through the voice-over narration is the Han girl's lack of confidence. If we place the image track side by side with the sound track, we see a clear elaboration:

IMAGE TRACK: Image of Dai girl Yibo.

VOICE-OVER: "Yibo is the most beautiful girl in the village; she makes me feel so unconfident."

IMAGE TRACK: Dai girls singing to attract the young men passing by.

VOICE-OVER: "The girls are flirting and attracting men's attention. But I myself look pathetic."

IMAGE TRACK: Shots of Dai girls swimming nude in the river.

VOICE-OVER: "I can only watch them because I don't have my swimming suit with me."

The conjunction of image and voice brings out two points. First, in the precise use of the voice-over narration we have access to the female protagonist's psychological world. "In the interior monologue," as Mary Ann Doane points out, "the voice and the body are represented simultaneously, but the voice, far from being an extension of that body, manifests its inner lining. The voice displays what is inaccessible to the image, what exceeds the visible: the inner life of the character. The voice here is the privileged mark of inferiority, turning the body inside-out."[22] As a result, the audience perceives Li Chun's unattractive image with her voice of frustration and self-doubt. Then, viewing the relation between body and voice carefully, one sees that while the Han body possesses the voice, the Dai body remains as the image. The minority other acts as a mirror image reflecting and reminding the Han self of her repressed sexuality and erased gender identity. In this way, "reading the other is turned into a confrontation with the self."[23] It is the minority female image rather than the dominance of Han culture that provokes the desire for identity transformation.

Second, the film problematizes the identity transformation by positioning the Han woman in relation to a Dai and a Han man simultaneously. At the beginning, Li Chun interprets the Dai girls' rejection as sociopolitical discrimination. She later learns that they refuse to associate with her because of her colorless, shapeless clothing. By adopting Dai hair and dress styles, Li Chun finally crosses racial and cultural lines. Her Dai dress, along with her Han knowledge, first win acceptance by the minority, then the attention of another sent-down young man. This "cross-dressing" or cross-identity, while allowing Li Chun to traverse borders, traps her in the dilemma of whether or not she can obtain a real Dai persona. The film suggests that this is impossible. As her doubled identity and newfound femininity attract both a Dai and a Han man, Li Chun takes pains to adjust her cultural, gender, and racial position. Her final decision to return to Han dress and leave the Dai village brings back her Han identity. The costs are considerable. Returning to the city, she moves away from the Dai nature, maternal love, enlightened femininity, and way of life free from Han restrictions. Left behind is the memory of sacrificed youth, a loss narrated from a woman's perspective and in a female voice, "those of the Han /Chinese ethnographer" who searches for a self in terms of the ethnic other.[24]

Fragments that mark feminine poetics unfortunately do not indicate feminist film production in China. Zhang Nuanxin's films after *Sacrificed*

Youth gradually show no further interest in a woman's perspective or female voice. Her *Good Morning Beijing* (Beijing ni zao, 1990) positions a female bus conductor at a moment of rapid socioeconomic transition in China. The young woman's changing relationship with three different male partners—a peer conductor, a driver, and a businessman—displays social attitudes and psychological choices altered under contemporary conditions. As a constant, each male character symbolizes a certain ideology and the female its signification. The perspective is social, and political voices speak for the group, not the individual. Zhang's other film, *Stories from Yunnan* (Yunnan gushi, 1994), is far from a woman's film but close to a commercial product. The landscape and the minority woman's way of giving birth become exotic and erotic selling points. Like many women directors, Zhang also declares that "I've never reminded myself that I'm a woman director and never have the intention of establishing a woman's perspective when I'm shooting a film."[25] She further explains that "a woman's text should be first and foremost personal rather than feminine. . . . As a female director, I speak as an artist, not as a woman. Art conceives no gender difference."[26]

The denial of the female perspective, language, and voice that are either embedded or concealed within women's works requires further examination. The work of another important female director, Li Shaohong, presents a different angle on the question of women's films and male authorship. Her *Family Portrait* (Sishi bu huo, 1992) is an excellent film in terms of narrative structure, psychological depth, and especially cinematography. Liu Heng, an acclaimed writer who works with well-known film directors, wrote the script. Discussions between the director and the scriptwriter led to an agreement that the film would be a psychological drama about a son's search for his father. As in many of Li Shaohong's films, her husband, Zeng Nieping, is the cinematographer. With control over pen and camera, male authorship emphasizes the father-son relationship and leaves little room for two female characters. The man's former wife appears in slide images, while the present wife inhabits the margins of domestic space.

The male protagonist, Cao Depei, a professional photographer, one day receives a phone call from the welfare office to report that his "son" has lost his way and is looking for him. Cao has never seen this son and knows nothing about him. Protagonist, audience, and the film narrative face the enigma of the past. The process of uncovering that past unfolds with the photographic images of the first wife. A trip to the far northeast, where the boy came from, makes Cao realize that the child is his son. His wife never told him that they had a son before they got divorced. With the wife recently dead from cancer, the boy comes to Beijing to find his father. The sudden appearance of the son puts the father in a difficult situation because he now has another son with his new wife. At a loss for what to do, Cao hides the boy in the darkroom he keeps in the basement of a building.

Inside the darkroom, the father turns on a slide projector and invites the son and the audience to see female images from the past. The photographs of the father's former wife and the son's mother take the film characters and the audience back into a history that remains only in the father's memories. The slides show a young woman in her sent-down youth uniform and in her loving relationship with the present male protagonist. Screening the past in terms of female images reveals a collective memory of the Cultural Revolution and a personal memory of a relationship. Nonetheless, with the woman as a mere image and the father and son as spectators, the cinematic structure of viewing-viewed enables the father figure to examine history while continuing the narrative. As the father-son bonding comes to terms through the photographed mother-wife image, the film is unable to define the woman. She is absent as a subject.

The slide screening is repeated three times. At the second viewing, the son is the only spectator. Seeing the young woman who later becomes his mother, the boy acknowledges at once the unknown history, the pre-Oedipal mother-son relationship, and finally the identification with the father figure. Finally, the film allows the male protagonist's present wife to witness the photographs of the female image that shares with her the mother-wife identities. Exposure to another woman as image prompts the present wife to accept the boy as her son, thus reinforcing the mother-wife identity. The moment when she calls her husband to suggest buying a double bed for the two boys, her eyes flood with tears. No one knows her psychological struggle. The film approaches the father-son relationship from a psychological perspective, or perhaps through retrospection from a woman's point of view, as the director explains.[27]

Another well-known film by Li Shaohong, *Blush* (Hong fen, 1994), concerns the campaign in the 1950s to reeducate prostitutes. The film, however, shows a counterinterpretation to the process of reeducation as the prostitute character clings to her old identity. *Blush* and the novella of Su Tong, from which the film was adapted, invite a reexamination of the official discourse of prostitution. The removal of prostitutes from brothels to workplaces and homes promised a transition in the status and meaning of the female body—from a diseased sexual symbol to a healthy, productive laborer. The Women's Labor Training Institute provided a social space in which the intended transformation was to occur. From the viewpoint of the communist regime, prostitution was symptomatic of the moral corruption of the capitalist system. The woman who sold her body acted as an unregulated worker, an agent of moral pollution, and her body symbolized the decadence of the traditional system to be supplanted by communism. Under the communists, however, former prostitutes continued to survive by the labor of their bodies—with their sexuality suppressed and their labor regulated by the state. The woman once engaged in the commerce of sex had not been truly liberated, only reassigned to a different, even more rigid role.

In addition to the sociopolitical implications, the director, through the process of shooting the film, realizes that the significance of handling a topic such as prostitution lies in how to *personalize* the female characters.[28] The film presents the life of a prostitute after reeducation as an embarrassing contradiction between the ideals and the realities of reform. The two prostitute figures in the film, Qiuyi and Xiao'e, embody the discourse of not only prostitution but also gender relations. Between them stands one male figure, Laopu, first Qiuyi's customer, then lover, and later Xiao'e's husband. Xiao'e completes her sojourn in the Training Institute but is unable

Blush, 1994

to completely wash away the mark of the prostitute from her body. Her insatiable appetite for luxury causes her to drive her new husband to crime and brings her family to a tragic end. Qiuyi, who manages to flee the Training Institute and avoid reeducation, by contrast, redeems her life by marrying an ordinary man. Yet all the while, she reserves her love for Laopu, executed by the government.

Unfortunately, the attempt to personalize the characters or achieve a feminine narration fails or is at least self-contradictory. In his analysis of both the novella and the film, Xu Jian ascribes the problems to the "disempowering" of the male protagonist, Laopu, and the female voice-over narration.[29] The voice-over does indicate a possible narration from a woman's point of view, yet the female narration fails to personalize either a female self or female spectatorship. The problem occurs because the voice-over appears to be third-person and omniscient. Such a position authorizes the voice to speak for the literary author and image maker. As the agent of omniscience, the voice supplies information missing from the diegetic field. Having privileged access to a character's inner world, the voice reveals unspoken thoughts and feelings.[30] The female and third-person narration in *Blush* speaks often for Qiuyi. As an explanative narrator, the voice tells what happens to the character(s). As a mind-thought observer, the voice exposes Qiuyi's psychological consciousness. As an authoritative commentator, the voice defines and differentiates Qiuyi from Xiao'e.

The voice-over narration inserted in *Blush*, nonetheless, is "disembodied voice," separated completely from the female body within the frame. "Disembodied, lacking any specification in space or time," as Doane says, "the voice-over is beyond criticism—it censors the question 'Who is speaking?' 'Where?' 'In what time?' and 'For whom?'"[31] With these questions in mind, we realize that the voice-over, dislocated from the female body as well as specific space/time, is assigned to the female character/body. The insertion marks either the literary author's original creation or the film director's adaptation. Thus a woman's own voice is missing. Omniscient and off-screen, the voice first leads the audience to an understanding of the two prostitute figures in the way it narrates. The voice then reminds the audience via textual construction where the sound track can speak for or dominate the image track.

The significance of using a female voice as the voice narration, however, does indicate gender consciousness on the part of the director. The question of how feminine a film can be when the scriptwriting and cinematography remain in the hands of men is open. Li Shaohong and other female directors realize the problems but have not yet come up with a satisfactory solution.

What is women's cinema? Are films that focus on women's experience or female perspective women's cinema? Or "should a film be categorized as women's cinema simply because it is made by a woman director?"[32] Questions such as these attract as well as confuse the female directors in China.

WOMEN'S FILMS WITHOUT WOMEN

The newly arrived woman director Ning Ying has attracted attention with her subtle vision of urban realities. One cannot easily label or categorize Ning Ying and her films. She has been Bernardo Bertolucci's student and assistant director for years. Yet her films show no evidence of Bertolucci's shadow. Ning Ying is a member of the so-called fifth-generation directors. But the absence in her films of national allegories and visual splendor has largely separated her from her peers. Her films concern local, everyday life, and her characters inhabit the margins of society. They differ, however, from the urban youth depicted by the independent directors or the troubled residents who figure in the urban politics of Huang Jianxin. Ning is an important female director. Yet interestingly none of her films focuses on women or inscribes a feminist perspective. Her distance from both the mainstream and feminism make me ask whether Ning is consciously subverting or simply ignoring the major figures, trends, and conventions. Is there a feminine perspective or aesthetics in a film where woman or gender takes no central concern?

Ning's films focus on ordinary urban dwellers. *For Fun* (Zhao le, 1992) presents a group of amateur Peking opera singers, retired from their professions yet seeking pleasure through opera singing. *On the Beat* (Minjing de gushi, 1995) exposes the boredom of local police officers as they spend their days either chasing dogs or tracking crimes. The significance of Ning's films lies in their capacity to convey extraordinary sociocultural insight in the guise of the most ordinary characters. Ning's camera anxiously captures vanishing social types and practices before they disappear from the urban scene. The representation of contemporary urban space reveals how commercial culture and modern reforms slowly erase a tradition, a people, an urban lifestyle. Her use of realistic or documentary devices, such as location shooting and reliance on nonprofessionals, strives for a visual authenticity apart from any explicit claim to social and political originality. Careful viewing of her films, however, helps us to trace an allegorical representation of an urban Beijing in the throes of cultural and economic transition.

The possibility of depicting urban realities with satirical undertones is owing too to Ning's feminine, if not feminist, vision. By "feminine vision,"

For Fun, 1992

On the Beat, 1995

I mean a perspective free from the conventions of sociopolitical discourses, as well as from gendered ideologies. Ning's method of directing is personal and subjective, neither defined by gender nor oriented to the mainstream. It concerns how the female subject feels rather than how she should feel. Ning's autonomy is evident in authorship and spectatorship. As author, Ning controls the articulation of her narrative and cinematic world. Moreover, she frees the spectator's gaze from the focus of sexual difference or sociopolitical narratives. As a result, Ning Ying's films raise significant sociocultural issues concealed in the wrap of everyday realities, only to subtly expose them to an ironical eye.

Narrative structure and characterization should be the point of departure for understanding Ning Ying's films. Her characters appear as faces from life. The retirees in *For Fun* and the local police in *On the Beat* are compelling examples. Nonetheless, these ordinary figures entail extraordinary meanings. They serve often as living signs to remind contemporary viewers of moments of transition where the old is vanquished and the new emerges. By positioning her characters in sociocultural transitions, Ning's films attempt to capture a slice of life that is disappearing.

Old Han and his fellow amateur opera singers in *For Fun*, for instance, are socially on the margins yet psychologically seeking a sense of identity. Peking opera thus becomes an art form, and public parks are transformed into places where the elderly can recreate a world of their own. Classical opera and the aging retirees reflect each other as cultural antiques soon to vanish or be forgotten. Ning Ying's camera attempts to seize the moment of disappearance and reveal their struggle for survival. In so doing, she does not dramatize the narrative but surprises the audience with her sense of humor and unexpected parodies. For instance, with Old Han's efforts, the group finds a space in the neighborhood cultural center to practice singing. The accomplishment of moving from the margins to the center, however, brings about a series of power struggles. First, the members vote to "institutionalize" their club and formulate regulations. Old Han, as the head of the club, kindly assists everyone to enjoy singing, yet he stubbornly practices his "power of authority." The possibility of getting a turn to sing means to seize the modes of expression or enunciation. The authority to decide who gets the next turn is power. The embodiment of such meanings within ordinary characters involves not only narrative satire, but also sociopolitical norms ascribed to individuals.

On the Beat stresses China's social, political, and economic transitions by taking the police bureaucracy and its officers as primary subjects. Like *For Fun*, however, sociopolitical implications are conveyed through the narrative of the policemen's everyday routines. Their daily responsibilities ironically include chasing dogs, searching for household pets, or interrogating "criminals." The criminals in the film include a card gambler who cheats customers, a peddler who sells posters of female nudes, and a puppy owner who has a bad attitude toward the police. The film does not mean to reveal merely the boredom of today's police, but rather the paradoxical situation in which they do not know how to adjust. Caught between the status of an instrument to party dictatorship in the past and an agent of law enforcement today, the ordinary policeman on patrol is confused.

As the nation-state undergoes economic reforms, the nature of police work inevitably shifts. The concept of the criminal changes from politically oriented counterrevolutionaries to an economically defined new criminal class, and the absolute power of the police seems to crumble. As Michael Dutton explains, "Politico-moral methods once used under Mao to improve police performance would give way to a series of money-based bonus systems, responsibility systems, and contractual arrangements."[33] For instance, the film begins with a bicycle tour, where the senior officer introduces the new officer to the residential area of responsibility. The film ends with an announcement of a suspended bonus because the senior police handled a case extralegally. The concept of money is the connection between the police and the "criminal." The number of dogs the police should collect and kill are their contractual assignments, and the extinction of one rabid dog brings honor and a bonus to the whole station.

As reforms change the system of policing and the image of the police, the old and familiar ruling structure has not yet disappeared. The coexistence of the old and the new creates a series of satirical moments. The film first mocks the question of whether the policing system can be independent from both the government and local customs. As the film shows, the neighborhood committee, composed of aging retirees, still functions as a mass-control organ. Seven grannies control almost every single corner of the residential community. They firmly and proudly state that living together without marriage is illegal and that tracking numbers of pregnancies or abortions is their duty. The film then ridicules the contemporary police. A charge is brought against a man who owns a dog that bites. Yet when the police interrogate the "criminal," they drone on with questions of family and class origin, political status, and information about all family members and social relations. They fail to realize that the police apparatus from the past can no longer assume complete control over the masses. As the puppy owner finally bursts out in anger, cursing the police as dirty dogs, the interrogator loses his composure and slaps the man's face. The film continues the satire by showing the police officers in their Jeep patrolling the neighborhood on a late and rainy night. The criminals for whom they are searching are not counterrevolutionaries but puppies of the residents. The scene might be amusing or satirical, but the question is penetrating: How can one define the police when their legal function is to collect and kill dogs?

Yet the director is not interested merely in the odd spectacle of old men singing operas or police chasing dogs. She pursues an autonomous way of constructing representation and selecting angles of view. Ning Ying self-consciously stresses that "when I write about or film the elderly, I actually search for myself and for the question of how to represent those characters from my perspective."[34] I see this "I" vision as a feminine, if not feminist, pursuit of authorial subjectivity and cinematic aesthetics. Indeed, the singularity of Ning's films comes from her handling of the editing, in addition to characterization. *On the Beat* begins with the opening credits rolling to a voice-over narration. As the image lures the viewer through a long take, we see a meeting room where the police chief is reading a political document while his officers "bury" themselves in cigarette smoke. The topic is how to coordinate police reform with the changing economic policies of the party. The film ends in the same setting, with the same voice-over. But this time the chief announces administrative and financial punishment against the senior officer. The same mise-en-scène carries different implications. The ideology of police reform that the officers have been faithfully following seems betrayed. As the reform policy leads to absurdity, the police chief feels confused and caught in the contemporary socioeconomic parody. The police do not benefit when dogs and puppies become the unfortunate "criminals" of urban society. "What are we doing here? I haven't been home for a whole week, only chasing dogs and dealing with this shit." The voice of confusion yet self-inquiry, while bringing the narrative to closure, mocks today's policing reforms.

A similar editing strategy is applied in *For Fun*. The members of the amateur opera singing group begin their daily entertaining activities in a public space, and they end up back there after a series of problems that occur after they move to the community cultural center. But in the time and space between the two end pieces, a narrative ripe with contradictions unfolds. Ning's telltale satire and social critique are embedded within the characters. On the one hand, the rising tide of modernity drives the elders away from the mainstream and into the margins. On the other hand, any possible return to the center will revive the bureaucratic power struggles. Ning Ying's satirical device, as Jerry White points out in his analysis of these two films, "exposes just how deeply engraved the propensity for power struggles is within human nature, not to mention Chinese society."[35]

Clearly, women are not Ning's central concern; they may be literally absent from her films. A subtle female consciousness or feminine vision, however, does impose a gendered implication. Her careful editing raises the concept of gender relations. After a sequence in which a group of police-men beats a rabid dog to death in *On the Beat,* the film cuts directly to a family scene. Does the editing attempt to moderate or reinforce the con-trast between the violence and tenderness? The familial scene occurs on an ordinary Sunday, with the whole family playing a game. At the little boy's request, the mother tells her son a story. In her made-up tale, she manages to "allegorize" her husband as a big tiger and the boy as a little tiger. She then complains how patriarchal the big tiger is since he refuses to share any housework. Thus the film enables the woman to insert her complaining voice and to indicate her position under contemporary social conditions. The contrast between the policeman's public duty and the domestic scene is elaborated in another sequence. After the police finish their task of col-lecting residential puppies, the film cuts again to the family. It is early in the morning, and the returning policeman disturbs his family. His wife expresses how hard it is to be a police officer's wife, and the husband stops her as he interrogates the criminals. In a third scene, the film does not use a cut but reveals how abruptly the officer hangs up on his wife's phone call as he goes to another assignment.

The brief association of the police officer with his family subtly reveals the conflict between public affairs and domestic interests and the hus-band's continuing authority over his wife. Indeed, Ning Ying does not need to make a feminist statement about her female character. Her articulation of the simple cut and a woman's voice exposes the family as socially defined space where gender difference comes into view as editing controls the screen time. First, we see the family, and the wife is able to deliver her story. Next, she can hardly finish her words as her husband yells at her to stop. Finally, the film mutes her voice and erases her presence because her domestic matters are interfering with public affairs. The camera's alternat-ing glimpses of familial scenes thus unravel the woman's subordinate posi-tion, as well as her expected multiple responsibilities.

For Fun reveals to us the world of elders living on the social margins. Woman remains absent. Nevertheless, in a careful viewing of the film one discovers how the concept of the look brings that absence into discourse. Old Han is packing his belongings as he retires from his post. Looking around his reception office, his eye stops at his wife's photo on the wall. At home the next morning, the retired Old Han rises on time only to realize that he does not need to go to work. The camera, assuming his vision, pans the room and stops again at the photo on the wall. The point-of-view shot links the man's vision with the woman's image. Her presence as an image yet absence as a woman suggests a past unknown to the audience yet alive in her husband's memory. But here, in contrast to the typical stance in Western feminist film theory, the concept of the look is not associated with female sexuality or pleasure in looking. For instance, on his way out, Old Han sees that the window to a women's public bathroom is open. He shuts it to prevent any possible looking. When he catches a glance of a calendar adorned with the image of a beautiful Western woman, Old Han turns away. One might take this as an old Chinese man's embarrassment around women. In a larger sense, the loss of the woman and the emptiness of the family account for Old Han's loneliness. The change in family structure isolates the elderly in urban reality.

If Old Han goes looking for "fun," other elders find in opera singing and their activity center a place apart from family. In addition to the sociocultural ignorance that drives the elders to the margins, the modern family is no longer a haven for older people. As the group responds to a journalist's interview, for instance, one man complains that the "child emperor" at home occupies center position. Another whines that no one at home likes the "noise" of his singing. They all share a passion for opera singing, confessing that their feet will "itch" if they miss one day of practice. The opera binds the old gentlemen together, and in the public space they find refuge from unfriendly families. Opera singing becomes a language they use to express and transcend their frustrations. The tragedy is that both opera and the elders are receding and will eventually disappear from the urban scene. This moment of transience is powerfully demonstrated through a mise-en-scène: high rises dominate the background of the frame, with dilapidated old houses in front and a flow of traffic running between.

Ning Ying's use of nonprofessional actors, location shooting, and quotidian situations creates a picture of contemporary urban reality. Yet with sociopolitical meanings embedded within the characterization and satirical implications woven into the narrative, Ning's films create a kind of reality that she defines as "surrealism." She tries to achieve the utmost realistic representation through editing. The convention of editing, the syntax of cinema, is inevitably mechanical and subjective. No matter how realistic they appear, the edited sequences are the outcome of (re)assembled materials. The power of Ning's films is to lure the spectator into an everyday reality without awareness of the editing process. As the image quietly fades in and fades out, meaning has already been imposed in the narrative. It would be impossible to produce such an effect without an authoritative control of the camera and the editing.

Compared with Zhang Yimou's *Not One Less,* a film that features the use of nonprofessional actors, location shooting, and rural reality, Ning's films demonstrate *feminine* vision and subjectivity. For instance, in Zhang's film, the socioeconomic subject, education amid poverty and the power of money, is clearly the central theme. The camera follows its central characters and reinforces the socioeconomic engagement between urban and rural space. The editing, such as superimposition, reveals its syntax and draws the audience into an emotional, melodramatic engagement with the character and the narrative. Ning, by contrast, emphasizes how she feels about her characters as she shoots the film and how the audience should engage in the experience *(ganshou)* rather than the story. A gender approach depends not on whether a man or a woman directs the film, but on how the film, its vision and structure, is constructed.

Chapter Nine

Desire in Difference

Female Voice and Point of View in Hu Mei's *Army Nurse*

IN FILMS MADE BY WOMEN directors, we find evidence of a female consciousness: the exploration of a self split between submission to sociopolitical ideology and allegiance to personal desire. In society, in cinema, and especially in military service, where the concepts of consensus and collectivity dominate and suppress individuality, a psychological conflict between the social and the personal becomes a point of departure from which the experience of female consciousness unfolds. As the female protagonist in women's films is torn between her obligation to fulfill social roles and her yearning to follow personal desires, the narrative structure is in turn split into a double discourse—a public discourse portraying women as social models and a private discourse exploring woman's inner world. In Hu Mei's *Army Nurse* (Nüer lou, 1985), the subjective assertion of woman's voice and perspective powerfully exemplifies the divided world and split self of woman. The double discourse of *Army Nurse* strives to accommodate female consciousness.

Taking the basic premise of Edward Branigan's theory of narration as a point of departure, where narrative refers to what is told by the story and narration refers to the process of telling the story, I will examine how the subject of female experience is constituted in terms of cinematic and gender codes.[1] Questions posited here include the following: Who is the speaking subject, and to whom is the narrator speaking? How does the film construct and control discourse through a woman's voice? What is the relationship between the teller and the tale? Do women's films achieve a female subjectivity by inserting a female voice?

Army Nurse, 1985

FILM SYNOPSIS

In representing female experience, *Army Nurse* portrays a character caught between private longings and military codes of behavior. At age fifteen, Xiaoyu is enlisted in the army as a nurse by her father. She suddenly realizes that leaving home this time is different from going to Granny's for summer vacation. A tracking shot of the train and a long take of the winter scenery show Xiaoyu and the other girls en route to a distant army hospital. Mountains and forests separate the girls from the outside world. At the hospital, male patients become the central concern of the girls' working duties, and the father figure, Commissar Lu, takes control of the girls' lives.

Life for a nurse in the hospital has its own rhythms: mopping the floor, distributing medicine, fetching hot water, washing test tubes. Years of unvarying work pass until one day Xiaoyu comes to know a new male patient. Their first encounter proves embarrassing for her. While distributing medicine as usual, Xiaoyu comes to a new name on the list and bungles its pronunciation. When the patient tells her that his name is Ding Zhu, Xiaoyu blushes and hides her embarrassment behind her large gauze mask. After she finishes her shift, she rushes to a dictionary to look up the meaning of the patient's name: "Zhu" refers to a soaring bird. From then on, Xiaoyu develops a passionate longing for Ding Zhu.

This unspoken passion (the army forbids dating) builds in dramatic tension until the day Ding Zhu asks Xiaoyu to change his bandage. They are alone, and as Xiaoyu unwraps and replaces the bandage around his chest, she feels overpowered by her nearness to him, as if the rest of the world had ceased to exist and her mind had been emptied of thought. This unvoiced but passionate first love moves Xiaoyu to follow the music from Ding Zhu's harmonica and to search for his figure every time she passes his ward. Xiaoyu's yearning for Ding Zhu to return her gaze and respond to her emotion is not answered until she receives a love letter from him long after he has left the hospital. With joy and fear, Xiaoyu runs to the bathroom so she can read the letter in privacy. But she barely finishes reading the letter when someone enters. Xiaoyu panics and flushes the letter down a toilet; she is left with only the envelope.

The experience of her first love flows away just like the letter thrown into the toilet because individuals must choose between personal desire and consensus values. At the moment when Xiaoyu ponders her choice between love and duty, Commissar Lu advises her that a young person should put study and work ahead of love. He promises Xiaoyu that when the proper time comes, the leaders and the party will see to her marriage. The most important goal, however, is to join the party, earn promotion, and not get sidetracked by personal affairs. Xiaoyu accepts Commissar Lu's words with complicated feelings; nevertheless, her sacrifice of love does bring her self-sufficiency. Xiaoyu is sent for advanced training and returns to head the nursing staff. Working hard and always helping others, Xiaoyu gains the reputation of a model nurse. As chief nurse, she becomes an authoritarian figure for the male patients, a model person for the new nurses, a mother figure for the young patients, and a friend to all her colleagues. But the mask of this model figure conceals Xiaoyu's inner loss and psychological imbalance.

At age thirty, Xiaoyu is introduced by a friend to a man, a potential husband whom the party leader checks out and approves as meeting army regulations. However, the arranged dating and proposed marriage fail to awaken Xiaoyu's emotions; she does not reexperience love. On the night before their wedding day, Xiaoyu is speechless and passionless as she stays with her fiancé in their new room. She realizes that she still loves the man and the time long ago lost. Without saying good-bye to the groom, Xiaoyu makes her way back to the hospital. The movie then ends with her voice-over comments: "I've lost so much over the past fifteen years. However, I can still see the longing eyes in the ward looking for me. I'm going back to my patients no matter where I have been."

PUBLIC/PRIVATE DISCOURSE

In the confrontation between public (dominant) and private discourse, the former constitutes the female protagonist as an ideological subject whereas the latter seeks the possibility of inserting a female voice. A poststructuralist analysis of discourse examines texts in terms of their linguistic and sociocultural dimensions and investigates how power or authority is distributed in the language in use. Among the many versions of discourse criticism, Louis Althusser's concepts of "interpellation" and "ideological state apparatuses" appear particularly helpful in the analysis of rhetorical confrontations between party ideology and female voice (silence) in *Army Nurse*.[2] For instance, in a foregrounding composition achieved by a wide-angle telephoto lens, the father figure of the political commissar sits against a huge poster. The poster bears quotations from Chairman Mao, white words painted on black, and suggests a political spatial environment. An extreme long take of the empty table with the commissar sitting at its head, Xiaoyu by the side, indicates a relationship between a political father and his pupil. The camera pan introduces one after another of the commissar's effects: notebook, pen, and glasses on the table symbolize the power of political education and announce the state's right to control an individual's private life. The conversation consists of the commissar's instruction and Xiaoyu's silent acceptance: "We are concerned about your promotion because you are a pacesetter here. You have a good future ahead of you, and we intend to send you to the nursing school. But you have been moody recently. As a girl, be careful about your private life. Put work and study first and devote yourself to your duty."

The commissar's political instruction indicates how a prevailing ideological discourse constitutes an individual as a social subject—a process of reproducing people willing to submit themselves to the social hierarchy. The construction of the subject, according to Althusser, results from the power of ideological apparatuses and through the process of "interpellation" or "hailing." Potential subjects such as Xiaoyu are hailed by institutions or political ideologies and offered appropriate identities to take up in the social formation. What ideology suggests, however, is contradictory—an "imaginary relationship of individuals to their real conditions of existence."[3] In other words, the imaginary relationship conceals the conditions and ways in which people are socioculturally constituted by ideological structures.

Althusser's ideologically constituted subjects *appear* to be autonomous individuals embodying freedom of choice and identity. A potential subject like Xiaoyu, however, is constituted in terms of an ideology of self-sacrifice for the greater glory of the state. In confronting the Chinese communist ideological apparatus, *Army Nurse* seeks to use self-representation to assert woman's personal voice against the dominant discourse. But power relations between dominant and private discourses are such that the effort is fraught with difficulties.

A FEMALE POINT OF VIEW

The self-representation that searches for female subjectivity and sexuality begins with a female point of view. The assertion of woman as a viewing subject, while declaring her access to point-of-view structure and narrative discourse, exemplifies the anxiety of female authorship in a women's film. The thematic exploration of female experience through a representation of self-consciousness raises several questions: How and under what conditions may a female character see? Can woman obtain her subjectivity and sexuality by taking the position of a viewing subject? What prevents woman from acknowledging her inner world? Even with a female protagonist positioned as seeing subject, why is making a women's film so difficult?

My investigation of these questions concerns woman's desire and her difficulties in seeing. Because of the conflict between personal desire and social duty that preoccupies female nurses in *Army Nurse*, the articulation of the look presents a double form: a public, collective look and a private, individual gaze. As viewing subjects, the female nurses look on an object as a group. Their collective look is framed within the public space of the workplace and confined by the ideal of duty. To see is to comprehend the knowledge of one's position as an army nurse.

As apprentice nurses, the girls' first lesson is to view a surgical demonstration. The process of teaching and learning is conveyed through a point-of-view structure. Unlike the normal point-of-view shot, however, where the camera first assumes the position of a subject and then shows us what the subject sees, all the point-of-view shots in *Army Nurse* reverse the conventional pattern to show the viewed object first. A body part in close-up on the operating table, for instance, introduces what the nurses will see. Xiaoyu and the other girls stand around the bed while the doctor surgically opens the body. In a reverse shot, the camera pans slowly from screen left to right as it reveals the fear and revulsion expressed through those gazing eyes. The camera pan stops on one girl about to throw up and then on Xiaoyu, hiding behind the girl next to her. The next lesson teaches how to care for patients. The nurses surround and focus their attention on a male patient lying in bed while the head nurse instructs them how to bathe the patient and how to take his urine. Xiaoyu exchanges glances with the girl next to her as if to say, "Is this what we are going to have to deal with every day?"

As the structure of seeing is socially constructed, the Chinese text again calls for careful cross-cultural analysis even as it raises issues familiar to Western film theory. The feminist assumption of woman as the object of man's voyeurism underlies a critique of cinematic ways of seeing and deriving pleasure. The articulation of looking in this Chinese film, however, is constructed on the ideological ground of duty. Whereas the narrative discourse of Hollywood films is typified by a pleasure in perceiving another person as an erotic object, *Army Nurse* represents an obligation to see another person as a social figure one needs to serve.

In exploring the relation between screen images and the audience, we find that the socially defined structure of looking further introduces a form of collective viewing position. As the point-of-view shot moves between the group of nurses and a single male patient, the trajectory of looking constitutes a collective viewing point. The placement of women as the seeing subject, taking the male patient as object, denies the audience the pleasure of looking at another person as an erotic object. Moreover, we are not allowed to identify with any individual subject but must share a collective viewing position, as if we were among the nurses. The lack of an individual point of view and the absence of woman as object-image of the look further emphasize the ideology of duty over desire and the value of consensus over difference.

The absence of sexual difference therefore creates a condition for desire—a narrative consciousness to unfold the repression and the existence of the desire. In the representation of woman in films in China, as Ann Kaplan suggests, is a desire either to represent what the state intends or what the state suppresses. If a nation does not have a preoccupation with sexual difference, it is likely to be obscuring this difference.[4] Beyond the articulations of looking within the diegesis and between the images and the audience lies an implied female authorship situated behind the camera. By revealing a female individuality through the cinematic construction of collective looking, the director asserts a controlling narrative device and instills gender awareness throughout the film. Her representation thus not only exposes the distinct social system in China, but also establishes a significant narrative discourse by which gender issues are approached.

Behind the public sphere a private self longs for romantic love. However, as the public discourse dominates personal life with an ideology of duty and submission, personal desire appears officially unspeakable. Intent on inserting woman's perspective into the discourse, the film director exposes her character's inner world through a retrospective point-of-view structure that reverses the order of the viewing subject and its object. The reversed order characterizes a significant condition for the female look. Under what conditions can a woman see? How does the camera manipulate the process of seeing? What does a woman see when she projects a personal look?

A key scene in *Army Nurse* that involves a silent encounter between Xiaoyu's passionate desire and the patient she loves is dramatized by the editing device of the cut. The cuts switch between psychological close-ups and narrative two-shots. In a quiet examination room, an establishing two-shot shows Xiaoyu about to change Ding Zhu's bandage. Since military regulations prohibit Xiaoyu from uttering her desire for Ding Zhu, the two-shot seems incapable of initiating their communication, even though it places them in the same frame. The scene is silent and still except for the white bandage being wrapped around Ding Zhu's chest, which serves as a visual and erotic bond tying Xiaoyu to him. In order to convey the female character's passion, the two-shot cuts to an extreme close-up of Xiaoyu with longing in her eyes. The camera then returns to its two-shot position and shows Xiaoyu unwrapping the bandage. As Ding Zhu stands up and Xiaoyu leans her body to his shoulder, the composition assumes an open form, with Ding Zhu's head cut from the upper frame. This suggests a temporary masking device, indicating the screen is too narrow in scope to express fully the moment of passion. By using two-shots for the image of dutifully changing the bandage and close-ups for expressing internal passion, the female director subtly insists on representing woman's desire.

Eager to see the man for whom she secretly longs, Xiaoyu peers inside the ward whenever she walks by. Seeing, however, always suggests an emptiness and loss. Each time Xiaoyu passes the ward, the camera gazes first into the room to reveal Ding Zhu's empty bed. Then a reverse shot turns to Xiaoyu to show her peeping nervously through the door. The point-of-view shots alternating between the empty bed in the ward and Xiaoyu's longing gaze through the door foreshadow a growing sense of loss. A persistent emptiness torments her innocent desire. After Xiaoyu learns that Ding Zhu is headed back to his labor team, she runs to the bus stop hoping to see him one more time. With a panning and tracking shot that intensifies the distance she has to run, the camera at first invites the audience to see what Xiaoyu will see: a quick tilting from the upper hill shows the empty road winding down. Then the camera allows Xiaoyu to look along the vacant road. Repeated images of emptiness make the sense of loss unbearable, so that seeing embodies no pleasure at all.

Through the retrospective point-of-view structure, the female protagonist experiences the opposite of what she desires. The placement of woman in the position of viewing subject establishes an origin from which the narrative discourse unfolds. A female consciousness arises in the possibility of seeing the object of desire. However, as the process of looking is framed within a social space and time (the nurse is on duty in the hospital), the desire to look becomes the repression of the desire. A point-of-view structure that focuses on the absence of the object of desire reinforces the sense of difficulty in approaching a female subjectivity. Such "narratives of subjectivity," Chris Berry has observed, "are very different from the Oedipal narrative where subjectivity is a positive goal to be attained through mastery over an object, thus dealing with the inevitable lack generated in the initial development of subjectivity. In these films the subjectivity that the main characters variously experience is simply a loss."[5] The reversed order of the point-of-view system not only stresses the film character's experience of loss, but also leads the audience to share those feelings. Whenever Xiaoyu looks, the camera will first invite the viewer to see what she is about to see. The audience then follows Xiaoyu's gaze. To gaze on absence brings the viewer into the discourse and the experience of loss.

By inviting one to see, the point-of-view structure calls for the spectator's participation in the film. In film theory, the concept of spectatorship describes a subjective viewing experience that is articulated in terms of double identifications.[6] The primary identification, or the spectator as subject, posits that the essential cinematic apparatus is constructed to meet the spectator's desire to see. The experience of seeing in turn confirms the audience's presumption that he or she is the subject of vision and the locus of the representation. In *Army Nurse*, for instance, we not only see what the female character sees, but through the camera eye we also realize what and why she fails to see. ("To see," of course, can be to perceive with the eye *and* to comprehend with the mind.) As a viewing subject spatially away from the diegesis yet subjectively participating in the discourse, the spectator is positioned as "the privileged, central, and transcendental subject of vision."[7]

Desire conveyed by the gaze seems to meet with nothing, and the subject remains unsatisfied. Why? An explanation can be broached in terms of the ideology of separated public and private spheres: establishing female subjectivity in *Army Nurse* is frustrated by the oppressive absence of private space. As private desires venture tentatively into public space, or as social space inhibits personal affairs, the female director represents woman's issues via spatial confinement.

Screen composition powerfully visualizes the idea of spatial divisions between social and personal or public and private worlds. In one scene, for example, the cross-hatching of a window frame divides the screen into foreground and background planes. Outside the window, in the far left background, a nurse reports a secret love affair to her supervisor. Inside, in the foreground, Xiaoyu surprisingly finds a letter to her on the table. As we hear the nurse's gossip ("It's such a shame that she hides the love letters everywhere. . . ."), we see Xiaoyu quickly and nervously shove the letter into her uniform pocket.

Division of the frame presents two opposing images in one space. The image track with Xiaoyu hiding the letter and the sound track with the phrase "hides the love letters" create a self-reflexive effect: while the dialogue comments on the image, the image visualizes the phrase. Thus a private issue is exposed to a public gaze. As the two actions unfold separately in the same visual field, the audience sees the foreshadowed implication— what Xiaoyu engages in (hiding a love letter) will play out as described by the nurse's gossip. The arrival of the love letter signals an anxiousness to locate a private place in which to read it.

A cut to a door with the large characters of "lavatory" on it suggests where Xiaoyu will read her letter. A public space for defecation becomes the private place for exposing one's internal secret. Locking the door temporarily shuts out the threat of exposure; the interior of the lavatory presents a closed form. The foreground composition is patterned with the square lines of ceramic tiles and unbalanced by a wall column. Against this tight framing, Xiaoyu nervously but happily reads her letter. A male voice-over narration recites the letter and confirms our suspicion that this is a love letter sent by Ding Zhu. Xiaoyu hardly finishes her reading, however, when the sound of someone knocking at the door intrudes. Xiaoyu rapidly balls up the letter and tosses it in the toilet. An immediate reverse cut to a close-up of the toilet's dark hole catches the moment the letter disappears with the flushing water. The dynamic image dramatizes a psychological panic—as if Xiaoyu had thrown someone's love in the sewer. The tight framing and the closed form constitute a cinematic imprisonment where private desire retreats before public intrusion and social prohibition. The temporary cooptation of the public lavatory into the private sphere comments on social conditions that force an individual to expose her private belongings only in the dark like a shameful thief.

Traditionally, from the Western point of view the public sphere has referred to the world of events and men, the private sphere to the world of domesticity and women. These public/private social divisions constitute the primary boundary of gender relations. On one side, the confinement of woman to the domestic sphere is both a spatial and a social control of female identity. The social division thus offers woman a choice: entry into the public world and a life not defined by family or husband, or submission to a domestic realm where her moral status and identity are secure. But the idea of separate spheres has become increasingly problematic in contemporary societies where women enter the public world in large numbers and where the boundaries between men and women that reinforce sexual differences and gender relations develop under various social conditions.

In contrast to the idea of separate spheres, woman in *Army Nurse* faces an absence of private space and lives a life defined by neither home nor husband. As the assertion of female desire against the absence of female space and the dominance of social space, female representation uncovers a subjectivity and sexuality related to impossibility. Woman's commitment to the state and her repression of desire create a conflict in psychological and cinematic representation. The spatial sequences analyzed above highlight and elaborate this point. The displacement of personal issues to the workplace (the nursing office) signals the prohibition. The act of reading a love letter in the lavatory intensifies the fear and restriction. The display of political power and concealment of personal desire in the meeting room symbolically announce the death of personal pursuit. After the public realm forces its way into the personal world, the experience of thinking and speaking as a woman becomes a matter of self-repression—how to sacrifice one's personal desire in the name of the state's ideology of duty and consensus.

As Western critics concentrate on the idea of boundaries, Chinese texts erase them into the absence of gendered spaces after women in China have entered the workforce and gained equality with men. However, behind the disappearance of gender boundaries lies the shadow of party institutions. The process of officially removing gender boundaries in China serves to present women as sexless social objects. In *Army Nurse,* the female character's object of desire—the man she loves—and the private world where she might be able to project her love are both absent. There are no scenes where the female protagonist needs to submit herself to father, husband, or son. Indeed, it seems that "women are no longer required to be obedient to men. But women and men together equally obey the sexless collectivity or its symbols."[8] If women in Western culture are treated as sexual objects for the pleasure of male desire, women in China are like screws fastened to the collective machine that reproduces social values but not personal desires. When the political commissar sits as the symbolic father figure on the throne of the patriarchal tradition, he fails to realize that when he treats Xiaoyu as a sexless being, he himself is already neutered by party ideology. Still, beyond the ideal of collectivity lies the consciousness of sexual differences. The immediate question is why the female director concentrates her film on the topic of female consciousness but leaves the female world in concealment.

As the absence of woman's personal life is replaced by her presence as a heroine and model worker, female representation contradicts itself with a narrative ambiguity: the desire to disclose woman's internal world may reveal her external identity as a disguise. The ambiguous narrative results from the problem of censorship. Can film directors produce a true women's film under the restrictions of political censorship? Ding Xiaoqi, the screen-writer for *Army Nurse* (and also the author of *Maidenhome*, the novella on which the movie is based), and the director of the film, Hu Mei, originally wanted the film to stress their protagonist's love experiences with three men and the spatial importance of the Maidenhome, a dormitory for single women doctors and nurses. It is a feminine place where women nurses can "hang their underwear to dry in the sun or be excused from morning exercise the first day of their periods."[9] It is a gendered territory with a strong sense of a women's world and a subjective self. If framed in the space of Maidenhome, the screen script would have introduced the female character in her love relationships with a teenage friend, then the patient, and finally the arranged suitor. Because there is no space for personal life and sexual description in the context of the military discipline that the director must depict approvingly, the Maidenhome is replaced by the military hospital. Rather than a woman involved in love relationships, the protagonist appears as an army nurse committed completely to her career. A film that might have explored female sexuality directly turns into a film seeking ways to address female sexuality while under the eye of censorship.

Because of the complexities of dealing with censorship, a women's film such as *Army Nurse* must pursue female subjectivity and sexuality under the guise of consensus ideology. Therefore, our interpretation of the film requires us to read in it an allegory, with knowledge of the cultural context that imparts meaning to events. After the film frustrates the female protagonist by supplanting love with ideology, a female voice serves as another important means to express the dilemmas of female representation.

FEMALE VOICE

Inserting a female voice to speak for woman's experience challenges film representation with an attempted female authorship. In *Army Nurse*, the use of flashbacks with voice-over narration constitutes not only an essential narrative structure, but also an anxious expression of female representation. Extensive use of voice-over and flashback seems to typify women's films. Thus the concept of woman's inner self is articulated with a personal voice embedded in a public domain.

As a cinematic adaptation of a work of fiction by a woman author, the film embodies affinities with and distinctions from the literary narrative form. Both fiction and film share a subjective concern for exploring woman's experience, psychologically as well as ideologically. The fiction concentrates on the heroine's three love relations and narrates the story from a third-person omniscient point of view. The film, however, owing to the limits of cinematic form and constraints of military censorship, faces a challenge of how to visualize conceptual consciousness and depict an inner life of turbulent emotions and pressing desires. In other words, what a narrative consciousness desperately desires to express is what the film medium can least promise; thus film represents the repression of a woman's personal desires.

Flashback, simply a narrative return to the past that is relevant to the present development of plot and character, provides temporal reference through which fragments of lived experience can be represented. Combined with flashback, voice-over narration links memory of the past with images on screen. We hear commentary by the voice of an unseen speaker situated in a space and time other than that being presented by the images on screen. Such elements of narration provide a means for suggesting a female subjectivity and sexuality in a women's film text. The speaking subject (Xiaoyu) in *Army Nurse* is both protagonist and narrator. As a first-person narrator self-consciously telling her life story, the personal and female voice of "I" initiates a subjective position. However, as her story is substantially introspective, the duality of external reality and subjective desire requires different channels of representation. Flashback images and sound track voice-overs thus create a double-level narration, with the former representing Xiaoyu's life story and the latter revealing her state of mind. Their juxtaposition further emphasizes the split and conflicting worlds of the female character.

In the image track, for instance, we see a succession of dissolves in flashback that reviews Xiaoyu's life transitions. For example, in a dissolve after the image of Xiaoyu reassembling the pieces of Ding Zhu's torn address slowly fades out, immediately fading in is an image of Xiaoyu in a nursing uniform looking at herself in the mirror. The dissolve conveys a temporal transition, indicating Xiaoyu's career promotion after her graduation from nursing school. A subsequent dissolve superimposes a series of images in which Xiaoyu lectures or supervises her colleagues. A further gradual fading-in frames Xiaoyu in the foreground ready to be honored as a model nurse. The final dissolve in this sequence adds a long shot of Xiaoyu receding from us along a hilly path. In conjunction with the image, we hear a voice-over narration on the sound track: "After graduating from nursing school, I wrote to him at the address he had given me. I waited for his response but received only a few words: 'Address unknown. Return to sender.' Over time, the address became a song in my mind. I saved it in my little notebook."

We notice a disjunction the moment the screen dissolves into flashback and we hear the voice-over narration. The disparities are striking, and our perception has to accommodate the different messages. On the one hand, the extensive use of dissolves symbolizes a smooth and successful transition in Xiaoyu's career and carries a tonal implication for the trajectory of one side of the character's life story. On the other hand, the voice-over narration refuses to explain the presentation of the scene before us but concentrates instead on revealing the nature of the character's inner world. While the temporal transition is indicated through the image track, we come to acknowledge that concealed beneath Xiaoyu's surface life lies an unspeakable desire of lost love.

The exploration of woman's split worlds in terms of dual channels of discourse employs a familiar narrative strategy to insert a female voice in a woman's text. Initially, to establish a female voice the character is made the first-person narrator to ensure her status as the speaking subject. As the "I" and using her own voice-over to reveal her thought, the character is able to turn the mind "inside out" and display what is "inaccessible to the image and what exceeds the visible."[10] In order to intensify the disjunction between the two worlds in which the female character lives and struggles, the second narrative strategy displaces her voice-over outside the fictional world introduced through flashback dissolves. The detachment of her inner thought from the here and now of external reality opens up a space for the voice of truth. By insisting forcefully on the displacement between voice/image, inner/outer, and desire/career, a female subjectivity becomes evident through the enunciation of her own voice.

When woman's personal voice self-consciously tells her own stories, it inscribes the female viewer as the recipient of the film's direct address.

Indeed, questions regarding to whom the narrator is speaking or how to address the audience have been conscious concerns of women's films. In *Army Nurse*, when Xiaoyu's personal voice takes the form of a voice-over narration coming from a space/time outside the diegesis, she is able to transform the story into discourse by exposing her internal thought directly to the public. As a form of direct address to the audience, the voice-over monologue produces several identifications for the female spectator. Because of the presence of a woman as the central character as well as a first-person narrator who composes and tells her story, the filmic narration provides the audience no alternative but to identify with the film character. Shared life experience initiates the female spectators' identification with the heroine. The female voice that speaks the silenced thoughts of the audience reinforces female spectatorship as the subject of film discourse.

By questioning the way things are, the female voice further calls for female spectators' recognition. A female inquiry echoed in the conjunction between sound and image subtly conveys a poetics of female representation. The image track shows that by her friend's arrangement Xiaoyu meets with a suitor, the soldier Tu Jianli. When the time comes for Tu to return to his unit, Xiaoyu agrees to see him off at the railway station. A crosscut shows Tu at the station waiting for Xiaoyu while she paces in her friend's apartment, hesitant to leave. As the cut enlarges the distance between the two characters, it reduces the distance between the separated locations. Tu waits in vain before rushing toward the train as it starts to leave the platform. Jumping up to the train door, he looks one more time in the hope that Xiaoyu will appear. At this moment, another crosscut to the station entrance shows Xiaoyu arriving. Barred outside the entrance by a tightly framed iron fence, Xiaoyu fails at the last minute to catch her potential candidate for marriage. By the time she finally reaches the platform, the train has gone and the station is empty. In conjunction with the images, we hear Xiaoyu's questioning voice-over: "At the railway station, all are rushing about their own business. Could they still make it if they were late? Is everything in the world like this? I don't know. But I want to pluck up my courage and try. Anyway, things should come to an end."

In this scene, the image track uses crosscutting to present us with a rhythm of external life that enhances the drama between the man who almost fails to catch his train and the woman who fails to see him off. The effect of increasingly shorter cuts between station/apartment, Xiaoyu's hesitance/Tu's anxiety, and departing train/arriving Xiaoyu creates an illusion of accelerated rhythm—the unrolling of fragments of life events. As Xiaoyu's voice-over narration comments on the events in the image track, she uses the real life clip as a metaphor to express her inner thoughts and psychological uncertainties. Her questions in voice-over about the difficulty of connecting and the need for courage are connotations extended from the visual denotation.

As the female voice transforms her life experience into a generic inquiry, the private turns into the public as the spectator is invited to question with her and expect explanations. Spectatorship, when exclusively engaged with women's questions, becomes both female and subjective. Feminist film theory, however, has paid far more attention to women as objects than to women as subjects. Beyond the standard concept of women as image, produced by and for men, there exists the possibility of viewing between women. As Linda Williams has observed, a film that constructs its spectator in a female subject position locked into a primary identification with a female subject on screen makes it possible for the spectator to impose her own feminist readings on the film.[11] Thus *Army Nurse* invites the female viewing subject to conduct her own readings.

An understanding of the disjunction between the image and the voice-over inspires the viewer to relate the narrative to a gender inquiry: why does the film foreground a female hero while consigning her inner voice to a sound track? This inquiry draws a second recognition: the limits imposed on woman's representation by ideology and censorship. The viewer begins to realize how the film discourse is constructed and why she is positioned as an ideal viewing subject. Reading, understanding, and interpreting contradictions in narrative and narration serve to ground and assure female spectatorship in a subject position.

Control of the discourse through the voice of a female narrator further exemplifies a gender consciousness. Female authorship faces a contradiction, however, between the ability to introduce a female voice and the difficulty of asserting its independence. Having examined the female voice at its narrative level, we might further ask, Is there a voice of the film behind the voice of the screen? And what is the relationship between the character as speaking subject and female authorship as subject of the enunciation? In order to approach these questions, we need to extend our comprehension of voice beyond the level of narratology. Susan Lanser describes voice as a narratological term that

> attends to the specific forms of textual practice and avoids the essentializing tendencies of its more casual feminist usage. As a political term, "voice" rescues textual study from a formalist isolation that often treats literary events as if they were inconsequential to human history. When these two approaches to voice

converge into "sociological poetics," it becomes possible to see narrative technique not simply as a product of ideology but as ideology itself: narrative voice, situated at the juncture of social position and literary practice, embodies the social, economic, and literary conditions under which it has been produced.[12]

From the broad view of both social and cinematic conditions in China, we hear different voices from Chinese female directors. In an interview, three well-known female directors respond differently to a question about the idea of "women's cinema." Zhang Nuanxin, the director of *Sacrificed Youth*, replies: "To be honest, I'm not that interested in women's cinema. . . . From my first days in filmmaking, I've been very interested in auteurism. I feel that for me film is like an author's pen. I want to use it to write the things I want to write." Peng Xiaolian, director of *The Women's Story*, responds: "Women's cinema should obviously be an expression of a woman's psychology." Finally, Hu Mei comments: "The most important thing is to stand in a position where one can see the world from what is completely a woman's angle."[13]

Listening to these female directors, we recognize several perspectives on the question of women and representation. Generally speaking, in filmmaking a female director primarily establishes herself as an author. She assumes the position of one who writes with the pen or films with the camera. In order to "hold the pen" as a man, female filmmakers have to degender themselves, so to speak, to claim that "I can make films as well as my male colleagues do." The ambition to enter the male-dominated mainstream of film production leads women directors to make films with a covert gender consciousness. This restrained gender consciousness, however, sometimes becomes overt when female experience contradicts social and political ideologies. The strong desire to represent female experience, coupled with the difficulty of finding a language or form in which to do so, often lends a cast of uncertainty to the work of women directors. Understanding a "woman's film" to mean the rendering of woman's psychological world from a subjective perspective leaves open the question of *how* to pursue a woman's angle and voice. A disjunction between voice and image is especially telling in regard to the question of female authorship in *Army Nurse*.

The notion of female authorship encompasses how a female voice and point of view emerge through different narrational modes. In this case, both fiction *(Maidenhome)* and film *(Army Nurse)* explore woman's experience, psychologically as well as ideologically. In contast to the first-person voice-over narration in the film, however, the fiction relies on a third-person, omniscient narrator to tell a woman's story. This third-person narrator represents a higher authority in relation to the narrative she relates. The narrator is a knower in every sense: of the character's innermost thoughts and feelings, as well as of the character's past and present. The consciousness that establishes and maintains this female, authorial third-person voice underscores the subjectivity of a female representation.

Narrated monologue is a specific narrative mode this third-person narrator employs. As defined by Dorrit Cohn, narrated monologue refers to "the technique for rendering a character's thought in his own idiom while maintaining the third-person reference and the basic tense of narration."[14] In reference to the Maidenhome, the narrated monologue reinforces the constitution of a female representation. As the narrator speaks for the woman's inner thoughts while remaining in a third-person position, the monologue dominates both the narrative (experience) and the narration (discourse).

In the corresponding sequence analyzed above in this chapter, one can see a contrasting narrational form from fiction, constituted through the narrated monologue:

> Ding Zhu asked Xiaoyu to change his bandage. As she wound the bandage around his neck, she could hear his heart thumping as though it was going to jump out of his chest. No doubt he could hear her heartbeat, too. She sensed his breathing becoming more labored and wished she hadn't agreed to put the bandage on. . . . She didn't know what would happen next; she just knew she wasn't breathing, her heartbeat had stopped, and the rest of the world had ceased to exist. She shut her eyes, her mind already empty of all thought. Was it a minute? No, longer; it seemed a lifetime in which she no longer belonged to herself. Yet it was so short, maybe only ten seconds, or even less; less time than it took for a single breath.[15]

In this passage, the third-person narration weaves in and out of the character's mind. The monologue describes the sequence of the characters' confrontation, speaks for the female character's inner thoughts, and renders an unspeakable desire or emotion. It is as if the narrator were formulating the thoughts in her own mind. The language, the voice of narration, speaks for the mind of the female protagonist. The inferred closeness between the narrator's voice and the character's mind makes us read the passage as transposed thought-quotations. Maintenance of the third-person narration, however, implies the presence of a woman's authorial voice in the narrative. Addressing the literariness of the scene, however, the unspeakable internal thoughts and emotions come across in the language of romantic cliché.

Cinematic rendering of this sequence, by contrast, underscores a silent confrontation between Xiaoyu and Ding Zhu. We receive neither words nor sounds from the sound track. We derive meaning exclusively from camera shots, mise-en-scène, and silence. In addition to the psychological close-ups and narrative two-shots discussed above, the interaction between silence and image constitutes the discourse of narration. The series of images unfolds against an almost absolute silence, so we concentrate on the two characters within the frame. Thus the silence creates a spatial sense of experience. As Xiaoyu unwraps the bandage from Ding Zhu's neck and chest, the camera exposes the male body in front of the female protagonist and the audience. We continue to feel the weight of silence when Xiaoyu emits a brief scream as Ding Zhu forcefully tears off the bandage. As Xiaoyu redresses Ding Zhu's wound, the silence persists, powerfully intensifying a temporal sense—creating a suffocating moment of desire and restraint. The silence fixes our vision to the only motion on the screen: the white bandage, placed by female hands onto a male chest. The silence of inexpressible passion forces us to imagine the sound of the would-be lovers' heartbeats. The sudden eruption of drumbeats and music, mimicking the rhythm of heartbeats, finally breaks the silence and heightens the characters' emotional climax.

The filmic counterpart to the voice in fiction is silence. In both forms of representation, female authorship inserts a voice into narrative: either the words of a narrator or the silence of image. In the latter, we *see* the bodies of lust and longing rather than hear of the encounter, as it were, secondhand.

In the final moments of *Army Nurse,* the protagonist's search for fulfillment through female desire ends with an unrealized dream. However, an awakened female consciousness brings her an understanding of who she is and what she truly desires. As Xiaoyu decides to end her relation with the arranged candidate, a sequence of close-up shots in conjunction with the voice-over narration reemphasizes the split female self: a death of the past and a rebirth for the future. An extreme close-up isolates Xiaoyu's diary on the screen and makes the characters of Ding Zhu's address visually dominant. The following close-up isolates Xiaoyu's hand as it grasps the torn pieces of the address and then lets them go. With the image track we hear a personal monologue from the sound track: "I never thought it would end like this. After I gave a long time to thought, I suddenly saw myself clearly for the first time. Over the past fifteen years, I've lost a lot." What Xiaoyu leaves behind her is a repressed female subjectivity and sexuality, yet the new destination toward which she heads, ironically, is her nursing career.

The female perspective explores women's experience and employs a poetics of female narration. "Female experience," Sally Robinson indicates, "is (at least) a twofold process through which one places oneself and is placed in discursive and social systems."[16] A self-consciousness of private longing and the socially determined role of model worker reflects precisely the endless articulation of woman's doubled placement in *Army Nurse*. The dilemma of trying to fulfill a social role hostile to personal desire forms such a compelling force that it causes lifelong torment for the female protagonist. The conflict between the compulsion to embody a representative citizen for the nation-state and the inner drive to search for a female self, therefore, underscores a significant process of female experience in the context of Chinese gender conditions.

Chapter Ten

Transgender Masquerading in Huang Shuqin's
Human, Woman, Demon

*Circumstances and opportunities have brought us many women directors. I
really appreciate what we have. Because I am a female director, but more
because I am a woman, I have always been concerned with the representation
of a female self in my works, life, and profession.*

—ZHANG NUANXIN

HUMAN, WOMAN, DEMON (Ren gui qing, 1987) is primarily concerned with the
subject of female experience.[1] Representing a woman's personal history
from childhood to adulthood, the film portrays its protagonist facing a
dilemma: her desire for and denial of a female identity. The dynamic of
rejecting a female identity stems from a mother-daughter conflict, initiated
when the adulterous mother fails to provide her daughter with an ideal role
model. The desire to secure a female identity, however, is evoked in the sexualized encounter with a male. In this oscillation between denial and desire,
she experiences an identity crisis. As an actor on the opera stage, she plays
male roles in masquerade. Off-stage, she carries out female roles as lover,
wife, and mother. Torn between different demands, the female protagonist
"marries" herself to the stage and identifies with her theatrical persona, the
male opera ghost.

Female experience as represented by women themselves posits a poetics of female self-representation. As defined by Sally Robinson, self-representation refers to "a process by which subjects produce themselves as
women within particular discursive contexts."[2] Since women have already

Human, Woman, Demon, 1987

been placed in sociocultural systems and "produced" by discursive narrative, self-representation has to seek new forms that articulate a difference
from normative constructions. Thus the process of narrative self-representation takes female experience as its focal point and pursues multiple subject positions concerning author, narrator, character, and reader. To read
and unravel the process of self-representation might therefore begin with
the question of how representation both reflects and produces female experience. In an analysis of representation, the nature of the speaking subject
becomes important: Who is the speaking subject in the text? From which
subject's perspective is experience represented? And who is the subject of
the text's address? Women who seek to render an authentic representation
of female experience—one truthful to a personal or shared reality—must,
as Robinson indicates, "concern themselves with the power of narrative to
(re)define the experience and gendered subjectivity."[3]

In basing my film analysis on the narrative subject of female identity
and the narrational structure of self-representation, I will consider the significance of self-representation as an articulation of female experience and
examine how the three orders of being—human, woman, demon—inform

the protagonist's journey toward selfhood. To do so, I will trace the female development of the character through three stages: her childhood and an Oedipal mother-daughter conflict, her youth and the concept of masquerading, and her adult life and the notions of desire and despair.

FILM SYNOPSIS

Drawing materials from the life of the opera actress Pei Yanling, the film portrays her passionate engagement with her role as the male ghost Zhong Kui. In flashbacks to her childhood and young womanhood that focus on the most conscious and sentimental moments of a woman's life, the film simultaneously evokes the drama of a personal life story and a poetics of female representation. The little girl known as Qiuyun grows up in an aristocratic opera family. She spends her childhood at the foot of the opera stage, watching as her father and mother perform the number "Zhong Kui Marries off His Sister." Constantly exposed to the opera, little Qiuyun even learns to notice whenever her father sings out of tune during a performance.

It is hard for Qiuyun to accept the fact that the parents she sees on-stage behave so differently off-stage. One evening, she happens to run into a barnyard, where she catches sight of her mother having sexual intercourse with a member of the opera troupe. Days later, her mother runs away with this man during the middle of an opera performance. As a girl abandoned by her mother, Qiuyun is taunted by her little friends and lives her childhood under a cloud of confusion, bewildered by her mother's flight.

With an editing cut, the narrative shifts from Qiuyun's childhood to her adolescence. Because of a chance opportunity (one of the male actors suddenly falls ill at the moment he is to go on-stage), Qiuyun is quickly made up as his substitute. Her wonderfully successful performance, however, does not spare her from a beating at the hands of her father. In hitting her with the sole of his shoe, the father attempts to stop Qiuyun from following in her mother's footsteps; he promises to send her to school instead. But Qiuyun stubbornly insists on pursuing a career on the stage. Qiuyun and her father agree, however, that she will play only male roles, so as to avoid the pitfalls to which female roles might be subject.

Qiuyun's talent and her arduous training in kung fu, singing, and acting win her a reputation as a prodigy, and she attracts a prominent opera teacher's attention. She is selected for the provincial opera troupe to train under the guidance of teacher Zhang, a well-known young male actor. Mesmerized by Qiuyun's acting talent and frustrated by his unhappy marriage, teacher Zhang expresses his passionate love for Qiuyun. With the real world and the opera world dominated by numerous devils and ghosts, this forbidden relationship leads to the forced resignation of teacher Zhang and a swirl of humiliating gossip about Qiuyun. Insulted and confused, Qiuyun tries to forsake her opera career and return home to farm with her father. But in contrast to the old days, when Qiuyun's father beat her to discourage her from learning opera, this time he threatens to beat her if she does not return to the troupe and continue her training.

To announce a temporal jump, the off-screen sound of a baby crying introduces the space and time of Qiuyun's married life. Her successful career contrasts with her troubled marriage. While she resumes her training after the Cultural Revolution and raises two children, her husband (an unseen character in the film) becomes attached to gambling. Remaining outside the home in his male world, the husband sends home pages of unpaid bills. So having failed to find fulfillment in a woman's role as daughter, lover, and wife, Qiuyun searches for an identity through her role of the ghost Zhong Kui. Donning Zhong Kui's mask, she feels that she is Zhong Kui, that Zhong Kui is she.

STRUCTURE OF NARRATION

The poetics of self-representation in *Human, Woman, Demon* involves a narrative structure based on a multiple diegesis. The autobiography of Pei Yanling, the legend of Zhong Kui, and the cinematic representation of the female actor's "betrothal" to the demon role she plays provide multiple registers for the construction of narrative form. "Multiple diegesis," according to Peter Wollen, refers to "heterogeneous narrative worlds" where different characters, languages, and coding systems within a film are interpolated into the main narrative structure. "Instead of a single narrative world," Wollen describes "an interlocking and interweaving plurality of worlds."[4] The structure of opera-within-the-film or film-within-the-opera in *Human, Woman, Demon* calls attention to the questions of how and why self-representation makes use of layered structures and multiple diegesis.

The narrative of Qiuyun's life experience constitutes the film's primary discourse. Covering the period from Qiuyun's childhood to her middle age, the film presents a series of life fragments arranged in a cause-and-effect pattern. The narrative focuses attention on the life episodes that best represent Qiuyun's female experience: her parents' bitter separation, her aborted first love, and her unfulfilling marriage. The insistent concern for women's issues manifests a female consciousness in self-representation, as well as a woman-centered inquiry into what constitutes and constrains the female experience. Women's film, like women's writing, distinguishes itself from the culture's male-oriented master narratives by stressing difference. The essential question of difference in women's writing is precisely the task of "gynocritics"—a critical discourse so labeled by Elaine Showalter.[5] This model of cultural critique interprets female experience in relation to social contexts, enabling us to see how female representation self-consciously places its protagonist in an endless process of finding her self-identity in social relations. The use of chronological order, for instance, clearly shows the psychological development of female experience. Editing to create a cause-and-effect pattern reveals the impasse between the search for identity and the refusal of recognition from the social hierarchy. Unlike Chen Kaige's *Farewell My Concubine*, where the narrative structure relies on China's social history, Huang's film eschews a historical framework and turns to the opera world for symbolic resonance.

In parallel with the film narrative, the opera discourse provides the film's second narrative diegesis. The myth of Zhong Kui is well known in Chinese history, literature, and theater. The opera number "Zhong Kui Marries off His Sister" draws on the legend of Zhong Kui's encounter with a gang of demons as he travels to Changan to take part in the imperial examination. They attack him with evil spirits and turn him into a strange and ugly figure. So ugly is his disfigurement that the lord refuses to offer him the title of *zhuang yuan* (topmost master), even though Zhong Kui wins top honors. Brokenhearted, Zhong Kui takes his life. When he later learns of Zhong Kui's innocence, the emperor ordains him the Lord of all Spirits. One day, the ghost Zhong Kui returns home to betroth his sister to the emperor in gratitude for his aid.[6]

Contrary yet complementary to the real world drama of the film, the opera discourse opens up an alternative time and space that enable the subject of female identity and female representation to be pursued from multiple perspectives. As a result of her frustration in searching for a female self, the protagonist identifies with the ghost figure Zhong Kui. Humiliations suffered in the social world move the heroine to seek values in the opera world, where playing a male role offers her expressive channels. The use of ritual myth to interpret reality and the opera ghost to signify the female player contributes a self-reflexive and interactive mode to the film's production of meaning. Thus, as cinematic images visualize the life drama and as opera numbers comment on those images, the dual registers (cinema and opera) self-reflexively interpret each other within the film diegesis.

As the double diegesis calls our attention to the filmic structure, the social power of language further explains the process of female experience.

Because of social constraints and cultural conventions, it is difficult for a woman to distance herself from her public image. The sociocultural drive in this women's film comes not from historical or political hegemonies but from the power of language. Surprisingly, we find that as the film narrative unfolds, the language of the powerful or the powerless functions as social discourse and rhetorical form defining or manipulating an individual's status. From this perspective, we see the difference between female and male representation. In Chen Kaige's *Farewell My Concubine,* where personal drama interweaves consistently with national upheavals, history as the dominant force provides the dynamics of narrative structure. In Huang Shuqin's *Human, Woman, Demon,* where female development progresses in a relational form, social discourse further problematizes female identity. Language-as-power confines the construction of the protagonist's identity and reinforces the overall narrative order. It is through language that social identities and positions for social subjects are constituted.[7]

A QUESTION OF IDENTITY

Qiuyun's transition from woman to male ghost and her inquiry into identity are evident from the film's opening credit sequence. The conscious, subjective questioning about woman as self and man as her mirrored other conveys a visual power that entraps the viewer immediately. In a foreground composition, a color montage of white, black, and red contained in three pigment bowls alerts us to the visual contrast of colors and to their possible symbolic meanings. In a parallel composition, three characters written in calligraphy roll onto the screen stroke by stroke, with "human" (*ren*) superimposed over the color white, "demon" (*gui*) over the color black, and "passion" (*qing*) over the color red. Following the film title, the opening sequence alternates between images of the female protagonist and introductory credits. In a pattern of transitions achieved by fade-outs and cut-ins, the metamorphosis from woman to male operatic persona proceeds shot by shot: a series of close-ups shows the woman sitting in front of a dressing mirror as she prepares for a performance. Fragmented images of applying makeup and putting on a costume fade in and out, alternating with credit lines. This sets the tone for the film story that follows. After the actress completes her transition from a woman into a male role, the camera pan introduces her and us into a hall of mirrors. By looking at the female character studying herself in the mirror, we see the image of the woman and the mirror reflection of the opera ghost refracted into superimposed fragments. As the camera pans horizontally, images of woman and ghost merge indistinguishably. Observing the woman before the mirror and the array of her reflections, we witness a process of transvestism. We wonder about her identity while she paints her face and dresses as a male ghost.

MOTHER-DAUGHTER CONFLICT

The exploration of gender identity in female representation emphasizes the changing consciousness that arises from female development. As *Human, Woman, Demon* knits together the fragments of the heroine's life from childhood to adulthood, our readings of the film become an engagement with the allegory of one woman's life story. The evolution of female identity appears to be a process biologically and socioculturally defined by the individual's relations with others. It is this relational discourse that enables the woman's story to be built upon and narrated from layered structures. Unlike Chen Kaige's *Farewell My Concubine*, which searches for an impersonated male identity through the discourse of national history, Huang Shuqin's *Human, Woman, Demon* reveals the character's personal world and invests that world with female consciousness.

The core relationships that entangle the heroine throughout her life involve male figures—her father, a male teacher, and her husband. However, the original base from which all further relationships derive is the mother-daughter bond, a powerful shadow always haunting the female protagonist. Because of the threat posed by the memory of maternal betrayal, the daughter's desire for a conventional, traditional female identity established in relation to a male figure fails at each stage of her development. To become someone not identified with her mother forms the heart of Qiuyun's lifelong struggle for selfhood. When the film flashes back to the time of Qiuyun's childhood, the mother-daughter relation initiates a conflict for the film's first narrative order—an encounter with maternal threat and a resistance to becoming the woman represented by her mother.

The conflict between daughter and mother starts from little Qiuyun's discovery of her mother's secret adultery. Playing hide and seek, Qiuyun runs into a hay-filled barn. In a composition of low-key lighting and tight framing, a point-of-view shot from Qiuyun's gaze shows two people engaged in sexual intercourse on the hay. The man on top remains unidentified, his face obscured, while the woman underneath appears to be Qiuyun's mother. After a series of confrontations between the girl's inquiring gaze and the woman's returning look, Qiuyun experiences a shock of recognition. As falling straw buries the bodies of the two figures, the girl, in a tracking shot, runs away screaming. Before Qiuyun understands what has happened, her mother decamps with the unknown man and leaves her daughter behind, motherless.

As a narrative strategy, female representation uses the maternal figure to signify the young girl's drive for identity, especially when the image of mother is that of a shameful adulteress. Rather than a nurturing and responsible maternal figure, Qiuyun's mother is exposed as immoral, caught in the act of violating a sexual taboo by the camera eye and by Qiuyun's gaze. Seeing her mother as a symbol of guilt, the little girl refuses to identify with her and runs away, in humiliation and confusion, toward her father. The image of the fallen mother therefore suggests a threat to woman's primary identity and self-concept. The maternal model is dramatized as a mirror image that the daughter fears to acknowledge yet cannot escape. During each transitional moment in Qiuyun's life, for instance, the absent mother shadows her like a specter. When Qiuyun insists on opera training, her father warns her that the fate of an actress has been foreshadowed by her mother's disgrace. When she enters a relationship with her opera teacher, subsequent gossip likens Qiuyun's situation to her mother's "shameful" deeds. Rendering the mother as an immoral figure and casting her in the shadows thus conveys a double message: rejecting the mother frees the daughter from an inherited social identity, and unfolding the mother-daughter myth reveals a female representation distinct from men's.

The ambivalence of daughter toward mother characterizes a female consciousness in women's films. Mother-daughter ties, while serving as a narrative device, provide a metaphorical mirror signifying a relationship between the female author and her character. To think of "the heroine as her author's daughter," as Judith Gardiner suggests, might open up a further possibility for us to comprehend the characteristics of female representation. Through the creation of a fictional daughter, a female author employs a double identification: with her own mother and with herself as a cared-for child.[8] Looking at herself through the fictional mother enables the female author to trace a history and narrative that has already been abandoned. Reexperiencing herself through her created heroine allows the female author to pursue or represent identities that are subjectively female. As the "mother" of a fictional daughter, the female author can depict female development with a freedom of selection, revision, and subjectivity. In Qiuyun's story as an example, the biography of Pei Yanling (on whom Qiuyun is based) reveals that Pei had three mothers: the first divorced from her father, the second dead of illness, and the third kind and supportive to her. When the mother is represented as a betrayer, psychic space opens, traumatically, for the daughter; the mold is broken. As a negative model, the image of the "bad mother" compels the daughter to search for an alternative identity. Erased from discourse, the absent mother shadows the presence of the daughter; the "death" of the mother makes possible the birth of the daughter.

The realm of language grows turbulent for Qiuyun, and her social identity becomes unmoored. After her mother runs off with the unknown man, Qiuyun becomes the scapegoat of the maternal "crime" and the target of public ostracism. The dramatic events of the adult world often have an aura of unreality in the mind of a child. But little Qiuyun senses that she and her mother have fallen into social disgrace as she listens to the gossip and bears the taunts. For instance, when Qiuyun's mother fails to appear for her performance, people pointedly question the girl: "Where is your mother? Why don't you watch for her carefully? That woman really has no shame." The outpouring of language from the people around her is strong enough to force Qiuyun to confront ugly social realities.

The self-realization of her degraded status in the community is further clarified and reinforced by the language of humiliation. In the scene following her mother's desertion, a medium and then a close-up shot presents Qiuyun molding clay figures from mud. A group of young boys arrives and destroys her work. Among them is a close playmate Qiuyun calls "brother." As she implores him to protect her, the "brother" hesitates but then embarrasses her by saying, "Who is your brother? Go and find your whore mother and father!" A brief utterance packs a forceful social message. The power of language splits the girl from her social group. As the source of utterance, the expresser of communal sentiment, the group confers and controls one's social identity. As the object of the words, the individual succumbs and bears the identity assigned to her. Thus female representation is exemplified by a girl confronting the collective force; the sound of crying (language of the powerless) is subordinated to the violence of vocal epithets (language of the powerful). Qiuyun embodies an identity and occupies a position that is socially and discursively enforced.

As the film narrative requires a transition from Qiuyun's childhood to her adolescence, the insertion of the opera provides a temporal and spatial bridge. The two diegeses convey filmic information, with the opera commenting indirectly on the cinematic images. As the narrative of Qiuyun's childhood concludes with the image of her humiliation at the hands of the boys, for instance, a new establishing shot transforms this screen image into an opera scenario where Zhong Kui performs the kung fu part of "catching the ghosts" and prepares to "marry off his sister." The symbolic suggestion of "catching the ghosts" implies that evil spirits are loose in the real world but that the ghost eliminator Zhong Kui is present as well. Zhong

Kui's preparations for his sister's marriage signify the ghost's sincere concern for Qiuyun's future life. Symbolic as well as mythical, the structure of opera-within-the-film blurs the distinction between theater and cinema. The two art forms in relation produce meaning.

Further interaction between visual images and opera numbers occurs in the parallel development of cinematic crosscuttings. Parallel editing, in Frank Beaver's definition, refers to "the development of two or more separate lines of action that are occurring simultaneously."[9] In a sequence shot, the crosscut switches from the image of Qiuyun in rigorous opera training to the stage presentation of Zhong Kui giving a kung fu performance. As hard training in real life parallels the performance on-stage, the former creates a life image while the latter explains that image. The crosscut continues to shift, from a life montage of Qiuyun and her father to Zhong Kui's performance on-stage; theatrical setting, acting, and lyrics all participate in the task of interpreting the cinematic devices. A series of crosscuts brings the image and the opera side by side:

IMAGE: Qiuyun and her father journeying on foot to look for an opera troupe that will accept Qiuyun.

OPERA: "The Road Is Rugged and Rough."

IMAGE: Qiuyun's father training her in the skill of turning.

ON-STAGE: Zhong Kui performing a series of acrobatic actions—turns, splits, and horse riding.

WOMAN AND MASQUERADING

Playing male roles on-stage yet maintaining female roles off-stage dramatizes the story of Qiuyun's youth as an identity crisis. The film narrative consistently points to the dilemma a woman faces. On the one hand, she declares her refusal to grow up with a supposed female identity. In so doing, she assumes ideal resolutions to the social humiliation and all the troubles that a woman has to confront. On the other hand, she cannot resist the hidden desire to retain her femininity and prove attractive to men. Several questions are raised: What identity is possible for a girl who rejects the mother and denies femininity? How can a woman enter the male world, and what happens to her if she does? Can the crossover identity bring the woman what she desires?

By dressing in men's costumes and pursuing knowledge in opera language, Qiuyun announces her gendered identity as a "man" in masquerade.

The concept of masquerade has been a problematic idea as applied in feminist and gender studies. From Joan Riviere's 1929 essay "Womanliness as a Masquerade," the assumption of masquerade emphasizes a central premise that femininity is constructed as a mask. Taking the mask or the veil as a particularly appropriate signifier, Riviere indicates that womanliness (femininity) can be seen as a mask that disguises female possession of masculinity or prevents punishment if she is found to possess it. Between womanliness and masquerade, there is no difference; whether radical or superficial, they are the same.[10]

Contrary to Riviere's concept of womanliness as a mask, the female protagonist in *Human, Woman, Demon* uses masculinity as a mask disguising her femininity. The masqueraded identity, however, engenders Qiuyun as neither a real man nor as a true woman. The uncertainty stems precisely from a transgressive doubleness: a self-denial of her femaleness and the social refusal of her masqueraded male identity. Qiuyun's rejection of her essential femininity in the desire to participate in the male world is challenged immediately in a love relationship with a man. During Qiuyun's training in the opera school, girls in her group like to playfully attract teacher Zhang's attention by displaying their feminine "charms." Her male role and facial mask keep Qiuyun distant from the teacher. In frustration and fantasy, Qiuyun sits in front of the mirror and paints her face with female makeup, attempting to recover her feminine beauty. A close-up shot of the mirror image shows Qiuyun in female makeup and costume. When teacher Zhang observes this private masquerading, we hear their conversation:

ZHANG: You look so beautiful. In this makeup, you could even play a coquette but never be Mei Lanfang. If you play a male role well, that would be really beautiful. You are perfect for the kung fu part. You are going to become famous if you concentrate on what you are playing. Why are you so depressed?

QIUYUN: You said I'm silly, and I think I'm ugly.

ZHANG: I didn't mean that. You are really a beautiful girl.

Questions about beauty and identity reinforce Qiuyun's ambivalence about her gender. In a belief that what role she plays will reflect her gender identity, Qiuyun wants to regain her female beauty by dressing and adorning herself as a beautiful woman. She longs to be as attractive to the teacher as are the other girls. The femininity that Qiuyun yearns for is an identity inseparable from costume and mask. By contrast, Zhang's interpretation of beauty depends on how well a woman can play a male role. In his eyes, gender and costume retain their distinctions. He sees her as a real woman even when she wears male costume; in fact, he *prefers* the woman to play male roles. Behind the mask and beneath the costume is concealed a non-identity for woman.

The conflict between playing male roles and remaining a true woman causes Qiuyun further ambivalence when the association between student and teacher develops into a love relationship. One evening, in the same barnyard where Qiuyun's mother committed adultery, Qiuyun practices kung fu skills. Teacher Zhang watches her in the darkness. As a zoom shot brings the two into a close-up, the boundaries between them begin to come down.

> QIUYUN: How did you know I was here?
>
> ZHANG: I've watched you many times. I can't stop watching you. You are so young, and I have something that I want to tell you. I've a wife and four children, but I have never known passion.

As Zhang holds Qiuyun's face in his hands, she suddenly bursts out, "I don't want to hear this!" In refusing Zhang's love, Qiuyun declares her fear of returning to a female identity. A tracking shot shows Qiuyun fleeing the barnyard, just as she once fled the scene of her mother's adultery. The encounter with Zhang brings Qiuyun to face her sexuality and reminds us of her mother's scandalous liaison.

Bringing the daughter back under the mother's shadow by framing the scene in the setting of the episode that defined the mother's life indicates the style of female representation. The dramatic device of repeating the scene with different characters intensifies the protagonist's dilemma with a profound irony. The daughter wishes to deny the mother's existence yet cannot escape the reach of the maternal shadow. The question of being and not being haunts the female protagonist; it reflects a double intention in the course of representation. In Mary Anne Doane's words, "masquerade doubles representation."[11] On the one hand, masquerade enables the transvestite to obtain a distance between herself and her image, therefore raising the possibility of resisting the socially assigned female position. On the other hand, the masqueraded identity appears as a mask under which a real sense of oneself has either been concealed or suppressed. For Qiuyun, success at playing male roles exacts a price: the failure to develop her female persona.

Being a male impersonator on-stage requires the suppression of female identity. The male persona, however, does not ensure acceptance into the social world of men. The ambivalence of identity confuses Qiuyun. This state of being, in essence neither man nor woman, suggests a nonidentity and subjectivity to the female protagonist. The audience applauds Qiuyun for her impersonation of various male heroes. These ideal stage heroes bring Qiuyun to a moment of identification with men. Off-stage, however, social conventions often remind her of her unstable identity. Her compatriots tease her, calling her a fake boy, and townspeople throw her out of the women's bathroom because of her boyish appearance. Social life does not accommodate a masqueraded gender identity.

Social pressure again manifests itself through spoken language—a form of gossip and rumor. The functional importance of scandal mongering and innuendo lies in the power of verbal communication to construct social relations among people. When rumor and gossip serve to manipulate behavior and define relationships, discourse helps to assert social conformity. For instance, the affair between Qiuyun and Zhang quickly spawns a rumor that spreads behind her back. In a conjunction of image and speech, the mode of filmic narration stresses the tenacious hold public language has over personal life. Before we hear the gossip, the compositional mise-en-scène introduces a social environment conducive to it: the camera pan leads a line of figures wearing various painted faces crossing the screen. As the camera enters the makeup room, the masked characters join in the excitement of gossiping. The room fills with the sibilant sounds of the "human ghosts": "They are having an affair. . . . They meet in the barn. . . . Her mother did the same thing. . . . Like mother like daughter." The power of gossip brings about Zhang's resignation from the opera troupe and Qiuyun's isolation from her peers. Gossip, while expressing the hatred and jealousy aroused by the female protagonist, tears off Qiuyun's mask and exposes her real gender identity. The social discourse situates Qiuyun in the traditional model of proper womanhood. The message behind the spoken words implies that a young girl cannot assume a man's position simply by learning to dress, gesture, and act like a man. The most powerful vehicle for ruining a woman is to enmesh her in the gossipy web of sexual scandal.

Confronting the invisible but audible sociolinguistic wall of isolation, Qiuyun remains speechless. The poetics of female narration, however, endeavor to speak for someone who is voiceless, to say that which is unspeakable. The visual motifs of camera work, composition, and lighting serve as a precise language for female expression. In a close-up shot with a Dutch angle, we see Qiuyun in front of the mirror painting her face half black, half red. She mixes the colors together, and her face becomes unrecognizable. The tilted view of Qiuyun's painted face visually suggests the disorientation of her mind. The projection of red and black paint onto a woman's face symbolizes the social shadow falling over and subsuming the individual. Qiuyun's psychological imbalance is further intensified by the visual motif of composition and lighting. She is framed at the edge of screen right, with only the ceiling as background dominating the rest of the frame. This compositional imbalance between character and ceiling suggests the uneven opposition between individual desire and collective will. Further intensified by an extreme low-angle shot—looking up at the character and the ceiling from a camera position set lower than our eye level—the ceiling looms up to swallow the character or to push her off the screen. In addition to the compositional weight, the sense of a striking imbalance in power is reinforced by the lighting system. A low-key spotlight provides the primary source of illumination. Directed to the character, it projects sharply defined shadows onto the ceiling. The fill light must come from a hanging light ball off-screen, swaying from side to side. As the swinging light enters and leaves the frame, the alternation between shadow and light makes the imbalanced mise-en-scène even more disproportional. Together, the visual motifs produced by low-angle shots, light from below, and shadow projected onto the ceiling portray the character's psychological turmoil in a suffocating social situation.

As the female protagonist, disgraced, withdraws from her social milieu, filmic representation turns the camera to the opera world, searching for explanations and understandings. From the image of Qiuyun, framed in humiliation, the camera crosscuts to the stage and invites Zhong Kui to the scene, as the opera lyrics intone: "Back to my home, see the courtyard in desolation. I intend to knock on the door but am afraid of frightening my sister. Tears fill my eyes before I start to speak. Don't cry; I am here." The use of the opera figure Zhong Kui to articulate the female character's inner emotion engenders an integrated narration. Intertextuality brings together the cinematic protagonist and theatrical character. As the former falls into silence, Zhong Kui emerges as a speaking agent, with the authority of one who can see into another's mind and reveal that mind to the audience. This reliance on a nonhuman figure to break the silence and on opera lyrics to express inner thoughts indicates both the strategy and difficulty in self-representation.

DESIRE AND DESPAIR

Beyond the role of daughter or sister, a further stage in a woman's life story is her marriage to a man. Having adopted identities as a wife, a mother, and a successful opera star specializing in playing male roles, Qiuyun still ponders the question of who she is. Her primary identification fluctuates between a familial relation with her husband and a passionate devotion to the opera role of Zhong Kui. Again, the frustrations of everyday life drive the female protagonist to see herself through a nonhuman ghost. Qiuyun's husband remains completely invisible within the film narrative. The idea of him and his relationship with Qiuyun come to us only through three conversations. In a domestic setting, Qiuyun has rushed back from a rehearsal to feed her baby. Her elder son returns from school, and a colleague arrives and tries to give her a hand. We hear first a conversation between Qiuyun and her son:

SON: Mom, Dad won't come home tonight.

MOM: Why?

SON: He's playing cards with his friends.

MOM: What are you looking for?

SON: Dad wants some good wine.

We next hear a conversation between Qiuyun and her woman colleague:

QIUYUN: We have just started to rehearse the old plays, but. . . .

COLLEAGUE: Doesn't he want you to act?

QIUYUN: Who knows? He's never at home. He thinks I'm ugly when I play male roles, but he feels upset if I play female roles.

COLLEAGUE: A man's heart is as narrow as the eye of a needle.

The invisible husband, however, embodies visible power through the presence of discourse. The utterance that "he thinks I'm ugly when I play male roles, but he feels upset if I play female roles" clearly announces that a female identity suffers under the regulating gaze of a male perspective. His comment, internalized and reproduced by Qiuyun, signifies the real presence of the absent husband. Disappointed in her marriage yet not able to challenge it directly, Qiuyun carefully expresses her frustrations to her colleague. Qiuyun embodies a series of contradictions: the mastery of man's language, in opera, with the silence of her own voice; a masterful role on stage, a subservient wife at home. Caught between home and career, Qiuyun, like many Chinese women, confronts a dilemma—how to remain herself in traditional roles while pursuing an unconventional profession for women.

In addition to pressure from her husband, public opinion continues to threaten the protagonist's stability. Comments and gossip no longer consist only of small talk or whispers but appear in print. In the third conversation, a man visits Qiuyun and introduces himself as her husband's friend. He tells Qiuyun that he holds much of her husband's considerable gambling debt. When Qiuyun responds that the matter is not her affair, the man presents a journal article titled "Qiuyun's Happy Family." He tells her that during the Cultural Revolution her husband did not betray her; indeed, he supported her opera career and thus "deserves part of your honors, awards, and money."

The disparity between the cinematic impression of Qiuyun's family life and the content of the printed story reinforces the dilemma embedded in both woman's life and the film narrative. Qiuyun longs for but does not enjoy the freedom of self-expression. In a social context, woman, especially a successful woman, bears the responsibility of exhibiting herself as a public model: the family life of an opera star must be a happy one. Printed discourse, while depicting male-female relations in accordance with social values, conceals a gender enigma behind the family door. In her position as a social model to the outside world and a wife-mother at home, Qiuyun faces the dilemma without comment as she returns the magazine to her visitor and silently looks away from the camera. Qiuyun's silence and her shift of vision indicate the difficulty of speaking for herself in the given social reality—that is, the difficulty of constituting a self-representation. Consciousness of self-representation becomes acute in the desire to utter the unspeakable.

A mood of solitude and despair further colors the film's exploration into psychological exploitation and gendered consciousness. The female protagonist experiences deep disappointment in her fruitless search for an ideal man. With a growing sense of solitude, she struggles to become an authentic self not determined by relations with men. This solitary female subject challenges the film director with the question of how to craft a representation focused on female experience. To trace how a woman moves from man's other to an isolated self, we need to begin with the question of woman's desperation. After briefly introducing Qiuyun's family life, the film narrative seems ready to reach its end, as if marriage signals the completion of a woman's life. The narrative repeatedly stresses the theme of woman's desperation about men. At each stage of Qiuyun's life, for instance, it is a man who drives Qiuyun to search for a new self-identity. Each male character breaks his promises to Qiuyun and then disappears. The man who runs off with Qiuyun's mother is never able to acknowledge that he is Qiuyun's real father. Qiuyun's young "brother" abandons her for a gang of boys. Her teacher expresses his love but leaves her rather than endure social stigma. Qiuyun's husband neglects the family but claims the right to condemn her career. What is the significance of these effaced male images in a women's film?

For many modern Chinese female intellectuals, a conscious quest for identity and the desire to articulate a female subjectivity prompts experimentation with multiple possibilities: either idealizing male figures through whom a woman wishes to have her desires expressed or creating female characters who seek success in professions from which they hope to find woman's positions and values in the social sphere. As Qiuyun's life experience has indicated, however, a female identity reliant on men or a self defined by profession will not bring women a completely autonomous subjectivity. The search for self-identity continues until the female subject recognizes her fantasy of submission to ideal male figures as benighted, and the social status of professional women conflicts with conventional expectations for a good mother and virtuous wife. Whereas Freud asked "What does woman want?" the Chinese woman intellectual asks who she might become when she is neither a mother's daughter nor a father figure's favored other. Only after painful alternations between hopeful ideals and disillusionment can a woman start to acknowledge a real sense of autonomous self, capable of expressing her own desires and situated subjectively in relation to men and to society. Unfortunately, this ideal self remains an unfinished project.

The absence or banishment of images of men calls for the female director to experiment with a self-representation that focuses mainly on female experience. The challenge of how to render subjectivity—psychological and sometimes unspeakable—requires narrative modes and visual motifs able to constitute and interpret states of consciousness. In addition to the multiple diegetic structure of film-within-opera, the mood effect of setting is another aesthetic of female representation used to express a character's thoughts. At the end of the *Human, Woman, Demon,* for example, the candle-lit banquet creates a realm where the composition of light and color shapes the screen space into a three-dimensional arrangement visually interpreting the character's psychological consciousness.

The candle flames act in the filmic composition as the primary lighting source, as well as an illuminated psychological realm. Tracking with the camera pans through the house, we see that the banquet has ended and the guests have left. Only hundreds of lit candles on many tables are scattered around every plane of the screen space. This three-dimensional arrangement of candles therefore imparts a spatial consciousness to our perception. Owing to the effect of depth of field, we see the screen space not only as a physical location where a banquet is held, but also as a psychological world suggesting the characters' potential thoughts and feelings. As the only lighting source, the orange-red flames, flickering against the dark shadows, fill the three-dimensional space with patterns of glittering dots. Surrounded by the luminous rings, Qiuyun in white and her father in black share their intimate comments on the opera role of Zhong Kui, to which father and daughter have devoted their lifelong passions.

QIUYUN: Father, tomorrow why don't you play Zhong Kui while I play his sister? You marry me off.

FATHER: All right. We'll present the complete piece of "Zhong Kui Marries off His Sister." I'd like to drive all the ghosts out of the world.

QIUYUN: Who is the ghost? The unknown is the real ghost. Zhong Kui is good at one thing. He is a matchmaker and wants to find good husbands for women. I think women should marry well.

FATHER: Men should marry well too.

The conversation between Qiuyun and her father offers different perspectives from which to read the father-daughter relationship. Qiuyun's proposal to present "Zhong Kui Marries off His Sister" with her father invites a possible transgression of position. The sight of the father playing Zhong Kui and Qiuyun playing Zhong's sister might convey the message that a brother-sister relation on-stage speaks better for the father-daughter relation in real life. From a daughter's point of view, Qiuyun looks to him after she rejects her mother. Viewing her father as a hero like Zhong Kui, Qiuyun seeks his protection when she faces humiliation and prohibition. From the father's perspective, he tries at first to prevent Qiuyun from becoming an opera player like her mother. Loving her like Zhong Kui cares for his sister, however, he eventually yields to Qiuyun's obsession and strives to "marry her off" to the stage and an opera career. After the daughter carries on her father's profession by playing the hero Zhong Kui, the relationship between father and daughter is no longer a conventional one of familial ties but a complementary signification of each other's desire.

The conversation declares that woman *should* marry well. The enunciation of what she desires from a woman's perspective surprises us with a female identity defined by a self in relation to the other. When the female subject concludes that a woman should marry well, the implicit feeling is one of despair rather than desire. Frustration about the realities of the limited possibilities for female self-realization causes her to turn to a nonhuman figure and an opera role for understanding and identity.

The film's spatial consciousness moves toward a visual summary of the female protagonist's life and a final closure between human/demon and woman/man. The application of jump cuts brings three separate locations—the candle-lit hall, the haystacks, and the theater stage—into a metaphor of spatial and temporal transition, thus providing a visual synopsis of the female protagonist's life trajectory. The camera introduces us first to the familiar image of the haystacks, lit in extreme low-key lighting, while the sound of a baby crying emanates from off-screen. At once a reminder to the female subject herself and an address to the audience, the cries recall the time when a little girl was born. The image of the haystacks represents again the space of sexuality where the parents' primal scene and the daughter's sexual encounter with her male teacher took place. Then the camera continues to pan from the haystacks to the theater stage, where Zhong Kui and the ghosts perform the finale of the opera: Zhong Kui marries off his sister. Three dislocations, when edited in the single camera pan, serve as a visual and spatial metaphor recapitulating a woman's life.

The poetics of representing female experience with a spatial consciousness finally intends to erase the boundaries between stage and reality, between opera player and woman. Against the total darkness of the screen space, Qiuyun in high-key lighting wanders among the shadows. The sharp contrast between the highlighted character and her shadowed surroundings further stresses the idea of Qiuyun's endless identity search. Juxtapositions by means of cuts finally bring together the character's world and the theatrical stage. In an extreme close-up two-shot, the stage ghost Zhong Kui, in costume, and his impersonator Qiuyun, in side-lighting, finally come face to face with a dialogue:

QIUYUN: Who are you?

ZHONG KUI: I'm you and you're me. We are always together. But you are a woman and I am an ugly ghost. You must be very tired. It's hard for men to play me and must be even harder for you to do so since you are a woman.

QIUYUN: I don't mind the hardship and I'm delighted to do it. I had hoped you'd save me.

As the conversation continues, Zhong Kui as a character disappears from on-screen space and emerges as a photographic image projected on the backdrop. In a composition contrasted by the enormous size of Zhong Kui's face on the background and the relatively tiny figure of Qiuyun in the foreground, the distance between human and ghost is again enlarged. The conversation, exchanged now as if between the ghost from heaven and the woman on earth, continues:

ZHONG KUI: I've come to marry you off.

QIUYUN: You've married me to the stage.

ZHONG KUI: Any regrets?

QIUYUN: No.

ZHONG KUI: Good-bye.

Lights suddenly come on and the image of Zhong Kui vanishes. The space revealed turns out to be a theatrical stage. Qiuyun, with her back toward us, keeps pacing on the stage. The shift from an imagined world, where the human character communicates with an opera ghost, to the exposed theatrical stage stresses the idea of life as opera and human character as a role. As the final credits are superimposed over the image of Qiuyun hovering on the stage in an empty theater, the question of—and quest for— a female subjectivity remains open. The desire to search for identity and the ambivalence toward confirming what constitutes a female self reveal a perplexing mood shared by many contemporary Chinese women.

From Qiuyun's story, we see that a woman's choice to play male roles and reject female identity embodies psychological and socio-ideological implications. The opportunity for women to enter men's world and speak their language exemplifies China's official gender system: women can do whatever men can do. However, the core question repeated throughout the film asks who woman is when she finds herself identifying with the masculine and negating her experience of becoming a woman. We see a confused female figure torn between mask and self. With the mask, she grasps a moment of freedom from her socially confined female identity. Leaving the mask and fulfilling female roles, however, she returns to the social position allotted to women. The unavoidable dilemma is that the mask of masculinity for woman is a take-it-*and*-leave-it proposition. One wears a supposed identity on the stage of social life *and* leaves it to fulfill the duties of the household. For decades, women under the socialist system in China have enjoyed the reputation of upholders of half the sky but have failed to recognize that this is a masquerade for which they pay a price. The process of self-representation thus discloses the awakening of female consciousness— woman's desire to be the subject of her own narrative and history.

Postscript

This book has examined the changing relations among gender, nation, and cinema in the framework of twentieth-century China. We have seen how cinema, a visual form, and gender, an analytical category, have served in representations of the nation-state. The changing history of the nation continually redefines gender identities and visual representations.

After Chinese audiences embraced foreign motion pictures as shadow-plays and filled the Western forms with their own narratives, early film production remained primarily a commercial enterprise and visual attraction. The 1930s witnessed the initial conversion that turned the film industry into a socionational instrument. The change followed in the wake of national turmoil stirred by Japanese aggression and the power struggle between the Communist Party and the nationalist government. The film industry became a contested terrain where the nationalists tried to consolidate control over the media through a censorship system, while the leftists attempted to infiltrate the field with their progressive strategies. In addressing urban mass audiences of the time, progressive films assumed a serious responsibility toward socionational conditions. In addition, the progressives asserted their dominance by writing screen scripts and film reviews.

In the process of saving the nation and awakening the masses, the cultural producers turned to woman for images. Women's emancipation was subordinated to national salvation, while the female body came to signify a motherland suffering from foreign invasions and domestic afflictions. The film *Goddess,* for instance, features a female identity split into a prostitute figure and virtuous mother. Thus the female body, debased and maternal, fulfills the distinctive discourses of both socionational crisis and traditional moral values. In the cinematic construction of the modern woman, and therefore the modern nation, *The New Woman* attempts to offer women new identities. Unclear about what "a new woman" means in the urban milieu and in visual representation, the created image is ambiguous, laden with the discursive clichés of emancipation from the patriarchal household and posed as the sexual object of male desire. To further reinforce socionational subjects in melodramatic forms, *The Spring River Flows East* casts the woman as a suffering figure of the war and the sacrificing wife/mother of the family. Again calling on the female body to represent national crisis and familial tragedy, the film encourages the mass audience to indulge in excessive emotion and associate this feeling with essential social realities.

Questions and problems arise as we summarize the tradition of early film productions. In addition to progressive or leftist film practices, what other productions did not take the nation as a core subject? How about Fei Mu's poetic films, for instance, or the mandarin ducks and butterflies genre?[1] Furthermore, while the screen image of woman signified the repressed, the suffering, and the modernized, how about the real lives of historical female stars? In the 1990s, Stanley Kwan's *Center Stage* addressed the second question from a postmodern perspective. Using a metanarrative structure and intertextual parody, the film links star image with star persona, thereby juxtaposing a film tradition in China in the 1930s with its remaking in Hong Kong in the 1990s. The fragmented female image and process of remaking reveals a deep concern for the uncertain relations between history and representation and postsocialist China and postcolonialist Hong Kong, as well as the theoretical contradictions between feminism and postmodernism.

As social consciousness and national narratives shaped early production, political interpellation through popular mass cultural form characterized socialist cinema. As an important part of the state apparatus and a vehicle for propagating ideology, filmmaking in the socialist era primarily served political interests and mass audiences. Mainstream productions were preoccupied with revolutionary history, socialist utopias, and model hero figures. The orthodox use of class difference and socialist realism as political criteria and aesthetic guidelines allowed little choice for directors and audiences. My investigation of socialist cinema is not a simple condemnation of it as an ideological tool for mass agitation, but an attempt to understand how and why a totalitarian state and its influential cinema could have found such popular acceptance among mass audiences. In other words, how does a socialist cinematic language system interpellate the viewing subject into ideology and a collective identity?

The power of interpellation depends on positioning the proletariat as both subject and object of the look. As a consequence, workers, peasants, and soldiers are framed as characters on the screen and addressed as audiences of the film. In so doing, the cinematic apparatus facilitates a matching identification between the film viewer and the screen heroes. Such an identification decisively assures the spectator that the screened other is a mirror image of oneself. We belong to the same class and encounter similar experiences. The spectators finally realize, however, that neither the proletarian characters with whom they identify nor the heroic models they find alluring are able to dominate the narration. Resolution to conflict must await the final emergence of communist discourses.

In addition to manipulating the spectator, socialist cinema takes the representation of gender seriously. The process of gender construction often begins with the representation of woman as a gendered other that is subject to social oppression and sexual violation. Then the emancipation of woman occurs when the communist liberator provides enlightenment. Primary transformation from someone subject to social and class oppression into the proletarian vanguard requires the erasure of one's gender identity. Only a genderless body can be absorbed by the collective body. In the form of communism, the collective takes the emancipation of the entire proletariat rather than individual men or women as its mission. Thus the question of whether gender difference persists in the absence of sexual difference prompts feminism to broaden its perspectives.

Two socialist classics, *The White-Haired Girl* and *Li Shuangshuang*, forcefully demonstrate the conversion of woman from a "ghost of the old society" into a "master of the new state." In the former, cross-positioning woman in class conflicts makes her a social victim calling for salvation and a sexual property exchanged between men. As class oppression turns the woman into a white-haired ghost, salvation for the poor and the suffering comes only from the collective strength of the communists. In the latter film, the emancipated woman, while glorifying the identity given through her participation in the socialist cause, feels confused about her traditional positions. In the public sphere, the woman is a model of productivity. At home she performs the conventional roles of wife and mother. The socialist filmic discourse attempts to blur the lines between social production and female reproduction, asking its female protagonist to shoulder a double load. Xie Jin's *The Red Detachment of Women* further elaborates socialist aesthetics and gender politics. As the film indicates, the primary criteria for constituting a revolutionary heroine are her class status followed by communist salvation. This double signification defines the woman as subordinate to two symbolic father figures: the patriarchy and communism. The transition in identity from class victim to model revolutionary is possible only when woman relinquishes her gender identity to the proletarian collectivity. The final image of the heroine is often politically sublime yet sexually neutral.

National cinema that initiated transnational engagement began with the new wave films, a term that is conveniently interchangeable with the fifth generation of film directors and their works. Their significant contribution to Chinese film history involves visual innovation and cultural reflection. The persistent pursuit of cinema as a subject and visuality as language is evident in a few avant-garde works like *Yellow Earth, One and Eight,* and *The Horse Thief.* Films released into the international market are works marked with cultural signs of China and distinctive visual modes of inducement. In a transnational framework, the production and perception of national cinema becomes a case where self-exhibition or self-Orientalizing meets international spectatorship. Restoring sexuality to the female image for the world gaze ensures the transnational engagement.

As a visual image constructed for a domestic audience, woman embodies social, political, and national meanings. For the international gaze, however, she presents an alluring site for the inscription of national trauma. Zhang Yimou's "iron house" series, *Ju Dou* and *Raise the Red Lantern,* relies precisely on this visually and sexually articulated female body/image.[2] By positioning her in a closed social frame and visual mise-en-scène, the director creates allegories of oppressive Chinese tradition. The spectators recognize non-Western sociocultural meanings and experience a distinctive pleasure in looking: the beautifully suffering body of that Chinese woman is exotic and erotic. Chen Kaige's *Farewell My Concubine* uses its epic form primarily to attract international interest. Fifty years of Chinese history, the classical art form of Peking opera, and the implied homosexual relationship of the two opera singers are woven into a dynamic representation. To reconstruct history and invite the audience, the film employs the unfolding process of female impersonation. The female impersonator's narcissistic identification with the role he plays enacts the director's persistent examination of self and history. When the opera king and his impersonated concubine assume all the key positions—in history, art, and gender—the film leaves little for women but to play the prostitute and add the market value of her sexuality.

Nonetheless, the new cinema could not sustain its international "fame" solely by producing national allegories. As film production became more and more enchanted by the pursuit of profits and critical acclaim, the fifth-generation directors, as a collective and privileged identity, began to recede. Although the title could still draw the attention of foreign investors and film festivals, the veterans faced the problem of what further subjects and forms they could explore. Finally, in the "masterpieces" of the fifth generation we have films that present to the world audience an *imagined* community, where fragments of female images signify the nation as an entity. For the question of whose community is imagined, however, our attention needs to turn to the interrelationships between women and the nation.

After examining woman as a spectacle articulated for national imaginations, I turn to women directors and their self-representations to seek feminine footprints in film history. As part of mainstream production, women's filmmaking has donned a masquerade of gender identity. Women's cinema as a different or counterdiscourse has hardly come into theory and practice. The terms "women's films" and "women's cinema" have distinct connotations. While the former refers either to films made by women directors or films that concentrate on women's issues, the latter suggests a cinema that self-consciously searches for an identity, language, and perspective that are gender specific. Of course in a nation where women's emancipation depends on national salvation, such a practice is unlikely. The sense of gender equality legitimated by the collective discourse offers women directors the pride of having a position in the mainstream. For decades, they might have realized but hesitated to admit that to join the mainstream one has to speak the given language and film accordingly. A female consciousness or perspective might arise occasionally but only to be suppressed in the interest of preserving one's status and affirming equality. The suppression originates, unfortunately, not only from the collective ideology, but also from women themselves. The problem is in part generational. Feminist assumptions and feminist identity sound alien to Chinese women of a certain age.

The pursuit of feminine—not feminist—representation challenges and enriches feminism with geopolitical or national differences. For decades, feminism has centered on the notion of difference to negotiate theoretical positions. Although today we speak of the multiplicity of difference, the concept remains largely within the realm of Western thinking about culture and gender. In order to comprehend gender politics in China, where sameness is valued more than difference, one must consider transnational feminism and the interactions among nations. Film production, as a cultural and commercial enterprise, relies inevitably on global entanglements: capital flows, distribution markets, and audience perceptions. The perspective of transnational feminism enables one to see first the geopolitical differences and then call for constructive conversations among nations. As a consequence, one realizes that gender relations under various national conditions cannot necessarily be understood in terms of feminism. In particular circumstances, theoretical assumptions on gender issues, especially feminism and nationalism, may engage in negotiations. In so doing, transnational interactions concerning feminist practices may transcend national boundaries and master narratives.

The perspective of transnational feminism enables women directors and self-representations to be examined against national conditions, as well as against feminist theories. For instance, Hu Mei's *Army Nurse*, Zhang Nuanxin's *Sacrificed Youth*, and Li Shaohong's *Blush* demonstrate the strong desire to assert a female voice through voice-over narration. Nonetheless, the protagonist in *Army Nurse* finds herself trapped when the woman's voice collides with official discourses and female desires conflict with social roles. In *Sacrificed Youth*, the voice, expressing a Han woman's awakened femininity, originates from her observation of Dai girls. Masquerading within the minority Dai identity helps the Han woman to possess both knowledge and femininity. When removed from the ethnographical reference, however, she returns to her original state. *Blush* attempts to articulate the voice of a prostitute. Yet the third-person, omniscient narration separates the voice from the prostitute body, thereby making a personal voice impossible. Huang Shuqin's *Human, Woman, Demon* forcefully visualizes a woman's identity crisis. Placing the female protagonist in the tension between opera stage and personal drama and between woman and male impersonator, the film uncovers the restrictive social conditions against which women have insistently questioned, Who am I as a woman? In Ning Ying's works, we have observed the mastery of film narratives and narration. Due to the nearly complete absence of woman as the subject of her films, however, the notions of female authorship and perspective seem to have been dislocated from this female director.

By the last decade of the twentieth century, the concepts of nationalism and national cinema in China had become much more than local and regional phenomena. The increasing global circulation of cultural products, from movies and music to commodities and ideas, called for a reimagining of the nation-state and a redefinition of national cinema. Film production in China had to deal with postsocialist political conditions and a transnational market economy. Thus, Lydia Liu suggests that "Transnationalism and postsocialism must be treated as a simultaneous process."[3] The engagement of the two acknowledges, on the one hand, the existence of socialist ideology and state apparatuses and, on the other, the transnational nature of capital flows, distribution channels, and audience perceptions. In the given circumstances, film producers, whether officially sanctioned or not, had to find the point where national discourses could elicit audience responses and gain commercial success.

In the late 1980s through the 1990s, the general audience outside China had yet to acknowledge that in contemporary China multiple film systems or trends coexist and collide. The mainstream of official film production maintained its hegemonic dominance, continuing as part of the state propaganda apparatus. In order to address a changing market and contemporary spectatorship, however, mainstream production struggled with the question of how to impose state nationalism or inspire nationalist sentiments while society underwent rapid commercialization. In the 1990s, a large number of films about revolutionary history and war entered the market under the aegis of state sponsorship. To make the past comprehensible and legitimate to a contemporary audience, revolutionary history had to be "depoliticized" and charismatic figures personalized. Nonetheless, as long as the political structure and the market economy remained contradictory, the commercial success of mainstream productions was not ensured.

Mainstream films then turned to depictions of a Western other to project nationalist sentiments and resentments. Titles such as *The Opium War* (1997), *My 1919, The National Flag,* and *The National Anthem* self-reflexively revealed how the film industry manufactured national symbols so as to forge national consolidations. Memories of Western imperialist invasions and unfair treaty agreements inspired nationalist resentment toward past humiliations and urged audiences to reject the dominant other. Moreover, the reassertion of national identity fed audiences patriotic images of nation and self. This self-other dichotomy effectively stimulated temporary feelings of national pride. The cinematic representations could appear contradictory, however, when the audience realized that after the Cold War the Western other signified a desirable ideal as well as a geopolitical antagonist.

In the process of creating such an engagement, the female image/body was divided between nation-self and foreign-other. Instead of a self-other relationship as one of aliens from different nations, romantic lovers crossed borders and narrative structures imitated or "Orientalized" Hollywood melodramas. *A Time to Remember* (Hongse lianren, 1998), for instance, looks back at the Chinese revolution and underground activists in the 1930s in Shanghai. The subject of revolution is depicted through a three-way relationship as an American doctor and a member of the communist underground pursue the same female lover. To the American, she represents Oriental beauty and mystery. The Oriental body entices him into a romantic fantasy as well as a revolutionary entanglement. For the mentally tormented communist hero, the woman acts as nurse, lover, and subaltern. She is always ready to nurse the hysterical patient or, eventually, to fulfill his sexual longing. The divided woman, with her love offered to the American doctor and her body given to the Chinese revolutionary, is a charged figure of transnational romance and a play for box office appeal. The revolution and its historical context are merely backdrops.

In addition to these macronarratives, mainstream films introduced new versions of model figures to the public and the market. Unlike the larger-than-life heroes created on socialist screens, the newly framed heroic images bore the identities of common people. One could compile a long list of such films, including *Jiao Yulu* (1990), *Kong Fansen* (1995), *The Days since I Left Lei Feng* (Likai Lei Feng de rizi, 1996), *Feng Huangqin* (1993), and *Fatal Decision* (Shengsi jueze, 2000). As these films demonstrate, the hero was no longer positioned in the vanguard of social change, ready to save the poor or enlighten the masses. The ordinary man or woman was caught between political faith and a swiftly changing society. With materialism supplanting idealism, the virtues that model figures could still hold were a persistent faith in and self-sacrifice toward political and moral values.

The Days since I Left Lei Feng, for instance, reveals how after decades of popularity the soldier-saint Lei Feng becomes a joke in the minds of contemporary consumers. The film first unveils the myth of Lei Feng's death, showing how Qiao Anshan, Lei Feng's comrade in arms, accidentally killed Lei Feng while backing up his truck. Qiao ever after lives a painful life of apology and regret because of the accident. The camera then follows Qiao Anshan to show how he acts as Lei Feng's living legacy and struggles against a rapidly changing socioeconomic environment. In a biting satire, Qiao's selfless deeds are seen as outdated; even the people he has helped now take advantage of him. It is precisely this displacement and contradiction—an icon politicized in the past and a pentitent overshadowed in the present—that dramatize as well as mediate narrative conflicts. The hero's vulnerability and persistence win the sympathy and respect of the audience. The absence of explicit political ideologies and the presence of self-sacrifice indirectly reinforce the legitimacy of state authority.

An important component of the official mainstream was the emergence of commercial films for and about the urban masses in a market economy. Perhaps the most successful director of this kind of film was Feng Xiaogang, who made a series of urban mass comedies and melodramas. In his films, ordinary characters with extraordinary desires create a world of fantasies and dreams that extend beyond national boundaries. *Be There or Be Square* (Bujian busan, 1998), for instance, engages the audience in a transnational fantasy. The story of two Beijingers in Los Angeles and their pursuit of the American dream subverts the representational convention that sees the Orient as a projection of the Western gaze. China/Chinese becomes the desiring subject, America/American the object to be desired and consumed. Such a turnabout poses its own problems, however, as America is stereotyped and fragmented to satisfy the Chinese imagination.

While directors like Feng Xiaogang ambitiously shot films in foreign locations, others anxiously brought Hollywood back home. The vogue for transnational subjects became a matter of marketing strategies as well as narrative resources. The Universal Pictures feature *Pavilion of Women* (Tingyuan li de nüren, 2001) demonstrates the transnational packaging. The film is a cinematic adaptation of Pearl Buck's novel of the same title. The crew includes Hollywood star Willem Dafoe as the male lead; Chinese actress Luo Yan as scriptwriter, producer, and female lead; and Yim Ho from Hong Kong as director. The film's shooting locale is set in Suzhou, China, because of its low overhead and its exotic visual beauty. Ironically, the film is another Hollywood representation of China. Set in the early twentieth century, the story concerns a frustrated Chinese woman, confined within a traditional marriage, who longs for personal salvation. An American missionary doctor offers help and they fall in love. With the interracial relationship as the narrative drive and transnational cooperation in marketing, gender and nation become subjects of global production and consumption.

Outside the mainstream, the emergence of independent film directors and their urban cinema quietly yet forcefully introduced unconventional narrative subjects and cinematic forms.[4] An individual subject positioned against the cityscape became the signature of independent or urban cinema. Persistence in narrating one's own stories from a personal perspective freed these directors from the restraining hand of official regulations and ideology. For the first time in the Chinese film tradition, we had a personal and subjective cinema where individual subjects in the everyday life of urban reality spoke for themselves rather than being spoken for by the nation-state. As representatives of a countercinema marginal to mainstream production, the mavericks endured official censorship and gained international notice. Unlike their fifth-generation predecessors, whose films attracted worldwide attention with national allegories and historical traumas, the independent producers fostered a new current of transnational engagement with their dissident identities and anti-official discourses. As a result, Western art house distributors and international film festivals welcomed a new "other" to succeed the fifth generation and to provide a new vocabulary for defining Chinese cinema. The pursuit of independent filmmaking faced an obstacle, however, as the directors realized that cinema cannot survive without cultivating both audience and market. While relocating to a position between the margins and the mainstream, the younger moviemakers began writing a new page of Chinese film history and deconstructing the notion of a nation-state.

For instance, Zhang Yuan's *East Palace, West Palace* (Donggong xigong, 1999), the first gay film from China, investigates the subject of homosexuality in the urban milieu. The significance of the film lies not so much in the gay images brought to the screen, but in the construction of gay discourse through encounters with the police apparatus. The film's discursive and cinematic construction of homosexuality represents a significant achievement in the field of gender/sexual discussions in China. From here, gender politics went beyond the conventions of difference. In addition to depicting homosexuality, the individual film practitioners subverted and rejected the dominance of law-of-the-father discourse. Jiang Wen's *In the Heat of the Sun* (Yangguang canlan de rizi, 1994) stages a revolutionary past set in urban space with an adolescent as the central figure. Authoritarian adult figures and the Cultural Revolution serve only as background. Adolescent ferment and idealistic heroism, subordinating history and politics, constitute a coming-of-age narrative. Unfortunately, these young directors soon understood that independent filmmaking could not sustain its independence against China's sociopolitical conditions and global consumer culture.

As contemporary China interacted ever more fully with the global marketplace of products and ideas, neither independent nor mainstream productions could secure a single identity. In 1995, China, after more than forty years of resistance, opened its market to Hollywood film imports. Even though limited to ten features a year, the profit on these films represented 70 percent of the entire market. The box office value earned from a single film, *Titanic*, equaled that of one hundred domestic productions. With China's entry into the WTO in 2001, the door to film imports opened wider. As Hollywood films gained more access to China's market, some Chinese feared that "the wolf is coming," and filmmakers worried about their own survival.[5] Nonetheless, the cultural import/export business cannot be defined simply as a kind of imperialist cultural invasion. Powerful representatives of both U.S. moviemakers and Chinese authorities (the Central Film Bureau) sit at the negotiation table. The former seek to expand the China market while the latter decide what can be imported. Thus the film market in China is subject to the competition between domestic productions and cooperative transnationalism.

Through the twentieth century, the narratives of nation and its cinematic representations underwent a tremendous transformation. The century saw the Chinese film industry move from shadow-play attractions to progressive films, from socialist mass products to new wave innovations, and from independent experiments to women's self-representations. In the process of narrating the nation, cinematic constructions relied heavily on gender, especially on woman as a discursive trope and visual code. After so many articulations through the camera lens, the significance of the female image continues to shift in the ongoing flux of nation and narration.

Filmography

The filmography includes films analyzed or mentioned in the book. Information for each film includes the English and Chinese titles, production studio or company, principal actors, director, cinematographer, screenwriter, and a brief annotation. Listings are arranged by the year of release.

SPRING SILKWORMS   CHUNCAN   春蠶

Shanghai: Mingxing Film, 1933

PRINCIPAL CAST	Xiao Ying, Yan Yuexian, Gong Jianong, Gao Qianping, Ai Xia
DIRECTOR	Cheng Bugao
CINEMATOGRAPHER	Wang Shizhen
SCREENWRITER	Xia Yan

Adapted from Mao Dun's story of the same title, this film was the first to adapt a May Fourth literary work to the screen. In addition to examining the subject of foreign domination of the local silkworm business, the film highlights a documentary style.

WILD TORRENTS   KUANG LIU   狂流

Shanghai: Mingxing Film, 1933

PRINCIPAL CAST	Hu Die, Gong Jianong, Xia Peizhen, Wang Xianzai
DIRECTOR	Cheng Bugao
CINEMATOGRAPHER	Dong Keyi
SCREENWRITER	Xia Yan

The first leftist film production, the film depicts class conflicts between peasants and landlords in 1932, when flooding along the Yangzi River swallowed southern China. The insertion of many documentary segments reinforces a sense of the social conditions of the time and establishes Xia Yan's reputation as a leading leftist screenwriter.

TWENTY-FOUR HOURS IN SHANGHAI
SHANGHAI ERSHISI XIAOSHI   上海二十四小時

Shanghai: Mingxing Film, 1933

PRINCIPAL CAST	Gu Lanjun, Gu Meijun, Zhao Dan, Zhu Qiuhen, Zhou Boxun
DIRECTOR	Shen Xiling
CINEMATOGRAPHER	Zhou Shimu
SCREENWRITER	Xia Yan

Framing an ordinary working day in a factory, the film crosscuts between the working class and the ruling capitalists. Using spatial dislocations, the film shows how the poor struggle to make a living while the rich enjoy the fruits of their exploitative practices.

GODDESS   SHENNÜ   神女

Shanghai: Lianhua Film, 1934

PRINCIPAL CAST	Ruan Lingyu, Zhang Zhizhi, Li Keng
DIRECTOR	Wu Yonggang
CINEMATOGRAPHER	Hong Weilie
SCREENWRITER	Wu Yonggang

Through the image of the prostitute, the film illustrates an oppressive social reality. Such an image, however, contains polar identities. She is a lowly prostitute selling herself on the street yet a virtuous mother exchanging her body to pay for her son's education. Doubly defined, she embodies social-gender meanings as well as moral conventions.

LIFE   RENSHENG   人生

Shanghai: Lianhua Film, 1934

PRINCIPAL CAST	Ruan Lingyu
DIRECTOR	Fei Mu
CINEMATOGRAPHER	Hong Weilie
SCREENWRITER	Zhong Shigen

In contrast to leftist film productions, Fei Mu's films use the female image to pursue philosophical issues rather than social criticism. The fragmentary life stories of females, from an abandoned orphan to a streetwalker, raise the question of how to define the purpose of life.

THE NEW WOMAN   XIN NÜXING   新女性

Shanghai: Lianhua Film, 1935

PRINCIPAL CAST	Ruan Lingyu, Zheng Junli
DIRECTOR	Cai Chusheng
CINEMATOGRAPHER	Zhou Daming
SCREENWRITER	Sun Shiyi

As the title suggests, the film continues the May Fourth inquiry into the nature of the new woman and what she can become after she flees the traditional household. The film portrays a modern woman, Wei Ming, characterized by her profession as a writer and by her individuality. In an urban milieu dominated by men and money, however, even a modern, independent woman cannot escape economic pressures; she ends up as a sexual commodity. The only way out, the film suggests, is to devote oneself to the collective force of revolution.

THE GIRL IN DISGUISE
HUASHEN GUNIANG 化身姑娘

Shanghai: Yihua Film, 1936

PRINCIPAL CAST	Yuan Meiyun, Lu Ming, Guan Hongda, Han Langen
DIRECTOR	Fang Peilin
CINEMATOGRAPHER	Wang Yusheng
SCREENWRITER	Huang Jiamo

This is one of the few films that represents soft-core film productions in the 1930s. Due to its plot twist drama of disguising a girl as a man, the film became the target of leftists, who accused it of ignoring social problems while indulging in vulgar romance.

STREET ANGEL MALU TIANSHI 馬路天使

Shanghai: Mingxing Film, 1937

PRINCIPAL CAST	Zhao Dan, Zhou Xuan, Wei Heling, Zhao Huishen
DIRECTOR	Yuan Muzhi
CINEMATOGRAPHER	Wu Yinxian
SCREENWRITER	Yuan Muzhi

The camera tilts to the bottom of a skyscraper and begins to reveal the life of urban dwellers at the lowest social stratum in Shanghai in the 1930s. The use of journalistic motifs indicates China's national condition at the time. Images of women as prostitutes as well as "angels" construct gender relationships defined by either male solidarity or ethical values. The film has become a classic leftist work owing to its thematic pursuit of gender and nation, as well as its cinematic awareness of Hollywood conventions and Soviet montage.

THE SPRING RIVER FLOWS EAST
YIJIANG CHUNSHUI XIANG DONGLIU 一江春水向東流

Shanghai: Kunlun Film, 1947

PRINCIPAL CAST	Bai Yang, Shu Xiuwen, Wu Yin, Shangguan Yunzhu
DIRECTOR	Cai Chusheng
CINEMATOGRAPHER	Wu Weiyun, Zhu Jinming
SCREENWRITERS	Cai Chusheng, Zheng Junli

This epic film centers on a family tragedy to reveal the eight-year war of resistance against the Japanese invasion. The suffering of old and young, along with the portrayal of a virtuous mother and sacrificing wife, are primary motifs in the nationalist discourse. The film's social message and melodramatic force give it an important place in the history of Chinese cinema.

The White-Haired Girl   Baimao nü   白毛女

Changchun: Northeast Film, 1950

PRINCIPAL CAST   Tian Hua, Li Baiwan, Zhang Shouwei, Chen Qiang
DIRECTOR   Shui Hua, Wang Bin
CINEMATOGRAPHER   Qian Jiang
SCREENWRITERS   Shui Hua, Wang Bin

One of the classics of socialist film production, the film displays the female body as a sexual and class signifier violated by oppressive landlords yet saved by the collective force of communism. The transformation of woman from a ghost of the old society to a master of the new state is the central theme.

The Story of Liubao Village
Liubao de Gushi   柳堡的故事

Beijing: August First Film, 1957

PRINCIPAL CAST   Tao Yuling, Liao Youliang
DIRECTOR   Wang Ping
CINEMATOGRAPHER   Cao Jinyun
SCREENWRITERS   Shi Yan, Huang Zongjiang

This is the female director Wang Ping's most acclaimed work, telling a tale of romance between a revolutionary army officer and a young village woman during wartime. The narrative brings to socialist film production the thematic pursuit of revolution-romance as well as feminine representation.

Song of Youth   Qingchun zhi ge   青春之歌

Beijing: Beijing Film, 1959

PRINCIPAL CAST   Xie Fang, Yu Yang, Yu Shizhi, Qin Wen, Qin Yi
DIRECTOR   Cui Wei, Chen Huaikai
CINEMATOGRAPHER   Nie Jing
SCREENWRITER   Yang Mo

A classic of socialist production, the film shows how communist ideology transforms the young woman, Lin Daojing, into a revolutionary follower. The explicit message is that emancipation of woman comes not from personal effort but from revolutionary enlightenment and collective action.

THE RED DETACHMENT OF WOMEN
HONGSE NIANGZIJUN　紅色娘子軍

Shanghai: Tianma Film, 1961

PRINCIPAL CAST	Zhu Xijuan, Wang Xingang, Chen Qiang
DIRECTOR	Xie Jin
CINEMATOGRAPHER	Shen Xiling
SCREENWRITER	Liang Xin

Another classic of socialist film production, the film depicts how a woman enslaved to a regional landlord follows the guidance of a communist leader and joins a revolutionary detachment. The woman is subordinated first to the repressive tradition of patriarchy, then to the collective symbol of communism. In this double identity, the woman signifies both class oppression and revolutionary emancipation.

LI SHUANGSHUANG　李雙雙

Shanghai: Haiyan Film, 1962

PRINCIPAL CAST	Zhang Ruifang, Zhong Xinghuo, Zhang Wenrong, Zhao Shuying
DIRECTOR	Lu Ren
CINEMATOGRAPHER	Zhu Jing
SCREENWRITER	Li Zhun

The film is a comedy that portrays a model peasant woman, Li Shuangshuang, in socialist China. Placing the female protagonist in the nexus of traditional patriarchal conventions and socialist ideologies, the film uses her as a mouthpiece for party policy while still confining her to the traditional role of submissive wife.

LOCUST TREE VILLAGE　HUAISHU ZHUANG　槐樹莊

Beijing: August First Film, 1962

PRINCIPAL CAST	Hu Peng, Sun Qipeng, Zhao Qiming
DIRECTOR	Wang Ping
CINEMATOGRAPHER	Cai Jiwei
SCREENWRITER	Hu Ke

One of female director Wang Ping's mainstream works, the film strives to create a revolutionary mother image. This maternal figure is inscribed with the political discourse of class struggle along with gendered connotations of female sacrifice.

SENTINELS UNDER THE NEON LIGHTS
NIHONGDENG XIADE SHAOBING　霓虹燈下的哨兵

Beijing: August First Film, 1964

PRINCIPAL CAST　　Tao Yuling, Lu Dacheng, Liao Youliang, Ma Xueshi
DIRECTOR　　　　　Wang Ping
CINEMATOGRAPHER　Huang Shaofen
SCREENWRITER　　　Shen Ximeng

Assigned to propagate the political doctrine of class struggle and the continuing revolution, the film depicts how an army officer, after entering the metropolis of Shanghai, faces the urban temptations of female sexuality and commercial materialism.

YELLOW EARTH　　HUANG TUDI　　黃土地

Nanning: Guangxi Film, 1984

PRINCIPAL CAST　　Xue Bai, Wang Xuexi
DIRECTOR　　　　　Chen Kaige
CINEMATOGRAPHER　Zhang Yimou
SCREENWRITER　　　Zhang Ziliang

A radical departure from tradition in Chinese cinema, the film marks the emergence of new wave cinema and the fifth-generation film directors. Bringing cultural signs—the Yellow River and yellow earth—into a visual mise-en-scène, the film questions whether communism can enlighten the nation and save the poor. International recognition of Chinese cinema began with the screening of *Yellow Earth*.

RED SORGHUM　　HONG GAOLIANG　　紅高粱

Xi'an: Xi'an Film, 1987

PRINCIPAL CAST　　Gong Li, Jiang Wen
DIRECTOR　　　　　Zhang Yimou
CINEMATOGRAPHER　Gu Changwei
SCREENWRITERS　　　Chen Jianyu, Zhu Wei, Mo Yan

Adapted from Mo Yan's novel, the film tells a story about the narrator's grandparents. The unfolding of the family history in terms of first-person narration involves a search for cultural roots and national identity. The directorial debut of Zhang Yimou, the film is marked with his visual signature: animated sorghum fields, the color red, and the image of Gong Li as his lead.

SACRIFICED YOUTH QINGCHUN JI 青春祭

Beijing: BFA Youth Film, 1985

PRINCIPAL CAST Li Fengxu, Guo Jianguo, Yu Ji, Feng Yuanzheng
DIRECTOR Zhang Nuanxin
CINEMATOGRAPHER Mu Deyuan, Deng Wei
SCREENWRITER Zhang Nuanxin

An important work of women's cinema, this film examines personal memory and China's political history from cultural and gender perspectives. A sent-down Han youth and a non-Han minority cross geopolitical and ethnic boundaries in a relationship that subverts mainstream narratives and inserts a female voice.

ARMY NURSE NÜER LOU 女兒樓

Beijing: August First Film, 1985

PRINCIPAL CAST Xu Hua, Li Qingqing, Hasi Bagen, Zhao Gang
DIRECTOR Hu Mei, Li Xiaojun
CINEMATOGRAPHER He Qing, Wu Fei
SCREENWRITERS Zhu Jianxin, Zhou Xiaowen

Another example of women's cinema, the film positions the female protagonist, an army nurse, at the crossroads between public and private discourse as she tries to be a social model while longing for personal love. Use of a female voice-over narration and point-of-view structure makes the film gender specific.

THE HORSE THIEF DAOMA ZEI 盜馬賊

Xi'an: Xi'an Film 1986

PRINCIPAL CAST Tseshang Rigzin, Dan Jiji
DIRECTOR Tian Zhuangzhuang
CINEMATOGRAPHER Hou Yong, Zhao Fei
SCREENWRITER Zhang Rui

A remarkable art film from a fifth-generation director, *The Horse Thief* vividly represents Tibet and its religion and people. As an ancient ritual is revealed, the film invites our vision not only to a marginalized culture, but also to a new way of filmmaking.

DISLOCATION CUO WEI 錯 位

Xi'an: Xi'an Film, 1986

PRINCIPAL CAST   Liu Zifeng, Yang Kun, Mou Hong
DIRECTOR   Huang Jianxin
CINEMATOGRAPHER   Wang Xinsheng
SCREENWRITERS   Huang Xin, Zhang Min

Known as a director of urban films, Huang Jianxin here uses the science fiction genre to satirize China's bureaucratic system. The film's protagonist creates a robot in his own image to stand in for him during endless, meaningless meetings. A series of conflicts escalates, however, when social problems seek technical solutions.

HUMAN, WOMAN, DEMON REN GUI QING 人鬼情

Shanghai: Shanghai Film, 1987

PRINCIPAL CAST   Xu Shouli, Pei Yanling, Li Baotian
DIRECTOR   Huang Shuqin
CINEMATOGRAPHER   Xia Lixing, Ji Hongsheng
SCREENWRITERS   Huang Shuqin, Li Ziyu, Song Guoxun

Considered the most feminist of Chinese films, *Human, Woman, Demon* shows a female opera player masquerading as a male ghost on-stage while following her wife/mother roles in reality. The given female experience, explored from a woman's perspective and in terms of a poetic narration, demonstrates a self-representation.

WHO IS THE THIRD PARTY?
SHEI SHI DI SAN ZHE 誰是第三者

Beijing: Beijing Film, 1987

PRINCIPAL CAST   Li Kechun, Zhang Jie, Li Rong
DIRECTOR   Dong Kena
CINEMATOGRAPHER   Zheng Yuyuan
SCREENWRITER   Yao Yun

An example of women's cinema, the film focuses on an affair between an art professor and his favored female student to raise the issue of extramarital relationships. Leaving the question of who is the real third party to the audience, the film foregrounds the wife and the lover to reinforce the drama.

THE WOMEN'S STORY NÜREN DE GUSHI 女人的故事

Shanghai: Shanghai Film, 1987

PRINCIPAL CAST	Zhang Wenrong, Zhang Min, Song Ruhui
DIRECTOR	Peng Xiaolian
CINEMATOGRAPHER	Liu Lihua
SCREENWRITER	Xiao Mao

The film focuses on three peasant women who step out of their traditional space and roles to go to town to earn money by selling yarn. Their journey from the countryside to the city arouses not only their commercial sense, but also their gender consciousness.

THE PRICE OF FRENZY
FENGKUANG DE DAIJIA 瘋狂的代价

Xi'an: Xi'an Film, 1988

PRINCIPAL CAST	Wu Yujuan, Li Qing, Xie Yuan, Chang Rong
DIRECTOR	Zhou Xiaowen
CINEMATOGRAPHER	Wang Xinsheng
SCREENWRITERS	Zhou Xiaowen, Lu Wei

In a gangster and thriller form, the film focuses on issues of rape and revenge. Tracking a young girl, the camera seizes the moment in a public shower room when she finds herself having her first period, then the moment of her rape. The girl's sister decides to capture the rapist to exact revenge. In following the process of finding the criminal, the director reveals the psychological torment where reason and emotion intertwine.

JU DOU 菊豆

Japan: Tokuma Shoten Publishing, 1989

PRINCIPAL CAST	Gong Li, Li Baotian, Li Wei
DIRECTOR	Zhang Yimou
CINEMATOGRAPHER	Gu Changwei
SCREENWRITER	Liu Heng

Set in a small village in the 1920s, the action follows a three-way relationship among the young wife, Ju Dou; the husband, a dye mill owner who abuses her for failing to bear a male heir; and the man's nephew, who lusts after her. The director uses closed film form, off-screen sound, and the color red to augment the repressive nature of the relations among the characters.

THE BLACK MOUNTAIN ROAD   HEISHAN LU   黑山路

Xi'an: Xi'an Film, 1989

PRINCIPAL CAST   Alia, Xie Yuan, Zhao Xiaorui
DIRECTOR   Zhou Xiaowen
CINEMATOGRAPHER   Zhou Xiaowen
SCREENWRITERS   Zhu Jianxin, Zhou Xiaowen

One of Zhou's early works, the film attempts to verify male identity and sexuality in a drama involving a woman and two men. Possessed by one man and desired by the other, the woman becomes the focus of the conflict between the male rivals. Resolution occurs with the death of the woman in a battle with the Japanese.

GOOD MORNING BEIJING   BEIJING NI ZAO   北京你早

Beijing: BFA Youth Film, 1990

PRINCIPAL CAST   Ma Xiaoqing, Wang Anquan, Jia Hongsheng, Jin Tiefeng
DIRECTOR   Zhang Nuanxin
CINEMATOGRAPHER   Zhang Xigui, Hua Qing
SCREENWRITER   Tang Danian

After her *Sacrificed Youth*, a work of feminine poetics, Zhang Nuanxin returns to a social perspective on gender relations. This film positions its female protagonist, a bus conductor, at a moment of rapid socioeconomic change in China. The unfolding of her relationships with three male partners reveals how social attitudes and personal choices are altered under contemporary conditions.

RAISE THE RED LANTERN
DAHONG DENGLONG GAOGAO GUA   大紅燈籠高高挂

Beijing: China Film coproduction, 1991

PRINCIPAL CAST   Gong Li, Ma Jingwu, He Saifei, Cao Cuifeng, Jin Shuyuan
DIRECTOR   Zhang Yimou
CINEMATOGRAPHER   Zhao Fei
SCREENWRITER   Ni Zhen

In a sealed-off mansion shot in a closed film form, the film shows how each day the master selects one of his four concubines with whom he will spend the night. The red lantern, which signifies the chosen woman, and the sounds of preparatory foot massage arouse as well as repress the sexual desires of those not chosen.

WOMAN, TAXI, WOMAN
NÜREN TAXI NÜREN 女人 TAXI 女人

Beijing: Beijing Film, 1991

PRINCIPAL CAST Ding Jiali, Pan Hong
DIRECTOR Wang Junzheng
CINEMATOGRAPHER Li Yuebing
SCREENWRITER Qiao Xuezhu

According to the director, the film is the product of her pursuit of feminism. The central narrative involves two female figures, one an intellectual and the other a taxi driver. In the course of taking her "professor" to different destinations, the driver first observes her customer's unspeakable experience in her personal and professional life, then offers friendship and encouragement. Gender difference, when framed between women themselves, demonstrates both the contrast between social classes and the sisterhood that can develop among women.

A SINGLE WOMAN DUSHEN NÜREN 獨身女人

Beijing: Beijing Film, 1991

PRINCIPAL CAST Pan Hong, Chen Xiguang
DIRECTOR Qin Zhiyu
CINEMATOGRAPHER Ru Shuiren
SCREENWRITERS Zhang Xian, Lin Yuan, Qin Zhiyu

Raising the question of the single woman in China, the film follows the female protagonist, a fashion designer and single mother, as she struggles to balance her career and her personal life.

FAMILY PORTRAIT SISHI BU HUO 四十不惑

Beijing: Beijing Film/Hong Kong: Era, 1992

PRINCIPAL CAST Li Xuejian, Song Dandan, Ye Qun
DIRECTOR Li Shaohong
CINEMATOGRAPHER Zeng Nieping
SCREENWRITER Liu Heng

A son's search for his father is the focus of the film. As the son-father relationship dominates the narrative, the female figures are left with little room. The father's former wife appears in slide show images, while the present wife inhabits the margins of domestic space. The film raises the question of whether the work of a woman director should necessarily be classified as a woman's film.

THE STORY OF QIUJU
QIUJU DA GUANSI 秋菊打官司

Hong Kong: Sil-Metropole/Beijing: BFA Youth Film, 1992

PRINCIPAL CAST   Gong Li, Liu Peiqi, Lei Luosheng, Yang Liuchun
DIRECTOR   Zhang Yimou
CINEMATOGRAPHER   Chi Xiaoning, Yu Xiaoqun, Lu Hongyi
SCREENWRITER   Liu Heng

A departure from the director's visual obsession with closed mise-en-scène and allegorical narratives, this film turns to a documentary film aesthetic. The use of a concealed camera, real-location shooting, and nonprofessional actors introduces the audience to a simple yet insistent peasant woman who seeks legal justice.

CENTER STAGE RUAN LINGYU 阮玲玉

Hong Kong: Golden Harvest, 1992

PRINCIPAL CAST   Maggie Cheung, Tony Leung, Waise Lee, Carina Lau
DIRECTOR   Stanley Kwan
CINEMATOGRAPHER   Pan Hengsheng
SCREENWRITER   Chiu Daian-ping

The film employs an intertextual form in which Maggie Cheung, a popular present-day actress, impersonates Ruan Lingyu, a silent screen star of the 1930s. A Hong Kong film crew transforms Ruan's archival film footage into a remake. The juxtaposition of past and present, anticipating the return of Hong Kong to China in 1997, indicates a concern for the disappearance and reconstruction of history.

FOR FUN ZHAO LE 找樂

Beijing: Beijing Film/Hong Kong: Vanke Film and Television, 1992

PRINCIPAL CAST   Han Shanxu, He Ming, Huang Wenjie, Huang Zongluo
DIRECTOR   Ning Ying
CINEMATOGRAPHER   Xiao Feng, Wu Di
SCREENWRITERS   Ning Dai, Ning Ying

Ning Ying's camera focuses on urban dwellers. The film presents a group of amateur Peking opera singers, retired from their professions yet seeking pleasure through opera singing. As retirees relegated to the social margins but who still find meaning in life, these ordinary citizens cling to a disappearing world.

FAREWELL MY CONCUBINE
BAWANG BIE JI　霸王別姬

Hong Kong: Tomson Film, 1993

PRINCIPAL CAST	Leslie Cheung, Zhang Fengyi, Gong Li
DIRECTOR	Chen Kaige
CINEMATOGRAPHER	Gu Changwei
SCREENWRITERS	Lilian Lee, Lu Wei

Marking a dramatic change in Chen Kaige's directing style, the film turns to history and narrative tradition in examining China's past and present. The film restages the classical opera piece "Farewell My Concubine" and centers on the personal drama of its players. As it portrays the social-gender transformation of a biological male into a cultural female, the film asks whether one can remain true to anything or anyone under the pressure of difficult circumstances.

THE BLUE KITE　LAN FENGZHENG　藍風箏

Hong Kong: Lonwick Film/Beijing: Beijing Film, 1993

PRINCIPAL CAST	Lu Liping, Puquanxin, Li Xuejian
DIRECTOR	Tian Zhuangzhuang
CINEMATOGRAPHER	Hou Yong
SCREENWRITER	Xiao Mao

Seen from a child's point of view and with a child's voice-over narration, this film, like *Farewell My Concubine* and *To Live*, continues the review of China's sociopolitical history. The film examines how ordinary individuals and families coped with the state during the oppressive 1950s and 1960s.

IN THE HEAT OF THE SUN
YANGGUANG CANLAN DE RIZI　陽光燦爛的日子

Hong Kong: Hong Kong Dragon Film/China Film Coproduction Corporation, 1994

PRINCIPAL CAST	Ning Jing, Xia Yu
DIRECTOR	Jiang Wen
CINEMATOGRAPHER	Gu Changwei
SCREENWRITER	Jiang Wen

Directed by Jiang Wen, a well-known actor in China, the film takes adolescents as central characters and views a revolutionary past from their perspective. The coming-of-age narrative subverts and rejects official discourse.

BLUSH　HONG FEN　紅粉

Hong Kong: Ocean Film/Beijing: Beijing Film, 1994

PRINCIPAL CAST	Wang Ji, He Saifei, Wang Zhiwen
DIRECTOR	Li Shaohong
CINEMATOGRAPHER	Zeng Nianping
SCREENWRITERS	Ni Zhen, Li Shaohong

The film invites a reexamination of the 1950s campaign to reeducate prostitutes. In showing the official policy of removing prostitutes from brothels to workplaces in an effort to transform them from diseased sexual bodies to healthy productive laborers, the film strives to depict the prostitute's experience sympathetically.

ERMO　二嫫

Shanghai: Shanghai Film/Hong Kong: Ocean Film, 1994

PRINCIPAL CAST	Alia, Liu Peiqi, Ge Zhijun, Zhang Haiyan
DIRECTOR	Zhou Xiaowen
CINEMATOGRAPHER	Lu Gengxin
SCREENWRITER	Lang Yun

The concept of modernity in a peasant woman's mind is signified by her desire to own a twenty-seven-inch television. To realize her dream, the film's protagonist, Ermo, travels from the village to the city, thereby from domestic traditions to public consumer culture. The cinematic representation of the female body and the process of noodle making bring female reproduction into relation with the social production of gender.

TO LIVE　HUOZHE　活著

Hong Kong: Era International, in association with Shanghai Film Studios, 1994

PRINCIPAL CAST	Ge You, Gong Li
DIRECTOR	Zhang Yimou
CINEMATOGRAPHER	Lu Yue
SCREENWRITERS	Yu Hua, Lu Wei

Comparable to Chen Kaige's *Farewell My Concubine* and Tian Zhuangzhuang's *The Blue Kite*, this film covers decades of modern Chinese history through a family's tragic melodrama. Framing children as the victims of different political campaigns (a son dies in the Great Leap Forward, a daughter during the Cultural Revolution), the film shows ordinary people struggling to survive under oppressive sociopolitical conditions.

ON THE BEAT   MINJING DE GUSHI   民警的故事

Beijing: Eurasia and Beijing Film, 1995

PRINCIPAL CAST   Li Zhanhe, Wang Liangui, Zhao Zhiming
DIRECTOR   Ning Ying
CINEMATOGRAPHER   Zhi Lei, Wu Hongwei
SCREENWRITERS   Ning Ying, Ning Dai

The film shows police officers, once the symbol of state power, now at a loss to cope with China's socioeconomic transition as they spend their days either chasing dogs or tracking crimes. Their everyday routines are exercises in boredom, and the satirical stance toward police reform is clearly conveyed through Ning's editing strategy.

TEMPTRESS MOON   FENGYUE   風月

Hong Kong: Tomson, 1995

PRINCIPAL CAST   Leslie Cheung, Gong Li, Kevin Lin, He Saifei
DIRECTOR   Chen Kaige
CINEMATOGRAPHER   Chris Doyle
SCREENWRITER   Shu Kei

The director searches for a psychological world where sexual impulse is the central drive. Ruling, yet confined in a rural mansion, Ruyi, an impetuous woman with an addiction to opium, desires to fall in love and taste sexual ecstasy. A star gigolo, Zhong Liang, having grown up in the same mansion before moving to Shanghai, enjoys seducing women and carousing in the city's dance halls. His return to the mansion lights Ruyi's emotional fire and thereby the film's drama. In contrast to the director's previous film, a connection is finally made between motion and emotion captured by the camera.

SHANGHAI TRIAD
YAO A YAO, YAO DAO WAIPO QIAO   搖啊搖搖到外婆橋

Shanghai: Shanghai Film, 1995

PRINCIPAL CAST   Gong Li, Li Baotian, Li Xuejian, Wang Xiaoxiao
DIRECTOR   Zhang Yimou
CINEMATOGRAPHER   Lu Yue
SCREENWRITER   Bi Feinian

The director experiments with a gangster film set in Shanghai in the 1930s. From a little boy's constant gaze, we are led into the private life of Jewel, a club singer and mistress of a gangster boss. The cinematography is beautiful and the characters exotic, yet emphasis is placed on depicting the world of the gangster.

KEEP COOL YOUHUA HAOHAO SHUO 有話好好説

Guangxi: Guangxi Film, 1997

PRINCIPAL CAST	Jiang Wen, Li Baotian, Qu Ying, Ge You, Zhang Yimou
DIRECTOR	Zhang Yimou
CINEMATOGRAPHER	Lu Yue
SCREENWRITER	Shu Ping

The film is a dramatic departure in both style and substance for Zhang, who turns his camera to the contemporary urban milieu of Beijing. Using the mobility of a hand-held camera, a telephoto lens on the characters, and unconventional editing, the director captures a moment of social transformation and complicated personal relationships.

THE DAYS SINCE I LEFT LEI FENG
YUANLI LEI FENG DE RIZI 離開雷峰的日子

Beijing: BFA Youth Film and Forbidden City Film, 1996

PRINCIPAL CAST	Liu Peiqi, Song Chunli
DIRECTOR	Lei Xianhe, Kang Ning
CINEMATOGRAPHER	Zhang Li
SCREENWRITER	Wang Xingdong

The legendary figure of Lei Feng has served for decades as an official political icon. The myth of his death and stories about him begin to unfold after a journalist finds and interviews Qiao Anshan, Lei Feng's comrade in arms. The film thus exposes the audience to the past, when Lei Feng was a model for everyone, as well as to the present, when Qiao Anshan represents Lei's living legacy. The great irony lies in the contrast between the idolatry lavished on the hero in the past and the ridicule heaped on him now by the masses in rapidly changing times.

A TIME TO REMEMBER HONGSE LIANREN 紅色戀人

Beijing: Forbidden City Film, 1998

PRINCIPAL CAST	Mei Ting, Leslie Cheung
DIRECTOR	Ye Daying
CINEMATOGRAPHER	Zhang Li
SCREENWRITER	Jiang Qitao

The film relies on romance and revolution as selling points for box office appeal. The female lead is positioned in relation to a young American doctor and an underground communist activist in Shanghai in the 1930s. The female body therefore fulfills the American's romantic fantasy as well as the communist's psychological/sexual needs.

Be There or Be Square   Bujian busan   不見不散

Beijing: BFA Youth Film and Forbidden City Film, 1998

PRINCIPAL CAST   Xu Feng, Ge You
DIRECTOR   Feng Xiaogang
CINEMATOGRAPHER   Zhao Fei
SCREENWRITER   Gu Xiaoyang

One of Feng Xiaogang's successful comedies, the film follows Beijingers who pursue their American dreams in the United States. The dislocation of the native Chinese to a foreign land turns the protagonists into desiring subjects and makes America into a commodity for urban Chinese audiences.

Not One Less
Yige dou buneng shao   一個都不能少

Guangxi: Guangxi Film, 1999

PRINCIPAL CAST   Wei Minzhi, Zhang Huike
DIRECTOR   Zhang Yimou
CINEMATOGRAPHER   Hou Yong
SCREENWRITER   Shi Xiangsheng

Continuing his experiment with the documentary form, Zhang creates a film cast entirely with nonprofessionals. A young substitute teacher, for the promise of 50 renminbi, takes responsibility for a class of village pupils. One escapes to town to become a child laborer, however, and the teacher's journey to find him then unfolds. The contrast between country and city, between poverty and prosperity, reveals contemporary China in the wake of economic reforms.

My 1919   Wode yijiu yijiu   我的一九一九

Xi'an: Xi'an Film/Beijing: Beijing Film, 1999

PRINCIPAL CAST   Chen Daoming
DIRECTOR   Huang Jianzhong
CINEMATOGRAPHER   Zhang Zhongping
SCREENWRITERS   Huang Dan, Tang Louyi

The film frames a historical moment in 1919 when a Chinese delegation and the Western powers negotiated the sovereignty of Shandong Province at the Versailles Peace Conference. The reconstruction of historical events intends to advocate today's nationalist sentiment as China considers its position in global politics.

THE NATIONAL ANTHEM GUOGE 國歌

Guangxi: Xiaoxiang Film, 1999

PRINCIPAL CAST   He Zhengjun, Chen Kun, Kong Wei, Fu Heng
DIRECTOR   Wu Ziniu
CINEMATOGRAPHER   Yi Huhe-wula
SCREENWRITERS   Fan Zhengming, Su Shuyang, Zhang Jiping

The film is the first mainstream project assigned to Wu Ziniu, a fifth-generation film-maker. Employing a conventional formula, the film represents the chapter of national history when Japan invaded China and the intellectual heroes Tian Han and Nie Er composed the national anthem.

LOVERS' GRIEF OVER THE YELLOW RIVER
HUANGHE JUELIAN 黃河絕戀

Shanghai: Yongle Film and Television, 1999

PRINCIPAL CAST   Ning Jing
DIRECTOR   Feng Xiaoning
CINEMATOGRAPHER   Feng Xiaoning
SCREENWRITER   Feng Xiaoning

The film foregrounds a romance narrative between an American pilot and a Chinese female soldier during World War II. The unusual liaison heightens nationalist anxiety at seeing the Chinese self through a Western other, and recognizes the need to strive for commercial viability.

EAST PALACE, WEST PALACE
DONGGONG XIGONG 東宮西宮

China/France: Quelqu'un D'Autre Productions, 1999

PRINCIPAL CAST   Hu Jun, Sihan
DIRECTOR   Zhang Yuan
CINEMATOGRAPHER   Zhang Jian
SCREENWRITERS   Zhang Yuan, Wang Xiaobo

A representative work of independent cinema, the film takes a gay relationship as its central theme. The confrontation between a state policeman and a gay man turns from one of authority against deviancy into a process of homosexual engagement. The gay voice, inserted to contest the official discourse, reveals the private history of the homosexual.

THE ROAD HOME
WO DE FUQIN MUQIN　我的父親母親

Guangxi: Guangxi Film/Beijing: Beijing New Picture Distribution, 2000

PRINCIPAL CAST	Zhang Ziyi, Sun Honglei, Zheng Hao, Li Bin
DIRECTOR	Zhang Yimou
CINEMATOGRAPHER	Hou Yong
SCREENWRITER	Bao Shi

In this film, Zhang Yimou returns to a love story and poetic narration. Through flashbacks and through the narrator's perspective, the memory of a romance between a village girl and an elementary school teacher (the narrator's parents) is revealed. A simple yet beautiful tale draws the audience into an innocent world where the passions of love overcome all obstacles.

PAVILION OF WOMEN
TINGYUAN LI DE NÜREN　庭院里的女人

China/United States: Universal Focus, 2001

PRINCIPAL CAST	Luo Yan, Willem Dafoe
DIRECTOR	Yim Ho
CINEMATOGRAPHER	Hang-Sang Poon
SCREENWRITERS	Luo Yan, Paul R. Collins

This Hollywood film presents a transnational project. With a Hong Kong director, it is set in Suzhou, China, and produced by a Chinese woman who is also the lead actor. The romantic story of a traditional Chinese woman who longs for personal salvation and the American missionary doctor who offers her enlightenment is designed for both narrative force and global consumption.

Notes

INTRODUCTION

1. Prasenjit Duara, *Rescuing History from the Nation: Questioning Narratives of Modern China* (Chicago: Univ. of Chicago Press, 1995), 4.
2. John Fitzgerald, *Awakening China: Politics, Culture, and Class in the Nationalist Revolution* (Stanford: Stanford Univ. Press, 1996), 348.
3. For further reference, see David E. Apter and Tony Saich, eds., *Revolutionary Discourse in Mao's Republic* (Cambridge, Mass.: Harvard Univ. Press, 1994).
4. Increasing interest in the relation between gender and nation has resulted in a number of constructive studies. See Gisela Brinker-Gabler and Sidonie Smith, eds., *Writing New Identities: Gender, Nation, and Immigration in Contemporary Europe* (Minneapolis: Univ. of Minnesota Press), for the helpful introduction.
5. Sheldon Hsiao-peng Lu, "Historical Introduction: Chinese Cinemas (1896–1996) and Transnational Film Studies," in S. H. Lu, ed., *Transnational Chinese Cinemas,* 21. Critics in and outside China use the phrase "gender erasure" to describe women of socialist China. For further reference, see Mayfair Mei-hui Yang, "From Gender Erasure to Gender Difference: State Feminism, Consumer Sexuality, and Women's Public Sphere in China," in *Spaces of Their Own: Women's Public Sphere in Transnational China,* ed. M. M. Yang (Minneapolis: Univ. of Minnesota Press, 1999), 35–67.
6. Brinker-Gabler and Smith, eds., *Writing New Identities,* 12.
7. In Laura Mulvey, *Visual and Other Pleasures* (Bloomington: Indiana Univ. Press, 1989).
8. Teresa de Lauretis, *Technologies of Gender: Essays on Theory, Film, and Fiction* (Bloomington: Indiana Univ. Press, 1987), 5.
9. Mary Ann Doane, Patricia Mellencamp, and Linda Williams, eds., *Re-Vision: Essays in Feminist Film Criticism* (Frederick, Md.: University Publications of America, 1984), 8.
10. Tania Modleski, *The Women Who Knew Too Much: Hitchcock and Feminist Theory* (New York: Methuen, 1988), 13.
11. See Judith Mayne, "Review Essay: Feminist Film Theory and Criticism," *Signs: Journal of Women in Culture and Society* 11, no. 1 (1985): 81–100.
12. Johnston, Flitterman-Lewis, and Dozoretz cited in ibid.
13. Teresa de Lauretis, ed., *Feminist Studies, Critical Studies* (Bloomington: Indiana Univ. Press, 1986), 13–14.
14. Gaylyn Studlar, *In the Realm of Pleasure: Von Sternberg, Dietrich, and the Masochistic Aesthetic* (Urbana: Univ. of Illinois Press, 1988), 10.
15. In Li Xiaojiang, Zhu Hong, and Dong Xiuyu, eds., *Xingbie yu zhongguo* (Gender and China) (Beijing: Sanlian shudian, 1994), 6–7.
16. Chris Berry, "Chinese 'Women's Cinema,'" *Camera Obscura: A Journal of Feminism and Film Theory* 18 (September 1988): 37.
17. Gayatri Chakravorty Spivak, *Outside in the Teaching Machine* (New York: Routledge, 1993), 256.

18. Recent publications on transnational feminism can be found in Inderpal Grewal and Caren Kaplan, eds., *Scattered Hegemonies: Postmodernity and Transnational Feminist Practices* (Minneapolis: Univ. of Minnesota Press, 1994); see also Caren Kaplan and Inderpal Grewal, "Transnational Feminist Cultural Studies: Beyond the Marxism/Poststructuralism/Feminism Divides," in *Between Woman and Nation: Nationalisms, Transnational Feminisms, and the State*, ed. Caren Kaplan, Norma Alarcon, and Minoo Moallem (Durham, N.C.: Duke Univ. Press, 1999), 349–363; Susan Stanford Friedman, *Mappings: Feminism and the Cultural Geographies of Encounter* (Princeton, N.J.: Princeton Univ. Press, 1998).

19. Spivak, *Outside in the Teaching Machine*, 278.

20. Grewal and Kaplan, eds., *Scattered Hegemonies*, 28.

21. See Fredric Jameson, "Third-World Literature in the Era of Multinational Capitalism," *Social Text* 15 (fall 1986): 82–104, and Edward Said, *Orientalism* (New York: Vintage Books, 1979).

22. Stephen Heath, *Questions of Cinema* (Bloomington: Indiana Univ. Press, 1981), 131.

23. Metz, Derrida, and Barthes cited in Robert Stam, *Film Theory: An Introduction* (Malden, Mass.: Blackwell, 2000), 185–191; Stam quote on p. 188.

24. Edward Branigan, *Point of View in the Cinema: A Theory of Narration and Subjectivity in Classical Film* (New York: Mouton, 1984), 73.

25. Ibid., 57.

26. Sandy Flitterman-Lewis, *To Desire Differently: Feminism and the French Cinema* (Urbana: Univ. of Illinois Press, 1990), 13.

27. Metz, "History/Discourse: A Note on Two Voyeurisms," in *Theories of Authorship*, ed. John Caughie (London: Routledge, 1981), 230.

28. Suzie Sau-Fong Young, "The Voice of Feminine Madness in Zhang Yimou's *Da Hong Deng Long Gao Gao Gua* (Raise the Red Lantern)," *Asian Cinema* 7, no. 1 (1995): 12.

CHAPTER ONE: FROM SHADOW-PLAY TO A NATIONAL CINEMA

1. For a discussion of the debate on the subject of national cinema studies, see Stephen Crofts, "Concepts of National Cinema," in *World Cinema: Critical Approaches*, ed. John Hill and Pamela Church Gibson (Oxford: Oxford Univ. Press, 2000), 1–10.

2. Anne McClintock, "No Longer in a Future Heaven: Nationalism, Gender and Race," in her *Imperial Leather: Race, Gender and Sexuality in the Colonial Contest* (New York: Routledge, 1995), 355.

3. For a detailed analysis of early Chinese cinema, see Zhang Zhen, "'An Amorous History of the Silver Screen': Film Culture, Urban Modernity, and the Vernacular Experience in China, 1896–1937" (Ph.D. diss., Univ. of Chicago, 1998). Also see Zhang Zhen, "Teahouse, Shadowplay, Bricolage: *Laborer's Love* and the Question of Early Chinese Cinema," in Zhang Yingjin, ed., *Cinema and Urban Culture in Shanghai*, 27–50.

4. Information collected from C. J. North, "The Chinese Motion Picture Market," *Trade Information Bulletin,* no. 467, U.S. Department of Commerce (Washington, D.C.: GPO, 1927): 1–41, and E. I. Way, comp., "Motion Pictures in China," *Trade Information Bulletin,* no. 722, U.S. Department of Commerce (Washington, D.C.: GPO, 1930): 7.

5. Ren Qingtai learned the skills of photography in Japan and opened his Fengtai Photography Studio in 1892.

6. Chen Xihe, "Zhongguo dianying meixue de zai renshi" (Reconsideration of the aesthetics of Chinese cinema), in Luo Yijun, ed., *Collected Essays,* 289–306.

7. Zhong Dafeng, "Yingxi lilun lishi suyuan" (Historical origin of the concept of Shadow-play), in Luo, ed., *Collected Essays,* 307–319.

8. Mary Ann Farquhar and Chris Berry, "Shadow Opera: Towards a New Archaeology of the Chinese Cinema," *Post Script: Essays in Film and the Humanities,* 20, no. 2/3 (winter/spring and summer 2001): 25.

9. Zhang Yingjin, "From 'Minority Film' to 'Minority Discourse': Questions of Nationhood and Ethnicity in Chinese Cinema," in S. H. Lu, ed., *Transnational Chinese Cinemas,* 87.

10. Tom Gunning, "The Cinema of Attractions: Early Film, Its Spectator and the Avant-Garde," in *Early Cinema: Space, Frame, Narrative,* ed. Thomas Elsaesser and Adam Barker (London: British Film Institute), 58.

11. Zheng Zhenqiu and Zhang Shichuan, two pioneering figures in Chinese film history, had a strong influence on early cinema. Zheng, a specialist in theater and scriptwriting, emphasized moral instruction and theatrical structure in his works. Zhang, a businessman and film director, was more concerned with a film's entertainment function and the visual force of the camera. Together, the two created classic films and launched a narrative/cinematic ontology that carried into later filmmaking.

12. Miriam Hansen, *Babel and Babylon: Spectatorship in American Silent Film* (Cambridge, Mass.: Harvard Univ. Press, 1991), 70. Hansen's chapters on American silent films and spectatorship inspired me to see early Chinese films from a fresh perspective.

13. Kirk A. Denton, ed., *Modern Chinese Literary Thought: Writings on Literature, 1893–1945* (Stanford: Stanford Univ. Press, 1996), 22.

14. Communist leadership and the leftist involvement in film production have guided the official writing on Chinese film history. The most important work is Cheng Jihua's monumental book, *Zhongguo dianying fazhan shi* (The history of the development of Chinese cinema), 2 vols. (Beijing Zhongguo dianying, 1963). In addition, the China Film Press has published works such as Chen Bo, ed., *Zhongguo zuoyi dianying yundong* (The leftist film movement in China) (Beijing: Zhongguo dianying, 1992); Chen Bo and Yi Ming, eds., *Sanshi niandai Zhongguo dianying pinglun wenxuan* (Chinese film reviews of the 1930s: An anthology) (Beijing: Zhongguo dianying, 1993); and Li Suyan and Hu Jubin, *Zhongguo wusheng dianying shi* (The history of Chinese silent films) (Beijing: Zhongguo dianying, 1996).

15. Works include Leo Ou-Fan Lee's early publication on Chinese cinema, "The Tradition of Modern Chinese Cinema: Some Preliminary Explorations and

Hypotheses" (in Berry, ed., *Perspectives on Chinese Cinema*), which examines the relation between film and literature and between historical trends and artistic forms of expression. Chinese film scholars, including Zhong Dafeng and Chen Xihe, provide a theoretical perspective on the engagement of modern filmmaking with traditional shadow-plays. Recent publications from Chinese film journals call for a conceptualization of China's "third cinema" or "Asian form." See, for instance, Ma Ning, "The Textual and Critical Difference of Being Radical: Reconstructing Chinese Leftist Films of the 1930s," *Wide Angle* 11, no. 2 (1989): 22–31, which presents a textual analysis of Hollywood and Russian influences on Chinese filmmaking.

16. Japan invaded Manchuria in 1931, bombed Shanghai in 1932, extended its territory to the north in 1933, and carried out the Rape of Nanking in 1937. From 1937 to 1945, China engaged in an eight-year war against Japanese aggression.

17. S. H. Lu, ed., *Transnational Chinese Cinemas*, 4.

18. Sergei Eisenstein and other Soviet filmmakers of the 1920s made montage editing the essence of film art. Rather than cut to continuity, Soviet montage emphasized editing individual shots into dynamic juxtapositions. The creation of meaning derived from juxtaposition rather than from single shots.

19. Screen scripts of the three films discussed here can be found in Xia Yan, *Xia Yan dianying ju benji* (Anthology of Xia Yan's film screenplays) (Beijing: Zhongguo dianying, 1985).

20. For the complete article, see Liu Naou, "Zhongguo dianying miaoxie de shendu wenti" (Questions of narrative depth in Chinese films)," in Chen Bo and Yi Meng, eds., *Chinese Film Reviews of the 1930s* (Beijing: Zhongguo dianying, 1993), 837–839.

21. Leo Ou-Fan Lee, *Shanghai Modern: The Flowering of a New Urban Culture in China, 1930–1945* (Cambridge, Mass.: Harvard Univ. Press, 1999), 92.

22. For further reference, see "The Historical Avant-Gardes," in Stam, *Film Theory*, 55–58.

23. In *Sanshi niandai Zhongguo dianying pinglun wenxuan*, Chen Bo and Yi Ming present a rich collection of essays published in the 1930s. Only six works written by the soft-core film critics are selected and are in an appendix.

24. Li Xiaojiang, *Xiawa de tansuo* (Eve's exploration) (Zhengzhou: Henan renmin, 1989), 157.

25. For further comments on these two literary and female gendered figures, see Meng Yue and Dai Jinhua, *Fuchu lishi dibiao* (Emerging from the horizon of history: Modern Chinese women's literature) (Zhengzhou: Henan renmin, 1989), 8–14.

26. L. O. Lee, *Shanghai Modern*, 37.

27. For a description of Shanghai as "the city of light" and "the city of darkness," see Zhang Yingjin, *The City in Modern Chinese Literature and Film: Configurations of Space, Time, and Gender* (Stanford: Stanford Univ. Press, 1996), 9–12.

28. Shannon Bell, *Reading, Writing, and Rewriting the Prostitute Body* (Bloomington: Indiana Univ. Press, 1994), 72.

29. Gail Hershatter, *Dangerous Pleasures: Prostitution and Modernity in Twentieth-Century Shanghai* (Berkeley: Univ. of California Press, 1997), 9.

30. Rey Chow, *Woman and Chinese Modernity: The Politics of Reading between West and East* (Minneapolis: Univ. of Minnesota Press, 1991), 170.

31. For a contextual explanation, see Vera Schearcz, "Ibsen's Nora: The Promise and the Trap," *Bulletin of Concerned Asian Scholars* 6 (January–March 1975): 3. Sophia, a female identity created through a woman's writing, originates in Ding Ling's story, "Miss Sophia's Diary." Using a foreign name to refer to Chinese women, however, bespeaks the desire of male intellectuals to voice women's issues for the urgency of national reform.

32. Cited in ibid.

33. Lu Xun cited in Lu Tonglin, ed., *Gender and Sexuality*, 4.

34. Ding Ling, "Miss Sophia's Diary," in *I Myself Am a Woman: Selected Writings of Ding Ling*, ed. Tani E. Barlow with Gary J. Bjorge (Boston: Beacon Press, 1989), 56.

35. Li Xiaojiang, *Xiawa de tansuo*, 271.

36. In her study, *Ding Ling's Fiction: Ideology and Narrative in Modern Chinese Literature* (Cambridge, Mass.: Harvard University Press, 1982), Yi-tsi Feuerwerker identifies an "inexplicable self," chaotic and psychologically tormented, burned by desire yet lost in words.

37. Tani Barlow argues that woman is used as a universal category for the construction of various patriarchal discourses: traditional and modern, as well as socialist and post-Mao, in "Theorizing Woman: Funü, Guojia, Jiating (Chinese Women, Chinese State, Chinese Family)," in Grewal and Kaplan, eds., *Scattered Hegemonies*.

38. Kristine Harris, "The New Woman Incident: Cinema, Scandal, and Spectacle in 1935 Shanghai," in S. H. Lu, ed., *Transnational Chinese Cinemas*, 297.

39. Frank Beaver, *Dictionary of Film Terms: The Aesthetic Companion to Film Analysis* (New York: Twayne, 1994), 229.

40. Nick Browne, "Society and Subjectivity: On the Political Economy of Chinese Melodrama," in Browne et al., eds., *New Chinese Cinemas*, 40.

41. Ibid., 41.

42. Paul G. Pickowicz, "Melodramatic Representation and the 'May Fourth' Tradition of Chinese Cinema," in *From May Fourth to June Fourth: Fiction and Film in Twentieth-Century China*, ed. Ellen Widmer and David Der-Wei Wang (Cambridge, Mass.: Harvard Univ. Press, 1993), 324.

43. Ibid., 305.

44. For an important discussion of Chinese family melodrama, see Ma Ning, "Symbolic Representation and Symbolic Violence: Chinese Family Melodrama of the Early 1980s," *East-West Film Journal* 4, no. 1 (1989): 79–112; passage quoted in text is on p. 79.

45. Robert Lang, *American Film Melodrama: Griffith, Vidor, Minnelli* (Princeton, N.J.: Princeton Univ. Press, 1989), 18.

46. Linda Williams, "Melodrama Revised," in *Refiguring American Film Genres: History and Theory*, ed. Nick Browne (Berkeley: Univ. of California Press, 1998), 44.

47. Lang, *American Film Melodrama*, 18.

48. A number of film scholars in China have called attention to the films of Fei Mu and have argued for the importance of his films in Chinese history.

Articles can be found in *Contemporary Cinema* (Dangdai dianying) 5 (1997): 4–47.

Chapter Two: Reconstructing History

1. Stanley Kwan, dir., *Center Stage* or *Actress* (Ruan Lingyu) (Hong Kong: Golden Harvest, 1992).
2. Ruan Lingyu (1910–1935) was an important silent screen star in early Chinese film history. During her ten-year film career, she portrayed a variety of female roles in twenty-nine films. She ended her life by suicide at age twenty-five owing to relentless social and media interference in her personal life.
3. Julian Stringer, "*Center Stage*: Reconstructing the Bio-Pic," *Cine Action* 42 (1997): 39.
4. Harris, "*The New Woman* Incident," 298.
5. For a discussion of feminism and postmodernism, see Barbara Creed, "From Here to Modernity: Feminism and Postmodernism," *Screen* 28 (1987): 47–67.
6. For further discussion of the postmodern condition in China, see *Boundary 2: An International Journal of Literature and Culture*, Special Issue: *Postmodernism and China* 24 (Fall 1997). Articles collected here express two major concerns: to explain Chinese postmodernism within the framework of its socioeconomic and cultural engagement with globalization, and to explore the usefulness of postmodern concepts for understanding contemporary Chinese societies. In considering *Center Stage* as a postmodern text, I see the poetics of postmodernism, when viewed under the sociocultural conditions specific to China and Hong Kong, as including intellectual consciousness, alternative perspectives, and self-reflexive visual forms.
7. For essays on Hong Kong at the moment of its sociohistorical transition, see *Public Culture: Society for Transnational Cultural Studies*, Special Issue: *Hong Kong 1997: The Place and the Formula* 23 (1997).
8. Ackbar Abbas, "The New Hong Kong Cinema and the *Déjà Disparu*," *Discourse* 16, no. 3 (1994): 65.
9. S. H. Lu, "Historical Introduction," 16.
10. As discussed in Abbas, "The New Hong Kong Cinema," 66.
11. Creed, "From Here to Modernity," 49.
12. Mary Ann Doane, "The Voice in the Cinema: The Articulation of Body and Space," in Weis and Belton, eds., *Film Sound*, 168.
13. Lianhua, one of China's leading film corporations in the 1930s, was well known for its capital management system and cinematic technical innovations. With its headquarters in Hong Kong and three film studios on the mainland, Lianhua released about one hundred films between 1930 and 1938. Many of these became Chinese classics.
14. Craig Owens, "The Discourse of Others: Feminists and Postmodernism," in *The Anti-Aesthetic: Essays on Postmodern Culture*, ed. Hal Foster (Port Townsend, Wash.: Bay Press, 1983), 59.
15. Anne Friedberg, *Window Shopping: Cinema and the Postmodern* (Los Angeles: Univ. of California Press, 1993), 175.

16. Linda Hutcheon, *The Politics of Postmodernism* (London: Routledge, 1989), 113.

17. Linda Hutcheon, *A Poetics of Postmodernism: History, Theory, Fiction* (New York: Routledge, 1988), 124–140.

18. Robert Stam, Robert Burgoyne, and Sandy Flitterman-Lewis, *New Vocabularies in Film Semiotics: Structuralism, Post-Structuralism and Beyond* (London: Routledge, 1992), 200.

19. Ibid.

20. Jacqueline Rose, "The Cinematic Apparatus: Problems in Current Theory," in *The Cinematic Apparatus*, ed. Teresa de Lauretis and Stephen Heath (London: Macmillan, 1980), 173.

21. Hutcheon, *The Politics of Postmodernism*, 117.

22. Patricia Waugh, *Metafiction: The Theory and Practice of Self-Conscious Fiction* (London: Methuen, 1984), 6.

23. Tony Wilson, "Reading the Postmodernist Image: A 'Cognitive Mapping,' " *Screen* 31 (winter 1990): 390–407.

24. Wheeler Winston Dixon, *It Looks at You: The Returned Gaze of Cinema* (Albany: State Univ. of New York Press, 1995), 3.

25. Mary Ann Doane, "Subjectivity and Desire: An(other) Way of Looking," in *Contemporary Film Theory*, ed. Antony Easthope (London: Longman, 1993), 171.

26. Hutcheon, *The Politics of Postmodernism*, 87.

27. Ibid., 92.

28. Waugh, *Metafiction*, 29.

29. Magali Cornier Michael, *Feminism and the Postmodern Impulse* (Albany: State Univ. of New York Press, 1996), 33.

CHAPTER THREE: CONSTRUCTING AND CONSUMING
THE REVOLUTIONARY NARRATIVES

1. The "Red wave" and "Mao fever" phenomena have drawn critical attention inside and outside China. Readers interested in the topic can start with Geremie R. Barme, *In the Red: On Contemporary Chinese Culture* (New York: Columbia Univ. Press, 1999); Wang Jing, *High Culture Fever: Politics, Aesthetics, and Ideology in Deng's China* (Berkeley: Univ. of California Press, 1996); and Dai Jinhua, "Redemption and Consumption: Depicting Culture in the 1990s," *Positions* 4, no. 1 (1996): 127–142.

2. Data from daily Chinese newspapers, such as *Beijing Morning News*, 25 August 1999, and *Yangcheng Evening News*, 2 October 1999.

3. As I was strolling in the streets of Beijing in 1991, the sound of revolutionary songs and the image of Mao made me wonder for a moment if China was returning to its socialist past or indulging in a commercial present.

4. Louis Althusser, *Lenin and Philosophy*, trans. Ben Brewster (London: New Left Books, 1971), 174–175. See also "Interpellation," *Encyclopedia of Contemporary Literary Theory: Approaches, Scholars, Terms*, ed. Irena R. Makaryk (Toronto: Univ. of Toronto Press, 1993), 567.

5. Althusser, *Lenin and Philosophy*, 567.

6. Bonnie S. McDougall, *Popular Chinese Literature and Performing Arts in the People's Republic of China, 1949–1979* (Berkeley: Univ. of California Press, 1984).
7. Li Xiaojiang, "Zouxiang nüren" (Toward women), *Nüxing ren* (Female being) 4 (1990): 256.
8. Meng Yue, "Female Images and National Myth," in Barlow, ed., *Gender Politics in Modern China*, 136.
9. Meng Yue and Dai Jinhua, *Fuchu lishi dibiao*, 31.
10. Stuart Schram, *The Thought of Mao Zedong* (New York: Cambridge Univ. Press, 1989), 32.
11. Meng Yue, "Female Images and National Myth"; Roxann Prazniak, "Mao and the Woman Question in an Age of Green Politics: Some Critical Reflections," in *Critical Perspectives on Mao Zedong's Thought*, ed. Arif Dirlik, Paul Healy, and Nick Knight (Atlantic Highlands, N.J.: Humanities Press, 1997), 23–58.
12. Judith Stacey, *Patriarchy and Socialist Revolution in China* (Los Angeles: Univ. of California Press, 1983).
13. Ibid., 209.
14. Chris Berry, "Sexual Difference and the Viewing Subject in *Li Shuangshuang* and *The In-Laws*," in Berry, ed., *Perspectives on Chinese Cinema*, 37.
15. For publications in Chinese, see Shu Xiaoming, "Chinese Cinema during the Cultural Revolution," in *Zhongguo dianying yishushi jiaocheng* (History of Chinese film aesthetics) (Beijing: Zhongguo dianying, 1996), 140–157, and Qu Jiannong, *Hongse wangshi: 1966–1976 nian de zhongguo dianying* (Red Retrospections: Chinese Cinema from 1966 to 1976), which provides production details and political background for each revolutionary model film.
16. See Chen Xiaomei, "The Marginality of the Study of Cultural Revolution: The Neglected and the Privileged in the Making of Imagined Communities," paper presented at the Historical Society for Twentieth-Century China symposium, Coeur d'Alene, Idaho, October 1997.
17. *Modern Chinese Literature and Culture* 12, no. 2 (fall 2000).
18. Francesca Dal Lago, "Personal Mao: Reshaping an Icon in Contemporary Chinese Art," *Art Journal* 58 (summer 1999).
19. Trevor Thomas Hay, "China's Proletarian Myth: The Revolutionary Narrative and Model Theater of the Cultural Revolution" (Ph.D. diss., Griffith University, 2000), 9.
20. Mary Gerhart, *Genre Choices, Gender Questions* (Norman: Univ. of Oklahoma Press, 1992), 5.
21. Ellen R. Judd, "Dramas of Passion: Heroism in the Cultural Revolution's Model Operas," in Joseph, Wong, and Zweig, eds., *New Perspectives on the Cultural Revolution*, 269–270.
22. Needeya Islam, "I Want to Shoot People: Genre, Gender and Action in the Films of Kathryn Bigelow," in *Kiss Me Deadly: Feminism and Cinema for the Moment*, ed. Laleen Jayamanne (Sydney: Power Publications, 1995), 96.
23. Barbara Mittler, "To Be or Not to Be: Making and Unmaking the *Yangbanxi*," paper presented at the annual meeting of the American Historical Association, Seattle, January 1998.

24. *Xipi* and *erhuang* are musical terms for conventional opera patterns that express strong emotion and deep feeling.

25. Paul G. Pickowicz, "Huang Jianxin and the Notion of Postsocialism," in Browne et al., eds., *New Chinese Cinemas*, 61.

26. Arif Dirlik, "Postsocialism? Reflections on 'Socialism with Chinese Characteristics,'" in Dirlik and Meisner, eds., *Marxism and the Chinese Experience*, 362–384.

27. Xu Ben, *Disenchanted Democracy: Chinese Cultural Criticism after 1989* (Ann Arbor: Univ. of Michigan Press, 1999), 29.

28. John Fiske, *Understanding Popular Culture* (Boston: Unwin Hyman, 1989), 15.

29. Dal Lago, "Personal Mao," 47.

30. I take red classics as cultural products (visual, written, or musical) that are politically oriented, ideologically censored, and produced for the masses under China's socialist system.

31. Xu Ben, *Disenchanted Democracy*.

32. Debates over postmodernism in China have attracted scholars across national boundaries and discursive disciplines. Such discussions create a constructive forum where different voices—Western, Chinese, Chinese in the West—can be heard. A shared concern focuses on "an anxiety of enunciation": what are the appropriate discourses for describing contemporary China? For essays on this subject, see Wang Hui and Yu Kwok-leung, eds., *Jiushi niandai de houxue lunzheng* (Post-ism in the nineties) (Hong Kong: Chinese Univ. of Hong Kong, 1998).

33. Allen S. Whiting, "Chinese Nationalism and Foreign Policy after Deng," *China Quarterly* 142 (June 1995): 295.

34. James G. Carrier, ed., *Occidentalism: Images of the West* (New York: Oxford Univ. Press, 1995), 1, and Chen Xiaomei, *Occidentalism: A Theory of Counter-Discourse in Post-Mao China* (New York: Oxford Univ. Press, 1995), 8.

35. Chen Xiaomei, *Occidentalism*, 8.

36. Carrier, *Occidentalism*, 8.

37. The film inspired such nationalistic sentiment that the delegates in the WTO negotiations imagined themselves in a position similar to those in the Versailles Peace Conference in 1919. The years 1919 and 1999 witnessed an ironic historical coincidence: the loss of sovereignty for Shandong in 1919 and the opening of the market for Hollywood in 1999.

38. "China can say no" was first raised in a book by Song Qiang, Zhang Zangzang, and Qiao Bian, eds., *Zhongguo keyi shuo bu* (China can say no) (Beijing: Zhonghua gongshang lianhe, 1996). The utterance reveals an antagonism toward American power and a patriotic allegiance to Chinese nationalism.

CHAPTER FOUR: GENDER POLITICS
AND SOCIALIST DISCOURSE
IN XIE JIN'S RED DETACHMENT OF WOMEN

1. Cora Kaplan, "Pandora's Box: Subjectivity, Class, and Sexuality in Socialist Feminist Criticism," in Greene and Kahn, eds., *Making a Difference*, 146.

2. De Lauretis, ed., *Feminist Studies, Critical Studies*, 14.

3. Xie Jin is one of the most important film directors in Chinese film history. Unlike the "fifth generation" of film directors, whose works constitute a radical reassessment of Chinese film tradition, Xie Jin and his films represent and preserve the tradition in terms of his virtuous subjects and melodramatic form.

4. Christine Roulston, "Discourse, Gender, and Gossip: Some Reflections on Bakhtin and *Emma*," in *Ambiguous Discourse: Feminist Narratology and British Women Writers*, ed. Kathy Mezei (Chapel Hill: Univ. of North Carolina Press, 1996), 40.

5. Claude Lefort, *The Political Forms of Modern Society: Bureaucracy, Democracy, Totalitarianism* (Cambridge: Polity Press, 1986).

6. See Meng, "Female Images and National Myth," 136.

7. Lu Tonglin, ed., *Gender and Sexuality in Twentieth-Century Chinese Literature and Society* (Albany: State Univ. of New York Press, 1993), 3.

8. Robert Con Davis and David S. Gross, "Gayatri Chakravorty Spivak and the Ethos of the Subaltern," in *Ethos: New Essays in Rhetorical and Critical Theory*, ed. James S. Baumlin and Tita French Baumlin (Dallas: Southern Methodist Univ. Press, 1994), 79.

9. Roulston, "Discourse, Gender, and Gossip," 43.

10. Apter and Saich, eds., *Revolutionary Discourse in Mao's Republic* 11.

11. Maxine Hong Kingston, *Woman Warrior: Memories of a Girlhood among Ghosts* (New York: Vintage International, 1989; originally published 1975).

12. Julia Kristeva, *About Chinese Women*, trans. Anita Barrows (New York: Urizen Books, 1977), 93, emphasis added.

13. Esther C. M. Yau, "Filmic Discourse on Women in Chinese Cinema (1949–65): Art, Ideology, and Social Relations" (Ph.D. diss., University of California, Los Angeles, 1990), 225.

14. Ibid.

15. Meng and Dai, *Fuchu lishi dibiao*, 268.

16. See Sigmund Freud, "The Dissolution of the Oedipus Complex," in *The Freud Reader*, ed. Peter Gay (New York: Norton, 1988), 661–666.

17. Robert Stam, *Subversive Pleasures: Bakhtin, Cultural Criticism and Film* (Baltimore: Johns Hopkins Univ. Press, 1989), 86, 95.

18. Ibid.

19. Susan Stanford Friedman, "Creativity and the Childbirth Metaphor: Gender Difference in Literary Discourse," in Warhol and Herndl, eds., *Feminisms*, 371.

20. Wang Ban, *The Sublime Figure of History: Aesthetics and Politics in Twentieth-Century China* (Stanford: Stanford Univ. Press, 1997), 133.

21. Althusser, *Lenin and Philosophy*.

22. Kaja Silverman, *The Subject of Semiotics* (New York: Oxford Univ. Press, 1983), 219.

CHAPTER FIVE: SCREENING CHINA

1. China reopened its colleges and universities and resumed a national entrance examination system in 1977, at the end of the Cultural Revolution. In 1982, the fifth-generation film directors became the first group to graduate from the Beijing Film Academy.

2. Wang Ban, "Trauma and History in Chinese Film: Reading *The Blue Kite* against Melodrama," *Modern Chinese Literature and Culture* 11, no. 1 (1999): 130.

3. A generation of "educated youth" was "sent down" to China's rural areas, factories, or military services to be reeducated by peasants, workers, and soldiers. Such political indoctrination and forced work left its marks on an entire generation.

4. Ma Ning, "New Chinese Cinema: A Critical Account of the Fifth Generation," *Cineaste* 17, no. 3 (1990): 32.

5. Yao Xiaomeng, "Zhongguo xin dianying: Cong yishi xingtai de guandian kan" (Chinese new cinema: From an ideological perspective), in *Zhongguo dangdai wenhua yishi* (Cultural consciousness in contemporary China) (Hong Kong: Joint Publishing, 1989), 198.

6. Zhang Xudong, *Chinese Modernism in the Era of Reforms: Cultural Fever, Avant-Garde Fiction, and the New Chinese Cinema* (Durham, N.C.: Duke Univ. Press, 1997), 205.

7. Ibid.

8. The idea of allegory as dialectical discourse appears in Walter Benjamin's "Allegory and Trauerspiel," in *The Origin of German Tragic Drama*, trans. John Osborne (London: NLB, 1977), 159–190. Also see Doris Sommer, "Allegory and Dialectics: A Match Made in Romance," *Boundary* 2 18, no. 1 (1991): 60–82.

9. See Yang Ping, "A Director Who Is Trying to Change the Audience: A Chat with Young Director Tian Zhuangzhuang," in Berry, ed., *Perspectives on Chinese Cinema*, 127.

10. Pickowicz, "Huang Jianxin and the Notion of Postsocialism," 68–69.

11. The titles of the short works of fiction or novels listed represent different literary trends during the 1980s and 1990s. Writings about the search for roots, cultural retrospection, or historical reconstruction, as well as avant-garde experiments, are just a few examples.

12. Rey Chow, *Primitive Passions: Visuality, Sexuality, Ethnography, and Contemporary Chinese Cinema* (New York: Columbia Univ. Press, 1995), 19–23.

13. Ibid., 23.

14. Ibid., 21.

15. Philip Lopate, "Odd Man Out," an interview with Tian Zhuangzhuang, *Film Comment* 30 (July–August 1994): 62.

16. Chow, *Primitive Passions*, 170.

17. Mark Freeman's comment on Edward Said's "Orientalism" in "Eastern Culture, Western Gaze: The Cinema of Zhang Yimou"; article online; cited 5 December 2000; available at http://home.vicnet.net.au/`freeman/theory/zhangyimou.htm.

18. Wang Yuejin, "The Cinematic Other and the Cultural Self? Decentering the Cultural Identity on Cinema," *Wide Angle* 11, no. 2 (1989): 36.

19. Stuart Klawans, "Zhang Yimou, Local Hero," *Film Comment* 31, no. 5 (1995): 11.

20. I think that *Ju Dou* offers an example of a gaze that transcends Laura Mulvey's classic definition of scopophilia: the desire and the pleasure in looking.

21. Thomas Elsaesser, *New German Cinema: A History* (New Brunswick, N.J.: Rutgers Univ. Press, 1989), 302.

22. Wang Hui and Leo Ou-Fan Lee, with M. J. Fischer, "Is the Public Sphere Unspeakable in Chinese? Can Public Space *(gonggong kongjian)* Lead to Public Spheres?" *Public Culture* 6 (spring 1994): 602.

23. Jameson, "Third-World Literature," 69.

24. David Holley, "China's Angry Old Men Crack Down Again," *Los Angeles Times*, 8 April 1991, sec. F.

25. Homi K. Bhabha, "The Commitment to Theory," in *Questions of Third Cinema*, ed. Jim Pines and Paul Willenmen (London: British Film Institute, 1989), 124.

26. E. Ann Kaplan, "Problematizing Cross-Cultural Analysis: The Case of Women in the Recent Chinese Cinema," *Wide Angle* 11, no. 2 (1989): 42, emphasis added.

27. Ibid., 42, emphasis added.

28. Ibid., 48.

29. Zhang Yingjin, "Rethinking Cross-Cultural Analysis: The Questions of Authority, Power, and Difference in Western Studies of Chinese Films," *Bulletin of Concerned Asian Scholars* 26, no. 4 (1994): 44.

30. Ibid., 49.

31. Ibid., 53.

32. Zhang Yingjin, "Review Essay: Screening China: Recent Studies of Chinese Cinema in English," *Bulletin of Concerned Asian Scholars* 29, no. 2 (1997): 61.

33. For an introduction to Italian neorealism, see Stam, *Film Theory*, 73.

34. Cited in Scarlet Cheng, "The Road Home," *Far Eastern Economic Review*, 6 April 2000, 53.

CHAPTER SIX: THE SEARCH FOR MALE MASCULINITY
AND SEXUALITY IN ZHANG YIMOU'S JU DOU

1. Jenny Kwok Wah Lau, "*Judou*—A Hermeneutical Reading of Cross-Cultural Cinema," *Film Quarterly* 45 (winter 1991–92): 2–10.

2. W. A. Callahan, "Gender, Ideology, Nation: *Ju Dou* in the Cultural Politics of China," *East-West Film Journal* 7, no. 1 (1993): 52–80.

3. Chow, *Primitive Passions*, 170–171.

4. Daniel Percheron, "Sound in Cinema and Its Relationship to Image and Diegesis," *Yale French Studies* 60, no. 1 (1980): 16–23.

5. Stacey, *Patriarchy and Socialist Revolution in China*, 39.

6. Mulvey, *Visual and Other Pleasures*.

7. Ibid., 18.

8. Callahan, "Gender, Ideology, and Nation," 57.

9. Leo Braudy, *The World in a Frame: What We See in Films* (New York: Anchor Press, 1976), 46.

10. Jonathan Dollimore, "Subjectivity, Sexuality, and Transgression: The Jacobean Connection," *Renaissance Drama* 17 (1986): 57.

11. Terry Eagleton, *Literary Theory: An Introduction* (Minneapolis: Univ. of Minnesota Press, 1983), 156.

12. Louis Giannetti, *Understanding Movies* (Englewood Cliffs, N.J.: Prentice-Hall, 1990), 132.

13. Jane Gallop, *Reading Lacan* (Ithaca, N.Y.: Cornell Univ. Press, 1985), 107.

14. Francis L. K. Hsu, "Eros, Affect and *Pao*," in *Rugged Individualism Reconsidered: Essays in Psychological Anthropology* (Knoxville: Univ. of Tennessee Press, 1983), 272.

15. Mencius (ca. 370–290 B.C.) was one of the founding fathers of the Chinese philosophy known as Confucianism. He believed in the "Mandate of Heaven": the rulers of a dynasty must remain virtuous to retain divine support. He also held that human nature is fundamentally good. Regarding filial piety, Mencius said, "There are three contraventions of the rules of filial piety, and of these the greatest is to have no progeny." See W. A. C. H. Dobson, ed., *Mencius: A New Translation Arranged and Annotated for the General Reader* (Toronto: Univ. of Toronto Press, 1963), 140.

CHAPTER SEVEN: SUBJECTED BODY AND GENDERED IDENTITY

1. Pauline Chen, "History Lessons," *Film Comment* 30 (March–April 1994): 85–87.

2. Jenny Kwok Wah Lau, "*Farewell My Concubine*: History, Melodrama, and Ideology in Contemporary Pan-Chinese Cinema," *Film Quarterly* 49, no. 1 (fall 1995): 17–27.

3. The opera *Farewell My Concubine* derives from a legendary love story set in the time of conflict between the King of Chu, Xiangyu, and the King of Han, Liubang, ca. 200 B.C. In the decisive battle between the two armies, the forces of the King of Chu face certain defeat. The king's beloved concubine, Yuji, after her final performance and wine service for the king, kills herself with his sword. She takes her life to express her loyalty to the king and to persuade him to flee and save himself. In the 1920s, Mei Lanfang, one of the greatest opera masters in China and a female impersonator himself, adapted the story to the stage and played the role of Yuji.

4. Terrence Rafferty, "Blind Faith," *New Yorker*, 11 October 1993, 122.

5. Kaja Silverman, *Male Subjectivity at the Margins* (New York: Routledge, 1992), 55.

6. Chow, *Primitive Passions*, 108–141.

7. Zhang Xudong, *Chinese Modernism*, 284.

8. Zha Jianying, "Shadows on the Screen," in Zha, *China Pop: How Soap Operas, Tabloids, and Best Sellers Are Transforming a Culture* (New York: New Press, 1995), 79–104.

9. Michel Foucault, *Discipline and Punish: The Birth of the Prison*, trans. Alan Sheridan (New York: Vintage Books, 1979), 34.

10. Cited in David D. Kim, "The Next Generation," *Village Voice*, 2 November 1993, 69.

11. Tim Edwards, *Erotics and Politics: Gay Sexuality, Masculinity and Feminism* (New York: Routledge, 1994), 3.

12. Elaine Showalter, "Critical Crossing: Male Feminists and the Woman of the Year," in *Raritan Reading*, ed. Richard Poirier (New Brunswick, N.J.: Rutgers Univ. Press, 1990), 371.

13. Jean E. Howard, "Cross-Dressing, the Theater, and Gender Struggle in Early Modern England," in *Crossing the Stage: Controversies on Cross-Dressing*, ed. Lesley Ferris (London: Routledge, 1993), 20–46.

14. Annette Kuhn, *Women's Pictures: Feminism and Cinema* (London: Verso, 1982), 10.

15. Cited in Kim, "The Next Generation," 69.

16. A prostitute or woman who engages in illegal sexual relations with men is often referred to as "worn shoes."

17. "To spill dog's blood" is a colloquial phrase indicating a flood of verbal outrage.

18. Joan Riviere, "Womanliness as a Masquerade," *International Journal of Psycho-Analysis* 10 (1929): 306.

19. Sally Robinson, *Engendering the Subject: Gender and Self-Representation in Contemporary Women's Fiction* (Albany: State Univ. of New York Press, 1991), 9.

20. Sandy Flitterman, "Woman, Desire, and the Look: Feminism and the Enunciative Apparatus in Cinema," in *Theories of Authorship*, ed. John Caughie (London: Routledge, 1993), 245.

21. Rafferty, "Blind Faith," 122.

CHAPTER EIGHT: FEMINISM
WITH CHINESE CHARACTERISTICS?

1. Rey Chow, *Writing Diaspora: Tactics of Intervention in Contemporary Cultural Studies* (Bloomington: Indiana Univ. Press, 1993), 99.

2. Interviews can be found in Berry, "Chinese 'Women's Cinema'"; Dai Jinhua and Mayfair Yang, "A Conversation with Huang Shuqin," *Positions* 3, no. 3 (1995): 790–805; and Wang Zheng, "Three Interviews: Wang Anyi, Zhulin, Dai Qing," in Barlow, ed., *Gender Politics in Modern China*, 159–208.

3. Cited in Dai and Yang, "A Conversation with Huang Shuqin," 792–798.

4. Cited in Wang Zheng, "Three Interviews," 164–165.

5. Cited in ibid., 193.

6. Li Xiaojiang, *Xiawa de tansuo*, 8. As the pioneer figure in the creation of women's studies in China, Li Xiaojiang is often cited as one of the most prominent feminist scholars in China, an identity she rejects.

7. See Li Xiaojiang, *Guanyu nüren de dawen* (Questions and answers about women) (Nanjing: Jiangsu renmin, 1998).

8. Li Xiaojiang, "With What Discourse Do We Reflect on Chinese Women?" in Yang, ed., *Spaces of Their Own*, 262.

9. Li Xiaojiang, *Guanyu nüren de dawen*, 61.

10. Ibid., 62–63.

11. Ibid., 63.

12. Harriet Evans, "The Language of Liberation: Gender and Jiefang in Early Chinese Communist Party Discourse," article on-line, cited 5 December 2000; available at http://www.sshe.murdoch.edu.au/intersections. This article presents critical references for anyone interested in the interrelationship between feminism and socialism.

13. Friedman, *Mappings*, 17–18.

14. See S. H. Lu, "Historical Introduction."

15. For Spivak's comments on transnational feminism, see Caren Kaplan and Grewal, "Transnational Feminist Cultural Studies," 350, 360.

16. Grewal and Kaplan, eds., *Scattered Hegemonies*, 28.

17. Data from Lu Le, Xi Shanshan, and Zhang Zhenqin, eds., *Caozong yinmu de nüxing: Zhongguo nüdaoyan* (Chinese women directors: Women who master the film screen) (Changchung: Beifang funü ertong, 1989), 2.

18. Dai Jinhua, "Bu kejian de nüxing: Dangdai zhongguo dianying zhongde nüxing yu nüxing dianying" (Invisible women: Contemporary Chinese cinema and women's films), *Dangdai dianying* (Contemporary cinema) 6 (1994): 58.

19. Cited in Berry, "Chinese Women's Cinema," 37.

20. Robinson, *Engendering the Subject*, 27.

21. For discussions of *Sacrificed Youth*, see Esther Yau, "Is China the End of Hermeneutics? Or, Political and Cultural Usage of Non-Han Women in Mainland Chinese Films," *Discourse* 11, no. 2 (1989): 115–136, and Zhang Yingjin, "From 'Minority Film' to 'Minority Discourse.'"

22. Doane, "The Voice in the Cinema," 168.

23. Yau, "Is China the End of Hermeneutics?" 117.

24. S. H. Lu, "Historical Introduction," 8.

25. Cited in Yang Yuanying, ed., *Tamen de shengyin: Zhongguo nüdaoyan de zisu* (Their Voices: Chinese women directors, self-expression) (Beijing: Zhongguo shehui, 1996), 108. The volume has interviews of Chinese women directors by Chinese critics.

26. Ibid.

27. Ibid., 211.

28. Ibid.

29. Xu Jian, "*Blush* from Novella to Film: The Possibility of Critical Art in Commodity Culture," *Modern Chinese Literature and Culture* 12, no. 1 (2000): 143–147.

30. On voice-over narration, also see Sarah Kozloff, *Invisible Storytellers: Voice-Over Narration in American Fiction Film* (Berkeley: Univ. of California Press, 1988), 80.

31. Doane, "The Voice in the Cinema," 168.

32. Yang Yuanying, ed., *Tamen de shengyin*, 214.

33. Michael Dutton, "The End of the (Mass) Line? Chinese Policing in the Era of the Contract," *Social Justice* 27, no. 2 (2000): 62.

34. Cited in Yang Yuanying, ed., *Tamen de shengyin*, 277.

35. Jerry White, "The Films of Ning Ying: China Unfolding in Miniature," *Cine Action* 42 (1997): 5.

CHAPTER NINE: DESIRE IN DIFFERENCE

1. Branigan, *Point of View in the Cinema*.

2. See Louis Althusser, "Ideology and Ideological State Apparatuses," in *Lenin and Philosophy*.

3. Ibid., 162.

4. E. Ann Kaplan, "Problematizing Cross-Cultural Analysis," 47.

5. Berry, "Chinese 'Women's Cinema,'" 16.

6. For further reference on double identification, see "Spectator" in Stam, Burgoyne, and Flitterman-Lewis, *New Vocabularies in Film Semiotics*, 146–158.

7. Jacques Aumont, Alain Bergala, Michel Marie, and Marc Vernet, *Aesthetics of Film*, trans. Richard Neupert (Austin: Univ. of Texas Press, 1983), 214.

8. Lu Tonglin, ed., *Gender and Sexuality*, 8.

9. Ding Xiaoqi, "Maidenhome," in *Maidenhome*, trans. Chris Berry (San Francisco: Aunt Lute Books, 1994), 3.

10. Doane, "The Voice in the Cinema," 68.

11. For the concept of female spectatorship, see Linda Williams, "Something Else Besides a Mother: *Stella Dallas* and the Maternal Melodrama," in Gledhill, ed., *Home Is Where the Heart Is*, 299–355.

12. Susan Sniader Lanser, *Fictions of Authority: Women Writers and Narrative Voice* (Ithaca, N.Y.: Cornell Univ. Press, 1992), 5.

13. Cited in Berry, "Chinese 'Women's Cinema,'" 21, 29, 36.

14. Dorrit Cohn, *Transparent Minds: Narrative Modes for Presenting Consciousness in Fiction* (Princeton, N.J.: Princeton Univ. Press, 1978), 100.

15. Ding Xiaoqi, "Maidenhome," 12–13.

16. Robinson, *Engendering the Subject*, 14.

CHAPTER 10: TRANSGENDER MASQUERADING IN HUANG SHUQIN'S *HUMAN, WOMAN, DEMON*

1. This chapter is dedicated to the memory of Zhang Nuanxin, a Chinese woman film director who passed away on 3 June 1995, at the age of fifty-three. She is one of the most important film directors in China, well known to both Chinese and Western audiences through her film *Sacrificed Youth* and her provocative use of film language. I met her in 1991 in Chicago, and she introduced me to the Beijing Film Academy, where I spent a term teaching American film genres. I have always been drawn to her films by their female consciousness and aesthetics of realism. The quotation cited above is from her last speech, given at a conference on female screenplay writers, directors, and artists. The obituary in *People's Daily*, 17 June 1995, said that she died from exhaustion.

2. Robinson, *Engendering the Subject*, 11.

3. Ibid., 16.

4. Peter Wollen, "Godard and Counter Cinema: Vent D'Est," in *Movies and Methods*, ed. Bill Nichols (Berkeley: Univ. of California Press, 1985), 2:505.

5. Elaine Showalter, "Toward a Feminist Poetics," in *The New Feminist Criticism: Essays on Women, Literature, Theory*, ed. Elaine Showalter (New York: Pantheon Books, 1985), 125–143.

6. Tom McHugh, trans., "Chung Kuei Gives His Sister in Marriage, a Ching Dynasty Kunchu Play," *Echo* 6, no. 7 (September 1977): 45–54.

7. Norman Fairclough, *Discourse and Social Change* (Cambridge: Polity Press, 1992), 64.

8. Judith Kegan Gardiner, "On Female Identity and Writing by Women," in *Writing and Sexual Difference*, ed. Elizabeth Abel (Chicago: Univ. of Chicago Press, 1982), 187.

9. Beaver, *Dictionary of Film Terms*, 272.
10. Riviere, "Womanliness as a Masquerade," 38.
11. Mary Ann Doane, "Film and the Masquerade: Theorizing the Female Spectator," *Screen* 23, no. 3/4 (1982): 82.

POSTSCRIPT

1. Likening lovers to mandarin ducks and butterflies, this literary genre popularized sentimental, romantic love stories in the early twentieth century. Seen to represent old-style fiction, the genre became a target of criticism with the advent of the May Fourth literary movement. During the 1920s and 1930s, however, many film adaptations drew on the mandarin ducks and butterflies literature.
2. The iron house metaphor derives from Lu Xun, who called Chinese tradition an iron house in which his sleeping countrymen were imprisoned and suffocating. The call to awaken and destroy the iron house is a primary theme in Lu Xun's writings.
3. Lydia H. Liu, "Beijing Sojourners in New York: Postsocialism and the Question of Ideology in Global Media Culture," *Positions* 7, no. 3 (1999): 765.
4. For a discussion of independent filmmaking, see Shuqin Cui, "Working from the Margins and outside the System: Independent Film Directors in Contemporary China," *Post Script* 20 (winter/spring 2001), 77–93.
5. Film directors and critics expressed serious concerns about the negotiations between China and the WTO. For comments and the data cited here, see Zheng Dongtian, "To Be or Not to Be: Concerns on the Survival of Chinese Cinema after China Joins WTO," *Film Art* 2 (2000), 4–8.

Works Cited

Western Sources

Abbas, Ackbar. "The New Hong Kong Cinema and the Déjà Disparu," *Discourse* 16, no. 3 (1994): 65–77.

Althusser, Louis. *Lenin and Philosophy and Other Essays.* Trans. Ben Brewster. London: New Left Books, 1971.

Apter, David E., and Tony Saich, eds. *Revolutionary Discourse in Mao's Republic.* Cambridge, Mass.: Harvard Univ. Press, 1994.

Aumont, Jacques, Alain Bergala, Michel Marie, and Marc Vernet. *Aesthetics of Film.* Trans. Richard Neupert. Austin: Univ. of Texas Press, 1983.

Barlow, Tani. "Theorizing Woman: Funü, Guojia, Jiating (Chinese Women, Chinese State, Chinese Family)." In Grewal and Kaplan, eds., *Scattered Hegemonies.*

———, ed. *Gender Politics in Modern China: Writing and Feminism.* Durham, N.C.: Duke Univ. Press, 1993.

Barme, Geremie R. *In the Red: On Contemporary Chinese Culture.* New York: Columbia Univ. Press, 1999.

Beaver, Frank E. *Dictionary of Film Terms: The Aesthetic Companion to Film Analysis.* New York: Twayne, 1994.

Bell, Shannon. *Reading, Writing, and Rewriting the Prostitute Body.* Bloomington: Indiana Univ. Press, 1994.

Benjamin, Walter. "Allegory and Trauerspiel." In *The Origin of German Tragic Drama.* Trans. John Osborne, 159–190. London: NLB, 1977.

Berry, Chris. "Chinese 'Women's Cinema.'" *Camera Obscura: A Journal of Feminism and Film Theory* 18 (September 1988): 5–41.

———. "Sexual Difference and the Viewing Subject in *Li Shuangshuang* and *The In-Laws.*" In Berry, ed., *Perspectives on Chinese Cinema,* 30–39.

———, ed. *Perspectives on Chinese Cinema.* London: British Film Institute, 1991.

Bhabha, Homi K. "The Commitment to Theory." In *Questions of Third Cinema.* Ed. Jim Pines and Paul Willenmen, 111–132. London: British Film Institute, 1989.

Branigan, Edward. *Point of View in the Cinema: A Theory of Narration and Subjectivity in Classical Film.* New York: Mouton, 1984.

Braudy, Leo. *The World in a Frame: What We See in Films.* New York: Anchor Press, 1976.

Brinker-Gabler, Gisela, and Sidonie Smith, eds. *Writing New Identities: Gender, Nation, and Immigration in Contemporary Europe.* Minneapolis: Univ. of Minnesota Press, 1997.

Browne, Nick. "Society and Subjectivity: On the Political Economy of Chinese Melodrama." In Browne et al., eds., *New Chinese Cinemas,* 40–56.

Browne, Nick, Paul G. Pickowicz, Vivian Sobchack, and Esther Yau, eds. *New Chinese Cinemas: Forms, Identities, Politics.* Cambridge: Cambridge Univ. Press, 1994.

Callahan, W. A. "Gender, Ideology, Nation: *Ju Dou* in the Cultural Politics of China." *East-West Film Journal* 7, no. 1 (1993): 52–80.

Carrier, James G., ed. *Occidentalism: Images of the West.* New York: Oxford Univ. Press, 1995.

Chatman, Seymour. *Story and Discourse: Narrative Structure in Fiction and Film.* Ithaca, N.Y.: Cornell Univ. Press, 1978.

Chen, Pauline. "History Lessons." *Film Comment* 30 (March–April 1994): 85–87.

Chen Xiaomei. "The Marginality of the Study of Cultural Revolution: The Neglected and the Privileged in the Making of Imagined Communities." Paper presented at the Historical Society for Twentieth-Century China symposium, Coeur d'Alene, Idaho, October 1997.

———. *Occidentalism: A Theory of Counter-Discourse in Post-Mao China.* New York: Oxford Univ. Press, 1995.

Cheng, Scarlet. "The Road Home." *Far Eastern Economic Review,* 6 April 2000.

Chow, Rey. *Primitive Passions: Visuality, Sexuality, Ethnography, and Contemporary Chinese Cinema.* New York: Columbia Univ. Press, 1995.

———. *Woman and Chinese Modernity: The Politics of Reading between West and East.* Minneapolis: Univ. of Minnesota Press, 1991.

———. *Writing Diaspora: Tactics of Intervention in Contemporary Cultural Studies.* Bloomington: Indiana Univ. Press, 1993.

Cohn, Dorrit. *Transparent Minds: Narrative Modes for Presenting Consciousness in Fiction.* Princeton, N.J.: Princeton Univ. Press, 1978.

Creed, Barbara. "From Here to Modernity: Feminism and Postmodernism." *Screen* 28 (1987): 47–67.

Crofts, Stephen. "Concepts of National Cinema." In *World Cinema: Critical Approaches.* Ed. John Hill and Pamela Church Gibson. Oxford: Oxford Univ. Press, 2000.

Cui, Shuqin. "Working from the Margins and outside the System: Independent Film Directors in Contemporary China." *Post Script* 20 (winter/spring 2001): 77–93.

Dai Jinhua. "Invisible Women: Contemporary Chinese Cinema and Women's Film." Trans. Mayfair Yang. *Positions* 3, no. 1 (1995): 255–280.

———. "Redemption and Consumption: Depicting Culture in the 1990s." *Positions* 4, no. 1 (1996): 127–142.

Dai Jinhua, and Mayfair Yang. "A Conversation with Huang Shuqin." *Positions* 3, no. 3 (1995): 790–805.

Dal Lago, Francesca. "Personal Mao: Reshaping an Icon in Contemporary Chinese Art." *Art Journal* 58 (summer 1999): 46–59.

Davis, Robert Con, and David S. Gross. "Gayatri Chakravorty Spivak and the Ethos of the Subaltern." In *Ethos: New Essays in Rhetorical and Critical Theory.* Ed. James S. Baumlin and Tita French Baumlin, 65–90. Dallas: Southern Methodist Univ. Press, 1994.

De Lauretis, Teresa. *Technologies of Gender: Essays on Theory, Film, and Fiction.* Bloomington: Indiana Univ. Press, 1987.

———, ed. *Feminist Studies, Critical Studies.* Bloomington: Indiana Univ. Press, 1986.

Denton, Kirk A., ed. *Modern Chinese Literary Thought: Writings on Literature, 1893–1945.* Stanford: Stanford Univ. Press, 1996.

Ding Ling. *I Myself Am a Woman: Selected Writings of Ding Ling.* Ed. Tani E. Barlow with Gary J. Bjorge. Boston: Beacon Press, 1989.

Ding Xiaoqi. "Maidenhome." In *Maidenhome.* Trans. Chris Berry, 1–49. San Francisco: Aunt Lute Books, 1994.

Dirlik, Arif. "Postsocialism? Reflections on 'Socialism with Chinese Characteristics.'" In Dirlik and Meisner, eds., *Marxism and the Chinese Experience.*

Dirlik, Arif, and Maurice Meisner, eds. *Marxism and the Chinese Experience: Issues in Contemporary Chinese Socialism.* New York: M. E. Sharpe, 1989.

Dixon, Wheeler Winston. *It Looks at You: The Returned Gaze of Cinema.* Albany: State Univ. of New York Press, 1995.

Doane, Mary Ann. "Film and the Masquerade: Theorizing the Female Spectator." *Screen* 23, no. 3/4 (1982): 74–87.

———. "Subjectivity and Desire: An(other) Way of Looking." In *Contemporary Film Theory.* Ed. Antony Easthope, 162–178. London: Longman, 1993.

———. "The Voice in the Cinema: The Articulation of Body and Space." In Weis and Belton, eds., *Film Sound,* 162–176.

Doane, Mary Ann, Patricia Mellencamp, and Linda Williams, eds. *Re-Vision: Essays in Feminist Film Criticism.* Frederick, Md.: Univ. Publications of America, 1984.

Dobson, W. A. C. H., ed. *Mencius: A New Translation Arranged and Annotated for the General Reader.* Toronto: Univ. of Toronto Press, 1963.

Dollimore, Jonathan. "Subjectivity, Sexuality, and Transgression: The Jacobean Connection." *Renaissance Drama* 17 (1986): 53–81.

Duara, Prasenjit. *Rescuing History from the Nation: Questioning Narratives of Modern China.* Chicago: Univ. of Chicago Press, 1995.

Dutton, Michael. "The End of the (Mass) Line? Chinese Policing in the Era of the Contract." *Social Justice* 27, no. 2 (2000): 61–105.

Eagleton, Terry. *Literary Theory: An Introduction.* Minneapolis: Univ. of Minnesota Press, 1983.

Edwards, Tim. *Erotics and Politics: Gay Sexuality, Masculinity and Feminism.* New York: Routledge, 1994.

Elsaesser, Thomas. *New German Cinema: A History.* New Brunswick, N.J.: Rutgers Univ. Press, 1989.

Evans, Harriet. "The Language of Liberation: Gender and Jiefang in Early Chinese Communist Party Discourse." Article online, cited 5 December 2000. Available at http://www.sshe.murdoch.edu.au/intersections.

Fairclough, Norman. *Discourse and Social Change.* Cambridge: Polity Press, 1992.

Farquhar, Mary Ann, and Chris Berry. "Shadow Opera: Towards a New Archaeology of the Chinese Cinema." *Post Script: Essays in Film and the Humanities* 20, no. 2/3 (winter/spring and summer 2001): 25–42.

Feuerwerker, Yi-tsi. *Ding Ling's Fiction: Ideology and Narrative in Modern Chinese Literature.* Cambridge, Mass.: Harvard Univ. Press, 1982.

Fiske, John. *Understanding Popular Culture.* Boston: Unwin Hyman, 1989.

Fitzgerald, John. *Awakening China: Politics, Culture, and Class in the Nationalist Revolution.* Stanford: Stanford Univ. Press, 1996.

Flitterman-Lewis, Sandy. *To Desire Differently: Feminism and the French Cinema.* Urbana: Univ. of Illinois Press, 1990.

———. "Woman, Desire, and the Look: Feminism and the Enunciative Apparatus in Cinema." In *Theories of Authorship.* Ed. John Caughie, 242–250. London: Routledge, 1993.

Foucault, Michel. *Discipline and Punish: The Birth of the Prison.* Trans. Alan Sheridan. New York: Vintage Books, 1979.

Freeman, Mark. "Eastern Culture, Western Gaze: The Cinema of Zhang Yimou." Article online; cited 5 December 2000. Available at http://home.vicnet.net.au/ 'freeman/theory/zhangyimou.htm.

Freud, Sigmund. "The Dissolution of the Oedipus Complex." In *The Freud Reader*. Ed. Peter Gay, 661–666. New York: Norton, 1988.

Friedberg, Anne. *Window Shopping: Cinema and the Postmodern*. Los Angeles: Univ. of California Press, 1993.

Friedman, Susan Stanford. "Creativity and the Childbirth Metaphor: Gender Difference in Literary Discourse." In *Feminisms*, Warhol and Herndl, eds., 371–403.

———. *Mappings: Feminism and the Cultural Geographies of Encounter*. Princeton, N.J.: Princeton Univ. Press, 1998.

Gallop, Jane. *Reading Lacan*. Ithaca, N.Y.: Cornell Univ. Press, 1985.

Gardiner, Judith Kegan. "On Female Identity and Writing by Women." In *Writing and Sexual Difference*. Ed. Elizabeth Abel, 177–192. Chicago: Univ. of Chicago Press, 1982.

Genette, Gerard. *Narrative Discourse*. Trans. Jane E. Lewin. Ithaca, N.Y.: Cornell Univ. Press, 1980.

Gerhart, Mary. *Genre Choices, Gender Questions*. Norman: Univ. of Oklahoma Press, 1992.

Giannetti, Louis. *Understanding Movies*. Englewood Cliffs, N.J.: Prentice-Hall, 1990.

Gledhill, Christine, ed. *Home Is Where the Heart Is: Studies in Melodrama and the Woman's Film*. London: British Film Institute, 1987.

Greene, Gayle, and Coppelia Kahn, eds. *Making a Difference: Feminist Literary Criticism*. London: Routledge, 1985.

Grewal, Inderpal, and Caren Kaplan, eds. *Scattered Hegemonies: Postmodernity and Transnational Feminist Practices*. Minneapolis: Univ. of Minnesota Press, 1994.

Gunning, Tom. "The Cinema of Attractions: Early Film, Its Spectator and the Avant-Garde." In *Early Cinema: Space, Frame, Narrative*. Ed. Thomas Elsaesser and Adam Barker, 56–62. London: British Film Institute, 1990.

Hansen, Miriam. *Babel and Babylon: Spectatorship in American Silent Film*. Cambridge, Mass.: Harvard Univ. Press, 1991.

Harris, Kristine. "*The New Woman* Incident: Cinema, Scandal, and Spectacle in 1935 Shanghai." In S. H. Lu, ed., *Transnational Chinese Cinemas*, 277–302.

Hay, Trevor Thomas. "China's Proletarian Myth: The Revolutionary Narrative and Model Theater of the Cultural Revolution." Ph.D. diss., Griffith University, 2000.

Heath, Stephen. *Questions of Cinema*. Bloomington: Indiana Univ. Press, 1981.

Hershatter, Gail. *Dangerous Pleasures: Prostitution and Modernity in Twentieth-Century Shanghai*. Berkeley: Univ. of California Press, 1997.

Holley, David. "China's Angry Old Men Crack Down Again." *Los Angeles Times*, 8 April 1991.

Howard, Jean E. "Cross-Dressing, the Theater, and Gender Struggle in Early Modern England." In *Crossing the Stage: Controversies on Cross-Dressing*. Ed. Lesley Ferris, 20–46. London: Routledge, 1993.

Hsu, Francis L. K. "Eros, Affect, and Pao." In *Rugged Individualism Reconsidered: Essays in Psychological Anthropology*. Knoxville: Univ. of Tennessee Press, 1983.

Hutcheon, Linda. *A Poetics of Postmodernism: History, Theory, Fiction*. New York: Routledge, 1988.

———. *The Politics of Postmodernism*. London: Routledge, 1989.

Islam, Needeya. "I Want to Shoot People: Genre, Gender and Action in the Films of Kathryn Bigelow." In *Kiss Me Deadly: Feminism and Cinema for the Moment.* Ed. Laleen Jayamanne. Sydney: Power Publications, 1995.

Jameson, Fredric. "Third-World Literature in the Era of Multinational Capitalism." *Social Text* 15 (fall 1986): 82–104.

Joseph, William A., Christine P. W. Wong, and David Zweig, eds. *New Perspectives on the Cultural Revolution.* Cambridge, Mass.: Council on East Asian Studies, Harvard Univ. Press, 1991.

Judd, Ellen R. "Dramas of Passion: Heroism in the Cultural Revolution's Model Operas." In Joseph, Wong, and Zweig, eds., *New Perspectives on the Cultural Revolution,* 265–282.

Kaplan, Caren, and Inderpal Grewal. "Transnational Feminist Cultural Studies: Beyond the Marxism/Poststructuralism/Feminism Divides." In *Between Woman and Nation: Nationalisms, Transnational Feminisms, and the State,* ed. Caren Kaplan, Norma Alarcon, and Minoo Moallem, 349–363. Durham, N.C.: Duke Univ. Press, 1999.

Kaplan, Cora. "Pandora's Box: Subjectivity, Class, and Sexuality in Socialist Feminist Criticism." In Greene and Kahn, eds., *Making A Difference,* 146–176.

Kaplan, E. Ann. "Problematizing Cross-Cultural Analysis: The Case of Women in the Recent Chinese Cinema." *Wide Angle* 11, no. 2 (1989): 40–50.

———, ed. *Feminism and Film: Oxford Readings in Feminism.* Oxford: Oxford Univ. Press, 2000.

Kim, David D. "The Next Generation." *Village Voice,* 2 November 1993, 68–69.

Kingston, Maxine Hong. *Woman Warrior: Memories of a Girlhood among Ghosts.* New York: Vintage International, 1989; originally published 1975.

Klawans, Stuart. "Zhang Yimou, Local Hero." *Film Comment* 31, no. 5 (1995).

Kozloff, Sarah. *Invisible Storytellers: Voice-Over Narration in American Fiction Film.* Berkeley: Univ. of California Press, 1988.

Kristeva, Julia. *About Chinese Women.* Trans. Anita Barrows. New York: Urizen Books, 1977.

Kuhn, Annette. *Women's Pictures: Feminism and Cinema.* London: Verso, 1982.

Lang, Robert. *American Film Melodrama: Griffith, Vidor, Minnelli.* Princeton, N.J.: Princeton Univ. Press, 1989.

Lanser, Susan Sniader. *Fictions of Authority: Women Writers and Narrative Voice.* Ithaca, N.Y.: Cornell Univ. Press, 1992.

Lau, Jenny Kwok Wah. "*Farewell My Concubine*: History, Melodrama, and Ideology in Contemporary Pan-Chinese Cinema." *Film Quarterly* 49, no. 1 (1995): 17–27.

———. "*Judou*—A Hermeneutical Reading of Cross-Cultural Cinema." *Film Quarterly* 45 (winter 1991–92).

Lee, Leo Ou-Fan. *Shanghai Modern: The Flowering of a New Urban Culture in China, 1930–1945.* Cambridge, Mass.: Harvard Univ. Press, 1999.

———. "The Tradition of Modern Chinese Cinema: Some Preliminary Explorations and Hypotheses." In Berry, ed., *Perspectives on Chinese Cinema,* 6–20.

Lefort, Claude. *The Political Forms of Modern Society: Bureaucracy, Democracy, Totalitarianism.* Cambridge: Polity Press, 1986.

Li Xiaojiang. "With What Discourse Do We Reflect on Chinese Women?" In Yang, ed., *Spaces of Their Own,* 261–277.

Liu, Lydia H. "Beijing Sojourners in New York: Postsocialism and the Question of Ideology in Global Media Culture." *Positions* 7, no. 3 (1999): 763–796.

Lopate, Philip. "Odd Man Out." Interview with Tian Zhuangzhuang. *Film Comment* 30 (July–August 1994).

Lu, Sheldon Hsiao-peng. "Historical Introduction: Chinese Cinemas (1896–1996) and Transnational Film Studies." In S. H. Lu, ed., *Transnational Chinese Cinemas*.

———, ed. *Transnational Chinese Cinemas: Identity, Nationhood, Gender*. Honolulu: Univ. of Hawai'i Press, 1997.

Lu Tonglin, ed. *Gender and Sexuality in Twentieth-Century Chinese Literature and Society*. Albany: State Univ. of New York Press, 1993.

Ma Ning. "New Chinese Cinema: A Critical Account of the Fifth Generation." *Cineaste* 17, no. 3 (1990): 32–35.

———. "Symbolic Representation and Symbolic Violence: Chinese Family Melodrama of the Early 1980s." *East-West Film Journal* 4, no. 1 (1989): 79–112.

———. "The Textual and Critical Difference of Being Radical: Reconstructing Chinese Leftist Films of the 1930s." *Wide Angle* 11, no. 2 (1989): 22–31.

Makaryk, Irena R., ed. *Encyclopedia of Contemporary Literary Theory: Approaches, Scholars, Terms*. Toronto: Univ. of Toronto Press, 1993.

Mayne, Judith. "Review Essay: Feminist Film Theory and Criticism." *Signs: Journal of Women in Culture and Society* 11, no. 1 (1985): 81–100.

McClintock, Anne. "No Longer in a Future Heaven: Nationalism, Gender and Race." In Anne McClintock, *Imperial Leather: Race, Gender and Sexuality in the Colonial Contest*, 353–389. New York: Routledge, 1995.

McDougall, Bonnie S. *Popular Chinese Literature and Performing Arts in the People's Republic of China, 1949–1979*. Berkeley: Univ. of California Press, 1984.

McHugh, Tom, trans. "Chung Kuei Gives His Sister in Marriage, a Ching Dynasty Kunchu Play." *Echo* 6, no. 7 (September 1977): 45–54.

Meng Yue. "Female Images and National Myth." In Barlow, ed., *Gender Politics in Modern China*, 118–136.

Metz, Christian. "History/Discourse: A Note on Two Voyeurisms." In *Theories of Authorship*, edited by John Caughie, 225–231. London: Routledge, 1981.

Michael, Magali Cornier. *Feminism and the Postmodern Impulse*. Albany: State Univ. of New York Press, 1996.

Mittler, Barbara. "To Be or Not to Be: Making and Unmaking the *Yangbanxi*." Paper presented at the annual meeting of the American Historical Association, Seattle, January 1998.

Modleski, Tania. *The Women Who Knew Too Much: Hitchcock and Feminist Theory*. New York: Methuen, 1988.

Mulvey, Laura. *Visual and Other Pleasures*. Bloomington: Indiana Univ. Press, 1989.

North, C. J. "The Chinese Motion Picture Market." *Trade Information Bulletin*, no. 467, U.S. Department of Commerce. Washington, D.C.: GPO, 1927.

Owens, Craig. "The Discourse of Others: Feminists and Postmodernism." In *The Anti-Aesthetic: Essays on Postmodern Culture*. Ed. Hal Foster, 57–82. Port Townsend, Wash.: Bay Press, 1983.

Percheron, Daniel. "Sound in Cinema and Its Relationship to Image and Diegesis." *Yale French Studies* 60, no. 1 (1980): 16–23.

Pickowicz, Paul G. "Huang Jianxin and the Notion of Postsocialism." In Browne et al., eds., *New Chinese Cinemas*, 57–87.

————. "Melodramatic Representation and the 'May Fourth' Tradition of Chinese Cinema." In *From May Fourth to June Fourth: Fiction and Film in Twentieth-Century China*. Ed. Ellen Widmer and David Der-Wei Wang, 295–326. Cambridge, Mass.: Harvard Univ. Press, 1993.

Prazniak, Roxann. "Mao and the Woman Question in an Age of Green Politics: Some Critical Reflections." In *Critical Perspectives on Mao Zedong's Thought*. Ed. Arif Dirlik, Paul Healy, and Nick Knight, 23–58. Atlantic Highlands, N.J.: Humanities Press, 1997.

Rafferty, Terrence. "Blind Faith." *New Yorker*, 11 October 1993, 121–123.

Riviere, Joan. "Womanliness as a Masquerade." *International Journal of Psycho-Analysis* 10 (1929): 303–313.

Robinson, Sally. *Engendering the Subject: Gender and Self-Representation in Contemporary Women's Fiction*. Albany: State Univ. of New York Press, 1991.

Rose, Jacqueline. "The Cinematic Apparatus: Problems in Current Theory." In *The Cinematic Apparatus*. Ed. Teresa De Lauretis and Stephen Heath. London: Macmillan, 1980.

Roulston, Christine. "Discourse, Gender, and Gossip: Some Reflections on Bakhtin and *Emma*." In *Ambiguous Discourse: Feminist Narratology and British Women Writers*. Ed. Kathy Mezei, 40–65. Chapel Hill: Univ. of North Carolina Press, 1996.

Said, Edward. *Orientalism*. New York: Vintage Books, 1979.

Schwarcz, Vera. "Ibsen's Nora: The Promise and the Trap." *Bulletin of Concerned Asian Scholars* 6 (January–March 1975).

Schram, Stuart. *The Thought of Mao Zedong*. New York: Cambridge Univ. Press, 1989.

Showalter, Elaine. "Critical Crossing: Male Feminists and the Woman of the Year." In *Raritan Reading*. Ed. Richard Poirier, 364–381. New Brunswick, N.J.: Rutgers Univ. Press, 1990.

————. "Toward a Feminist Poetics." *The New Feminist Criticism: Essays on Women, Literature, Theory*. Ed. Elaine Showalter, 125–143. New York: Pantheon Books, 1985.

Silverman, Kaja. *Male Subjectivity at the Margins*. New York: Routledge, 1992.

————. *The Subject of Semiotics*. New York: Oxford Univ. Press, 1983.

Sommer, Doris. "Allegory and Dialectics: A Match Made in Romance." *Boundary 2* 18, no. 1 (1991): 60–82.

Spivak, Gayatri Chakravorty. *Outside in the Teaching Machine*. New York: Routledge, 1993.

Stacey, Judith. *Patriarchy and Socialist Revolution in China*. Los Angeles: Univ. of California Press, 1983.

Stam, Robert. *Film Theory: An Introduction*. Malden, Mass.: Blackwell, 2000.

————. *Subversive Pleasures: Bakhtin, Cultural Criticism and Film*. Baltimore: Johns Hopkins Univ. Press, 1989.

Stam, Robert, Robert Burgoyne, and Sandy Flitterman-Lewis. *New Vocabularies in Film Semiotics: Structuralism, Post-Structuralism and Beyond*. London: Routledge, 1992.

Stringer, Julian. "*Center Stage*: Reconstructing the Bio-Pic." *Cine Action* 42 (1997): 28–39.

Studlar, Gaylyn. *In the Realm of Pleasure: Von Sternberg, Dietrich, and the Masochistic Aesthetic*. Urbana: Univ. of Illinois Press, 1988.

Wang Ban. *The Sublime Figure of History: Aesthetics and Politics in Twentieth-Century China.* Stanford: Stanford Univ. Press, 1997.

———. "Trauma and History in Chinese Film: Reading *The Blue Kite* against Melodrama." *Modern Chinese Literature and Culture* 11, no. 1 (1999): 125–156.

Wang Hui and Leo Ou-Fan Lee, with Michael M. J. Fischer. "Is the Public Sphere Unspeakable in Chinese? Can Public Space *(gonggong kongjian)* Lead to Public Spheres?" *Public Culture* 6 (spring 1994): 598–605.

Wang Jing. *High Culture Fever: Politics, Aesthetics, and Ideology in Deng's China.* Berkeley: Univ. of California Press, 1996.

Wang Yuejin, "The Cinematic Other and the Cultural Self? Decentering the Cultural Identity on Cinema." *Wide Angle* 11, no. 2 (1989): 32–39.

Wang Zheng. "Three Interviews: Wang Anyi, Zhulin, Dai Qing." In Barlow, ed., *Gender Politics in Modern China.*

Warhol, Robyn R., and Diane Price Herndl, eds. *Feminisms: An Anthology of Literary Theory and Criticism.* New Brunswick, N.J.: Rutgers Univ. Press, 1993.

Waugh, Patricia. *Metafiction: The Theory and Practice of Self-Conscious Fiction.* London: Methuen, 1984.

Way, E. I., comp. "Motion Pictures in China." *Trade Information Bulletin,* no. 722, U.S. Department of Commerce. Washington, D.C.: GPO, 1930.

Weis, Elisabeth, and John Belton, eds. *Film Sound: Theory and Practice.* New York: Columbia Univ. Press, 1985.

White, Jerry. "The Films of Ning Ying: China Unfolding in Miniature." *Cine Action* 42 (1997): 2–10.

Whiting, Allen S. "Chinese Nationalism and Foreign Policy after Deng." *China Quarterly* 142 (June 1995): 295–315.

Williams, Linda. "Melodrama Revised." In *Refiguring American Film Genres: History and Theory.* Ed. Nick Browne, 42–88. Berkeley: Univ. of California Press, 1998.

———. "Something Else Besides a Mother: *Stella Dallas* and the Maternal Melodrama." In Gledhill, ed., *Home Is Where the Heart Is.*

Wilson, Tony. "Reading the Postmodernist Image: A 'Cognitive Mapping.'" *Screen* 31 (winter 1990): 390–407.

Wollen, Peter. "Godard and Counter Cinema: Vent D'Est." *Movies and Methods,* Ed. Bill Nichols, 2: 500–509. Berkeley: Univ. of California Press, 1985.

Xu Ben. *Disenchanted Democracy: Chinese Cultural Criticism after 1989.* Ann Arbor: Univ. of Michigan Press, 1999.

Xu Jian. "*Blush* from Novella to Film: The Possibility of Critical Art in Commodity Culture." *Modern Chinese Literature and Culture* 12, no. 1 (2000): 115–163.

Yang, Mayfair Mei-hui. "From Gender Erasure to Gender Difference: State Feminism, Consumer Sexuality, and Women's Public Sphere in China." In Yang, ed., *Spaces of Their Own,* 35–67.

———, ed. *Spaces of Their Own: Women's Public Sphere in Transnational China.* Minneapolis: Univ. of Minnesota Press, 1999.

Yang Ping. "A Director Who Is Trying to Change the Audience: A Chat with Young Director Tian Zhuangzhuang." In Berry, ed., *Perspectives on Chinese Cinema.*

Yau, Esther C. M. "Filmic Discourse on Women in Chinese Cinema (1949–65): Art, Ideology, and Social Relations." Ph.D. diss., Univ. of California, Los Angeles, 1990.

———. "Is China the End of Hermeneutics? Or, Political and Cultural Usage of Non-Han Women in Mainland Chinese Films." *Discourse* 11, no. 2 (1989): 115–136.

———. "*Yellow Earth*: Western Analysis and a Non-Western Text." *Film Quarterly* 41, no. 2 (1987/88): 22–33. Reprinted in Berry, ed., *Perspectives on Chinese Cinema*, 62–79.

Young, Suzie Sau-Fong. "The Voice of Feminine Madness in Zhang Yimou's *Da Hong Deng Long Gao Gao Gua* (Raise the Red Lantern)." *Asian Cinema* 7, no. 1 (1995): 12–23.

Zha Jianying. "Shadows on the Screen." In *China Pop: How Soap Operas, Tabloids, and Best Sellers Are Transforming a Culture*. New York: New Press, 1995.

Zhang Xudong. *Chinese Modernism in the Era of Reforms: Cultural Fever, Avant-Garde Fiction, and the New Chinese Cinema*. Durham, N.C.: Duke Univ. Press, 1997.

Zhang Yingjin. *The City in Modern Chinese Literature and Film: Configurations of Space, Time, and Gender*. Stanford: Stanford Univ. Press, 1996.

———. "From 'Minority Film' to 'Minority Discourse': Questions of Nationhood and Ethnicity in Chinese Cinema." In S. H. Lu, ed., *Transnational Chinese Cinemas*, 81–104.

———. "Rethinking Cross-Cultural Analysis: The Questions of Authority, Power, and Difference in Western Studies of Chinese Films." *Bulletin of Concerned Asian Scholars* 26, no. 4 (1994): 44–53.

———. "Review Essay: Screening China: Recent Studies of Chinese Cinema in English." *Bulletin of Concerned Asian Scholars* 29, no. 2 (1997).

———, ed. *Cinema and Urban Culture in Shanghai, 1922–1943*. Stanford: Stanford Univ. Press, 1999.

Zhang Zhen. "'An Amorous History of the Silver Screen': Film Culture, Urban Modernity, and the Vernacular Experience in China, 1896–1937." Ph.D. diss., Univ. of Chicago, 1998.

———. "Teahouse, Shadowplay, Bricolage: *Laborer's Love* and the Question of Early Chinese Cinema." In Y. Zhang, ed., *Cinema and Urban Culture in Shanghai*, 27–50.

Zheng Dongtian. "To Be or Not to Be: Concerns on the Survival of Chinese Cinema after China Joins WTO." *Film Art* 2 (2000).

CHINESE SOURCES

Chen Bo 陳播, ed. *Zhongguo zuoyi dianying yundong* 中國左翼電影運動 (The leftist film movement in China). Beijing: Zhongguo dianying, 1992.

Chen Bo 陳播 and Yi Ming 伊明, eds. *Sanshi niandai Zhongguo dianying pinglun wenxuan* 三十年代中國電影評論文選 (Chinese film reviews of the 1930s: An anthology). Beijing: Zhongguo dianying, 1993.

Chen Jianyu 陳劍雨, Zhang Guohuan 張國還, and Zhang Mingtang 張銘堂, eds. *Lun Xie Jin dianying* 論謝晉電影 (Comments on Xie Jin's films). Beijing: Zhongguo dianying, 1998.

Chen Kaige 陳凱歌. *Shaonian Kaige* 少年凱歌 (Young Kaige). Beijing: Renmin wenxue, 2001.

Chen Xiaoming 陳曉明. "Yiwai de hemou: Jingying yu dazhong de chongdie yingxiang" 意外的合謀: 精英與大眾的重疊影像 (Superimposed images: An unexpected conspiracy between the elite and the masses). *Today* 3 (1995): 64–80.

Chen Xihe 陳犀禾. "Zhongguo dianying meixue de zai renshi" 中國電影美學的再認識 (Reconsideration of the aesthetics of Chinese cinema). In Luo, ed., *Collected Essays*, 289–306.

Cheng Jihua 程季華. *Zhongguo dianying fazhan shi* 中國電影發展史 (The history of the development of Chinese cinema). 2 vols. Beijing: Zhongguo dianying, 1963.

Dai Jinhua 戴錦華. "Bu kejian de nüxing: Dangdai zhongguo dianying zhongde nüxing yu nüxing dianying" 不可見的中國女性: 當代中國電影中的女性與女性電影 (Invisible women: Contemporary Chinese Cinema and women's films). *Dangdai dianying* 當代電影 (Contemporary cinema) 6 (1994): 37–45.

———. *Wuzhong fengjing: Zhongguo dianying wenhua 1978–1998* 霧中風景中國電影文化一九七八至一九九八 (Chinese film culture: 1978–1998). Beijing: Beijing Univ. Press, 2000.

Ding Yaping 丁亞平. *Yingxiang zhongguo: Zhongguo dianying yishu 1945–1949* 影像中國: 中國電影藝術 (Signs of China: Chinese film aesthetics, 1945–1949). Beijing: Wenhua yishu, 1998.

Jiang Wen 姜文. *Yibu dianying de dansheng* 一部電影的誕生 (The birth of a film). Beijing: Huayi, 1997.

Ke Lin 柯靈. "Shiwei wusi yu dianying hua yi lunkuo" 試為五四與電影畫一輪廓 (Framework for the May Fourth movement and Chinese cinema). In Chen Bo, ed., *The Leftist Film Movement in China*, 902–913.

Li Suyuan 酈蘇元 and Hu Jubin 胡菊彬. *Zhongguo wusheng dianying shi* 中國無聲電影史 (The history of Chinese silent films). Beijing: Zhongguo dianying, 1996.

Li Xiaojiang 李小江. *Guanyu nüren de dawen* 關於女人的答問 (Questions and answers about women). Nanjing: Jiangsu renmin, 1998.

———. *Xiawa de tansuo* 夏娃的探索 (Eve's exploration). Zhengzhou: Henan renmin, 1989.

———. "Zouxiang nüren" 走向女人 (Toward women). *Nüxing ren* (Female being) 4 (1990): 255–266.

Li Xiaojiang 李小江, Zhu Hong 朱虹, and Dong Xiuyu 董秀玉, eds. *Xingbie yu Zhongguo* 性別與中國 (Gender and China). Beijing: Sanlian Shudian, 1994.

Liu Huaishun 劉懷舜, ed. *Zhongguo dianying tuzhi* 中國電影圖誌 (Illustrated annals of Chinese film). Guangzhou: Zhuhai, 1995.

Liu Naou 劉吶鷗. "Zhongguo dianying miaoxie de shendu wenti" 中國電影的描寫深度問題 (Questions of narrative depth in Chinese films). In Chen Bo and Yi Ming, eds., *Chinese Film Reviews of the 1930s*, 837–839. Also reproduced in Luo Yijun, ed., *Collected Essays*, 256–261.

Lu Le 魯勒, Xi Shanshan 奚姍姍, and Zhang Zhenqin 張震欽, eds. *Caozong yinmu de nüxing: Zhongguo nüdaoyan* 操縱銀幕的女性: 中國女導演 (Chinese women directors: Women who master the film screen). Changchun: Beifang funü ertong, 1989.

Lu Xun 魯迅. "Lun renyan kewei" 論人言可畏 (On gossip as a fear thing). In *Complete Works of Lu Xun*. Beijing: Renmin wenxue, 1958.

Luo Yijun 羅藝軍, ed. *Zhongguo dianying lilun wenxuan* 中國電影理論文選 (Collected essays of Chinese film theory: An anthology). Beijing: Wenhua yishu, 1992.

Ma Junxiang 馬軍驤. "Minzu zhuyi suo suzao de xiandai zhongguo dianying" 民族主義所塑造的現代中國電影 (Modern Chinese films in the construction of nationalism). In *Nationalism: Its Interaction with Modernization in China*, ed. Liu Qingfeng, 521–532. Hong Kong: Chinese Univ. of Hong Kong, 1994.

Meng Yue 孟悦 and Dai Jinhua 戴錦華. *Fuchu lishi dibiao* 浮出歷史地表 (Emerging from the horizon of history: Modern Chinese women's literature). Zhengzhou: Henan renmin, 1989.

Ni Zhen 倪震. *Gaige yu zhongguo dianying* 改革與中國電影 (Reform and Chinese cinema). Beijing: Zhongguo dianying, 1994.

Qu Jiannong 瞿建農. *Hongse wangshi: 1966–1976 nian de zhongguo dianying* 紅色往事一九六六至一九七六年的中國電影 (Red retrospections: Chinese cinema from 1966 to 1976). Beijing: Taihai, 2001.

Shu Xiaoming 舒曉明. *Zhongguo dianying yishushi jiaocheng* 中國電影藝術史教程 (History of Chinese film aesthetics). Beijing: Zhongguo dianying, 1996.

Song Qiang 宋強, Zhang Zangzang 張藏藏, and Qiao Bian 喬邊, eds. *Zhongguo keyi shuo bu* 中國可以說不 (China can say no). Beijing: Zhonghua gongshang lianhe, 1996.

Wang Hui 汪暉 and Yu Kwok-leung 余國良, eds. *Jiushi niandai de houxue lunzheng* 九十年代的後學論爭 (Post-ism in the nineties). Hong Kong: Chinese Univ. of Hong Kong, 1998.

Wang Yichuan 王一川. *Zhang Yimou shenhua de zongjie: Shenmei yu wenhua shiye zhong de Zhang Yimou dianying* 張藝謀神話的終結: 審美與文化視野中的張藝謀電影 (The end of the Zhang Yimou myth: Zhang Yimou's films from the perspectives of culture and aesthetics). Zhengzhou: Henan renmin, 1998.

Xia Yan 夏衍. *Xia Yan dianying jubenji* 夏衍電影劇本集 (Anthology of Xian Yan's film screenplays). Beijing: Zhongguo dianying, 1985.

Yang Yuanying 楊遠嬰, ed. *Tamen de shengyin: Zhongguo nüdaoyan de zisu* 她們的聲音: 中國女導演自述 (Their voices: Chinese women directors' self-expression). Hebei: Zhongguo shehui, 1996.

Yao Xiaomeng 姚曉濛. "Zhongguo xin dianying: Cong yishi xingtai de guandian kan" 中國新電影: 從意識形態的觀點看 (Chinese new cinema: From an ideological perspective). In *Zhongguo dangdai wenhua yishi* 中國當代文化意識 (Cultural consciousness in contemporary China), ed. Gan Yang 甘陽. Hong Kong: Joint Publishing, 1989.

Yin Hong 尹鴻. *Shiji zhuanzhe shiqi de zhongguo yingshi wen hua* 世紀轉折時期的影視文化 (Chinese film and television culture at the turn of the century). Beijing: Beijing chuban, 1998.

Zhong Dafeng 鍾大豐. "Yingxi lilun lishi suyuan" 影戲理論歷史溯源 (Historical origins of the concept of shadow-play). In Luo, ed., *Collected Essays*, 307–319.

Index